Fod
Vie
the Danube
Valley

CW00921344

Reprinted from *Fodor's Austria*

Fodor's Travel Publications, Inc.
New York • Toronto • London • Sydney • Auckland

Fodor's Vienna & the Danube Valley

Editor: Kristen Perrault
Area Editor: George W. Hamilton
Contributors: Alan Levy, Delia Meth-Cohn, Paula Consolo, Katherine Kane, Marcy Pritchard, Earl Steinbicker, George Sullivan
Creative Director: Fabrizio La Rocca
Cartographer: David Lindroth, Eureka Cartography
Illustrator: Karl Tanner
Cover Photograph: Robert Lightfoot III/Nawrocki Stock Photo

Design: Vignelli Associates

Contents

Maps

Foreword

We would like to thank the directors of the Austrian National Tourist Offices in Vienna and in New York—especially Gabriele Wolf—and the individual tourist offices for each of the provinces for their generous and considerable assistance in preparing this new edition. Werner Fritz and the staff of the Austrian National Tourist Office in London have been of further help.

While every care has been taken to ensure accuracy of the information in this guide, tourism in Austria is a dynamic industry and changes will occur; consequently, the publisher can assume no liability for errors.

All prices and opening times quoted in this guide are based on information supplied to us at press time. Hours and admission fees may change; call ahead to avoid disappointment. Fodor's wants to hear about your travel experiences, both pleasant and unpleasant. When a hotel or restaurant fails to live up to its billing, let us know, and we will investigate the complaint and revise our entries where warranted.

Send your letters to the editors of Fodor's Travel Publications, 201 E. 50th St., New York, NY 10022.

Highlights and Fodor's Choice

Highlights

Politics and the Economy Out of the ashes of World War II, Austria has quietly developed into one of Europe's most prosperous countries. Its economic growth rate this year will top Germany's, in part because of its flourishing tourism. At the same time, inflation has been held to moderate levels. Visitors from the United States will not find Vienna cheap, but the problem has more to do with the dollar-schilling exchange rate than with Austrian prices. The country has not been spared the general European economic turndown, however, and behind the scenes, Austria is going through a structural transition triggered as much as anything by the unexpected opening of the former Eastern Bloc. This has meant industrial closures and unemployment.

When the four occupying powers—the United States, the United Kingdom, France, and the Soviet Union—left the country in 1955, Austria pledged "perpetual neutrality" in return for its sovereignty. In today's very different world, the Austrians are finding neutrality a hard concept to define, particularly as the country presses its application for membership in the European Community. EC membership could come as early as 1995.

Travel Tourism officials realize that unlimited growth could spoil the country's main attractions: sensational scenery, unpolluted air and water, safe cities, and easy accessibility. With tourism among Austria's top industries, care is being taken to preserve lakes, forests, and wilderness from overexploitation. Mountain bikes are forbidden in some areas, and white-water rafting is restricted to streams where any ecological damage will be minimal. The Austrians don't want to limit your fun, but they do want to make certain that the environment can support mass activities and still leave something for the next generation.

Starting this year, parking in the center of Vienna is restricted (whole squares have been cleared of cars), and tour buses are limited to specific routes. All of this means that you should be prepared to walk—which is, indeed, the best way to see Austria.

The hotel industry is seeing changes, too. Hotel construction is booming, but most new hotels are in the four- and five-star categories and are part of major chains. The surplus of high-priced rooms in the larger cities has led to substantial discounting, so don't be afraid to ask for the best possible price in a top hotel, particularly off season.

Travelers in Austria again face problems with credit cards this year. Some travel agents will accept only Diner's Club cards. Many establishments—even some pricey restaurants—now refuse to take any cards, and some hotels and restaurants will take one or two, but not all.

The Arts   Musical events begin with the New Year's concert of the Vienna Philharmonic, Laurin Maazel conducting, and a performance of Beethoven's Ninth by the Vienna Symphony; both events take place in Vienna on New Year's Eve and again on New Year's Day. The main musical events of the Vienna Festival Weeks from mid-May through mid-June take place this year in the Musikverein. The fall musical season will be minus the opera, as the Staatsoper opera house is undergoing renovation. It will reopen on December 15 with a new production of the Giordano opera *Fedora*. In November, the Theater an der Wien will present Mozart's *Così fan tutte*.

Highlights of the ball season will include the Philharmonic Ball on January 20 in the Musikverein and the Opera Ball on February 10, which takes place in the elegantly decorated opera house. The main ball season runs through *Fasching*, the carnival period, which ends with a great parade around the Ring in Vienna on April 2. The Imperial Ball in the Hofburg wraps up the year in style on December 31.

Sports   Cycling is in, and bicycle routes now parallel the full length of the Danube in Austria. Route maps and information brochures identify restaurants and hotel stopover possibilities along the way. The National Tourist Office has organized a "Cycling Spring in Austria" campaign. Bicycle rental is an easy matter at railroad stations throughout the country.

Fodor's Choice

No two people will agree on what makes a perfect vacation, but it can be fun and helpful to know what others think. We hope you'll have a chance to experience some of Fodor's Choices yourself while visiting Austria. For detailed information on individual entries, see the relevant sections of this guidebook.

Times to Remember

High Mass on Sunday in the Augustinerkirche

The New Year's Day concert in Musikverein

Works of Art

Bosch's *Last Judgment*

Brueghel's *Hunters in the Snow*

Carved wood altar (Kefermarkt)

Cellini's gold saltcellar

Klimt's *The Kiss*

Schiele's *The Family*

Vermeer's *Allegory of the Art of Painting: the Artist in his Studio*

Museums

Belvedere Palace

Historisches Museum der Stadt Wien (Museum of Viennese History)

Kunsthistorisches Museum (Museum of Art History)

Sights to Remember

St. Charles's church by night

Chestnut trees in blossom along the Praterallee

The Naschmarkt and Flea Market on a Saturday morning

Memorable Drives

The Wachau along the Danube when the apricot trees are in blossom

Taste Treats

Sampling wine at a romantic *Heuriger*

Architectural Gems

Art Deco buildings along the Linke Weinzeile
Ferstel Palace and Café Central
Gloriette (Schönbrunn Palace Gardens)
Hundertwasserhaus
Looshaus
Secession building

Hotels

Briston
Burg Bernstein
Palais Schwarzenberg
Pension Zipser

Cafés

Central
Hawelka
Schwarzenberg

Churches and Abbeys

Karlskirche
St. Charles'
St. Stephen's

Parks and Gardens

Belvedere
Burggarten
Schönbrunn
Stadtpark

Austria

SLOVAKIA

CZECH REPUBLIC

HUNGARY

SLOVENIA

ITALY

SWITZERLAND

LIECHTENSTEIN

GERMANY

Danube (Donau)

Neusiedler See

BURGENLAND

Vienna

Hainburg

Bruck

Eisenstadt

Poysdorf

Stockerau

Mödling

Baden

Wiener Neustadt

Neunkirchen

LOWER AUSTRIA (NIEDERÖSTERREICH)

Horn

Waidhofen

Zwettl

Krems

Melk

St. Pölten

Gmünd

Scheibbs

Mariazell

Mürzzuschlag

Hartberg

Fürstenfeld

Bruck a. d. Mur

STYRIA (STEIERMARK)

Kapfenberg

Leoben

Knittelfeld

Judenburg

Liezen

Graz

Feldbach

Bad

Gleichenberg

Radkersburg

Bad

Mura

Drava

SLOVENIA

St. Veit

CARINTHIA (KÄRNTEN)

Klagenfurt

Villach

Feldkirchen

Spittal

Drau

Heiligenblut

Bad Gastein

EAST TIROL

Lienz

Matrei

SALZBURG

Bischofshofen

Radstadt

Bad Aussee

Bad Ischl

Gmunden

St. Wolfgang

Salzach

Salzburg

St. Johann

Zell am See

Saalfelden

Kitzbühel

Kufstein

Jenbach

Mayrhofen

Innsbruck

TIROL

Landeck

St. Anton

Imst

Reutte

Zürs

Lech

Feldkirch

Bregenz

Dornbirn

Bludenz

VORARLBERG

Boden See

Danube (Donau)

Linz

Enns

Steyr

Wels

Eferding

Ried

Braunau

Schärding

UPPER AUSTRIA (OBERÖSTERREICH)

Vöcklabruck

Freistadt

Inn

Enns

Enns

MUR

Drau

N

50 miles

75 km

Vienna

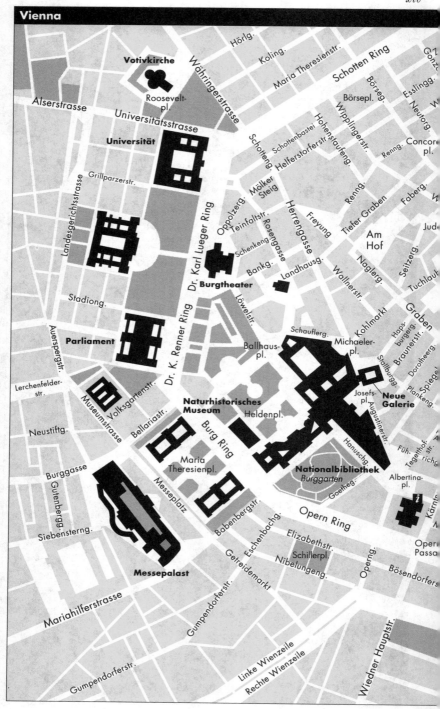

Votivkirche

Roosevelt-pl.

Hörlg.

Koling.

Maria Theresienstr.

Schotten Ring

Gonz.

Börseg.

Börsepl.

Esslingg.

Wipplingerstr.

Neutorg.

W

Alserstrasse

Universitätsstrasse

Hohenstaufeng.

Renng.

Concore
pl.

Universität

Schotteng.

Schottenbastei

Schottenring

Halferstorferstr.

Freyung

Tiefer Graben

Faberg.

W

Grillparzerstr.

Oppolzerg.

Mölker
Steig

Teinfaltstr.

Herrengasse

Am
Hof

Jude

Landsgerichtsstrasse

Schenkeng.

Rosengasse

Renng.

Naglerg.

Setzerg.

Bankg.

Landhausg.

Wallnerstr.

Tuchlaut

Stadiong.

Burgtheater

Löwelstr.

Kohlmarkt

Graben

Schauflerg.

Michaeler-
pl.

Haps-
burgerg.

Braunerstr.

Dorotheeg.

Spiegel

Dr. Karl Lueger Ring

Dr. K. Renner Ring

Parliament

Auerspergstr.

Ballhaus-
pl.

Stallburgg.

Plankeng.

Josefs-
pl

Neue
Galerie

Lerchenfelder-
str.

Volksgartenstr.

Naturhistorisches
Museum

Heldenpl.

Augustinerstr.

Neustiftg.

Museumstrasse

Bellariastr.

Burg Ring

Hanuschg.

Füh-
richg.

Tegethoff-
str.

Burggasse

Maria
Theresienpl.

Nationalbibliothek

Burggarten

Albertina-
pl.

Gutenbergg.

Messeplatz

Goetheg.

Kärnt

Siebensterng.

Opern Ring

Babenbergstr.

Elizabethstr.

Opern
Passa

Messepalast

Getreidemarkt

Eschenbachg.

Schillerpl.

Operng.

Bösendorfers

Mariahilferstrasse

Gumpendorfstr.

Nibelungeng.

Gumpendorferstr.

Linke Wienzeile

Rechte Wienzeile

Wiedner Hauptstr.

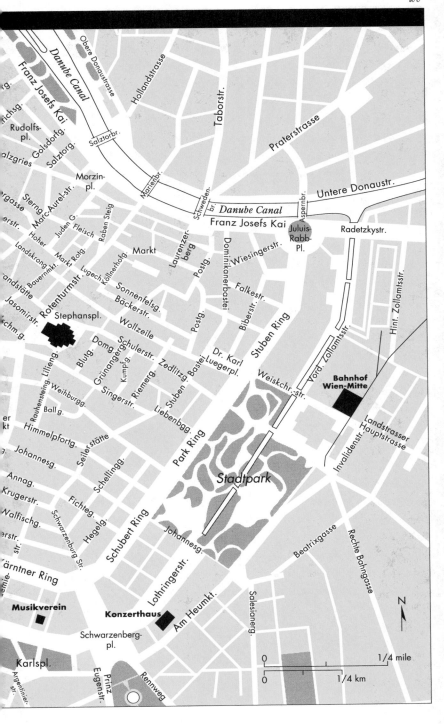

World Time Zones

Numbers below vertical bands relate each zone to Greenwich Mean Time (0 hrs.). Local times frequently differ from these general indications, as indicated by light-face numbers on map.

Algiers, **29**
Anchorage, **3**
Athens, **41**
Auckland, **1**
Baghdad, **46**
Bangkok, **50**
Beijing, **54**

Berlin, **34**
Bogotá, **19**
Budapest, **37**
Buenos Aires, **24**
Caracas, **22**
Chicago, **9**
Copenhagen, **33**
Dallas, **10**

Delhi, **48**
Denver, **8**
Djakarta, **53**
Dublin, **26**
Edmonton, **7**
Hong Kong, **56**
Honolulu, **2**

Istanbul, **40**
Jerusalem, **42**
Johannesburg, **44**
Lima, **20**
Lisbon, **28**
London (Greenwich), **27**
Los Angeles, **6**
Madrid, **38**
Manila, **57**

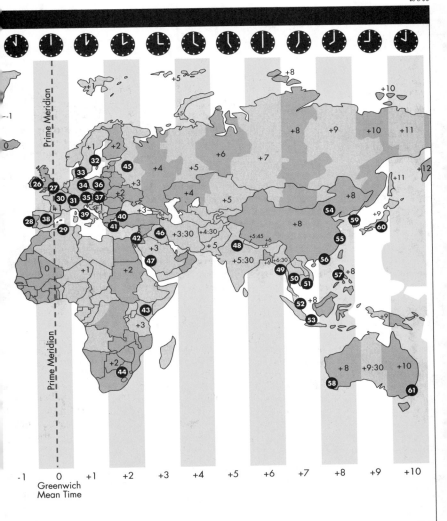

Introduction

By Alan Levy

Now editor-in-chief of the Prague Post, *Alan Levy lived in Vienna for 20 years.*

Today's Austria—and in particular its capital, Vienna—reminds me of a formerly fat man who is now at least as gaunt as the rest of us, but still allows himself a lot of room and expects doors to open wide when he goes through them. After losing two world wars and surviving amputation, annexation, and occupation, a nation that once ruled Europe now endures as a tourist mecca and a neutralized, somewhat balkanized republic.

It takes any foreign resident in Austria, even a German or Swiss, the whole first year to find out what questions one should be asking. It takes the second year to start getting answers; beginning with the third year, one can sift the merits of the answers. This is why I tell our friends from embassies, agencies, banks, and businesses—people doing two- or three-year stints in Austria—that they need a minimum of five years here to liquidate the investment of effort and utilize the contacts they've made. To tourists, I have just three words of advice: "Don't even try." Were you to succeed in thinking like the Viennese, for example, you would be a prime candidate for Doctor Freud's couch at Berggasse 19; but he and it aren't there anymore—the house is now the Sigmund Freud Museum, and the couch is in London.

Sitting in a loge in the Vienna State Opera in the 1970s, my wife and I gasped with dismay when a young ballerina slipped and fell, but while we applauded the girl's quick recovery, the ancient dowager next to me merely murmured: "In the days of the monarchy, she'd have been taken outside and shot."

I hope it was hyperbole, but she had a point. In a world of tattered glitter and tacky taste, jet-lagged superstars and under-rehearsed choruses, opera and operetta aren't what they used to be (though Viennese ballet has climbed steadily uphill in the decades since that girl's fall).

Still, there are oases of perfection, such as those Sunday mornings from September to June, when—if you've reserved months in advance—you can hear (but not see) those "voices from heaven," the Vienna Choir Boys, sing Mass in the marble-and-velvet royal chapel of the Hofburg. Lads of eight to thirteen in sailor suits, they peal out angelic notes from the topmost gallery, and you might catch a glimpse of them after Mass as you cut across the Renaissance courtyard for the 10:45 performance of the Lippizaner Stallions in the Spanish Riding School around the corner. Beneath crystal chandeliers in a lofty white hall, expert riders in brown uniforms with gold buttons and black hats with gold braid put these aristocrats of the equine world through their classic paces.

Just past noon, when the Spanish Riding School lets out, cross the Michaelerplatz and stroll up the Kohlmarkt to No. 14: Demel's, the renowned and lavish pastry shop founded shortly after 1848 by the court confectioner. It was an instant success with those privileged to dine with the emperor, for not only was Franz Josef a notoriously stodgy and paltry eater, but, when he stopped eating, protocol dictated that all others stop, too. Dessert at Demel's became a must for hungry higher-ups. Today's Demel's features a flawless midday buffet offering venison en croûte, chicken in pastry shells, beef Wellington, meat tarts, and frequent warnings to "leave room for the desserts."

Closer to the less-costly level of everyday existence, my family and I laid on a welcoming meal for visitors just off plane or train: a freshly baked slab of *Krusti Brot* to be spread with *Liptauer*, a piquant paprika cream cheese, and *Kräuter Gervais*, Austria's answer to cream cheese and chives, all washed down by a youngish white wine. Such simple pleasures as a jug of wine, a loaf of bread, and a spicy cheese or two are what we treasure as Austrian excellence in democratic days. Though our visitors managed to live well back home without Grüner Veltliner and Rheinriesling to drink or Liptauer and Kräuter Gervais to eat, they did find it hard to rejoin the outside world of white bread that wiggles. And if they really carried on about our wine, we could take them on the weekend to the farm it was from, for going to the source is one of the virtues of living in this small, unhomogenized land of 7½ million people that is modern Austria.

"Is it safe to drink the water?" is still the question I'm asked the most by visitors to Vienna. "It's not only safe," I reply, "it's recommended." Sometimes they call back to thank me for the tip. Piped cold and clean via Roman aqueducts from a couple of Alpine springs, the city's water has been rated the best in the world by such connoisseurs and authorities as the Austrian Academy of Sciences and an international association of solid waste–management engineers. Often on a summer evening, when our guests looked as though a cognac after dinner might be too heavy, I brought out a pitcher of iced tap water, and even our Viennese visitors smacked their lips upon tasting this refreshing novelty. But don't bother to try for it in a tavern; except for a few radical thinkers and the converts I've made, virtually all Viennese drink bottled mineral water, and few waiters will condescend to serve you any other kind.

People say that after two decades in Vienna one must feel very Viennese, and maybe they're right, because here I am chatting about food and drink, which is the principal topic of Viennese conversation. So let me call your attention to three major culinary inventions that were all introduced to Western civilization in Vienna in the watershed year of 1683: coffee, the croissant, and the bagel.

That was the year the second Turkish siege of Vienna was at last repelled, when King Jan Sobieski of Poland and Duke Charles of Lorraine rode to the rescue, thereby saving the West for Christianity. The Sultan's armies left behind their silken tents and banners, some 25,000 dead, and hundreds of huge sacks filled with a mysterious brownish bean. The victorious Viennese didn't know what to make of it—whether to bake, boil, or fry it. But one of their spies, Franz George Kolschitzky, a wheeler-dealer merchant who had traveled in Turkey and spoke the language, had sampled in Constantinople the thick black brew of roasted coffee beans that the Turks called *"Kahve."* Though he could have had almost as many sacks of gold, he settled for beans—and opened history's first Viennese coffeehouse. Business was bad, however, until Kolschitzky tinkered with the recipe and experimented with milk, thus inventing the *mélange:* taste sensation of the 1680s and still the most popular local coffee drink of the 1990s.

While Kolschitzky was roasting his reward, Viennese bakers were celebrating with two new creations that enabled their customers truly to taste victory over the Moslems: a bun curved like a crescent, the emblem of Islam (what Charles of Lorraine might have called *croissant*, Austrians call *Kipferl*), and a roll shaped like Sobieski's stirrup, for which the German word was *Bügel*. The invention of the bagel, however, proved less significant, for it disappeared swiftly and totally, only to resurface in America centuries later, along with Sunday brunch.

Though Vienna's is more a wine culture than a beer culture, in its hundreds of *Heurige* (young-wine taverns identified by a bush over their door) the Viennese male indulges in a beer-garden ritual that I call "airing the paunch." With one or two buttons open, he exposes his belly to sun or moon or just passing admiration. One would be hard put to tell him that Wien (the German name for the capital) is not the navel of the universe, let alone of Austria, but the person who could tell it to him best would be a Vorarlberger. The 305,600 citizens of Austria's westernmost province live as close to Paris as they do to Vienna, which tries to govern them; their capital, Bregenz, is barely an hour's drive from Zurich, but eight or more from Vienna, and the natives sometimes seem more Swiss than Austrian.

1 Essential Information

Before You Go

Government Tourist Offices

By George W. Hamilton

A 30-year resident of Vienna, George Hamilton writes on industry and economy as well as travel and tourism.

In the United States the primary source of information for anyone planning a trip to Austria is the **Austrian National Tourist Office,** 500 5th Ave., 20th floor, New York, NY 10110, tel. 212/944–6880; 11601 Wilshire Blvd., Suite 2480, Los Angeles, CA 90025, tel. 310/477–3332. **In Canada** the offices are at 2 Bloor St. E., Suite 3330, Toronto, Ontario M4W 1A8, tel. 416/967–3381; 1010 Sherbrooke St. W, Suite 1410, Montreal, Quebec H3A 2R7, tel. 514/849–3709; 200 Granville St., Suite 1380, Granville Sq., Vancouver, BC V6C 1S4, tel. 604/683–5808 or 683–8695. **In the United Kingdom,** check with the tourist office at 30 St. George St., London W1R 0AL, tel. 071/629–0461. Ask for the *Holiday Hotline* for the latest resort and price information.

The U.S. Department of State's **Citizens Emergency Center** issues Consular Information Sheets, which cover crime, security, and health risks as well as embassy locations, entry requirements, currency regulations, and other routine matters. For the latest information, stop in at any passport office, consulate, or embassy; call the interactive hotline (tel. 202/647–5225); or, with your PC's modem, tap into the Bureau of Consular Affairs' computer bulletin board (tel. 202/647–9225).

Tours and Packages

Should you buy your travel arrangements to Vienna packaged or do it yourself? There are advantages either way. Buying packaged arrangements saves you money, particularly if you can find a program that includes exactly the features you want. You also get a pretty good idea of what your trip will cost from the outset. Generally, you have two options: fully escorted tours and independent packages. Escorted tours are most often via motorcoach, with a tour director in charge. They're ideal if you don't mind having limited free time and traveling with strangers. Your baggage is handled, your time rigorously scheduled, and most meals planned. Escorted tours are therefore the most hassle-free way to see a destination, as well as generally the least expensive. Independent packages allow plenty of flexibility. They generally include airline travel and hotels, with certain options available, such as sightseeing, car rental, and excursions. Independent packages are usually more expensive than escorted tours, but your time is your own.

While you can book directly through tour operators, you will pay no more to go through a travel agent, who will be able to tell you about tours and packages from a number of operators. Whatever program you ultimately choose, be sure to find out exactly what is included: taxes, tips, transfers, meals, baggage handling, ground transportation, entertainment, excursions, sports or recreation (and rental equipment if necessary). Ask about the level of hotel used, its location, the size of its rooms, the kind of beds, and its amenities, such as pool, room service, or programs for children, if they're important to you. Find out the operator's cancellation penalties. Nearly everyone charges them, and the only way to avoid them is to buy trip-cancellation insurance (*see* Trip Insurance, *below*). Also ask about the single supplement, a surcharge assessed to solo travelers. Some operators do not make you pay it if you agree to be matched up with a roommate of the same sex, even if one is not found by departure time. Remember that a program that has features you won't use, whether for rental sporting equipment or discounted museum admissions, may not be the most cost-wise choice for you.

Fully Escorted Tours   Escorted tours are usually sold in three categories: deluxe, first-class, and tourist or budget class. The most important differences are the price, of course, and the level of accommodations. Some operators specialize in one category, while others offer a range.

Contact **Abercrombie & Kent** (1520 Kensington Rd., Oak Brook, IL 60521, tel. 800/323–7308 or 708/954–2944), **Maupintour** (Box 807, Lawrence, KS 66044, tel. 800/255–4266 or 913/843–1211), and **Tauck Tours** (11 Wilton Rd., Westport, CT 06881, tel. 800/468–2825 or 203/226–6911) in the deluxe category; **American Express Vacations** (300 Pinnacle Way, Norcross, GA 30093, tel. 800/241–1700), **Austrian Airlines** (tel. 800/843–0002), **Brendan Tours** (15137 Califa St., Van Nuys, CA 91411, tel. 800/421–8446 or 818/985–9696), **Caravan** (401 N. Michigan Ave., Suite 3325, Chicago, IL 60611, tel. 800/227–2826 or 312/321–9800), **Delta Dream Vacations** (tel. 800/872–7786), **DER's Europabus Division** (11933 Wilshire Blvd., Los Angeles, CA 90025, tel. 800/937–1234 or 213/479–4140), **European Train Travel** (contact your travel agent), **Globus-Gateway** (95025 Queens Blvd., Rego Park, NY 11374, tel 800/221–0099 or 718/268–7000), **Olson-Travelworld** (Box 10066, Manhattan Beach, CA 90266, tel. 800/421–2255 or 310/546–8400), and **Trafalgar Tours** (21 E. 26th St., New York, NY 10010, tel. 800/843–0103 or 212/689–8977) in the first-class category; and **Cosmos**, a sister company of Globus-Gateway (*see above*), in the budget category.

Most itineraries are jam-packed with sightseeing, so you see a lot in a short amount of time (usually one place per day). To judge just how fast-paced the tour is, review the itinerary carefully. If you are in a different hotel each night, you will be getting up early each day to head out, travel to your next destination, do some sightseeing, have dinner, and go to bed, then you'll start all over again. If you want some free time, make sure it's mentioned in the tour brochure; if you want to be escorted to every meal, confirm that any tour you consider does that. Also, when comparing programs, be sure to find out if the motorcoach is air-conditioned and has a restroom on board. Make your selection based on price and stops on the itinerary.

Independent Packages   Independent packages, which travel agents call FITs (for foreign independent travel), are offered by airlines, tour operators who may also do escorted programs, and any number of other companies from large, established firms to small, new entrepreneurs.

Contact **Abercrombie & Kent, Austrian Airlines, Brendan Tours,** and **DER Tours** (*see above*), as well as **British Airways** (tel. 800/247–9287) and **Continental Airlines' Grand Destinations** (tel. 800/634–5555).

Their programs come in a wide range of prices based on levels of luxury and options—in addition to hotel and airfare, sightseeing, car rental, transfers, admission to local attractions, and other extras. Note that when pricing different packages, it sometimes pays to purchase the same arrangements separately, as when a rock-bottom promotional airfare is being offered, for example. Again, base your choice on what's available at your budget for the destinations you want to visit.

Special-interest Travel Special-interest programs may be fully escorted or independent. Some require a certain amount of expertise, but most are for the average traveler with an interest and are usually hosted by experts in the subject matter. When the program is escorted, it enjoys the advantages and disadvantages of all escorted programs; because your fellow travelers are apt to be passionate or knowledgeable about the subject, they can prove as enjoyable a part of your travel experience as the destination itself. The price range is wide, but the cost is usually higher— sometimes a lot higher—than for ordinary escorted tours and packages, because of the expert guiding and special activities.

Train Travel **Abercrombie & Kent** and **European Train Travel** (*see above*) offer programs through Austria on the restored vintage Venice Simplon Orient-Express.

Music **Dailey-Thorp** (330 W. 58th St., New York, NY 10019, tel. 212/307–1555) offers classical music and opera programs to Salzburg and Vienna.

Biking **Backroads** (1516 5th St., Suite Q333, Berkeley, CA 94710-1740, tel. 800/245–3874 or 510/527–1555) offers a bike trip through Germany and Austria with stays at inns or at campsites.

When to Go

Vienna has two main tourist seasons. The weather usually turns glorious around Easter to mark the start of the summer season and holds until about mid-October, often later. May and early June, September, and October are the pleasantest months for travel; there is less demand for restaurant tables, and hotel prices tend to be lower.

An Italian invasion takes place between Christmas and New Year's Day and over the long Easter weekend, and hotel rooms in Vienna are at a premium; otherwise July and August and the main festivals are the most crowded times.

Climate Vienna has four distinct seasons, all fairly mild. In winter it's wise to check with the automobile clubs for weather conditions, since mountain roads are often blocked, and ice and fog are hazards.

The following are average monthly maximum and minimum temperatures for Vienna:

Jan.	34F	1C	May	66F	19C	Sept.	68F	20C
	25	- 4		50	10		52	11
Feb.	37F	3C	June	73F	23C	Oct.	57F	14C
	27	- 3		57	14		45	7
Mar.	46F	8C	July	77F	25C	Nov.	45F	7C
	34	1		59	15		37	3
Apr.	59F	15C	Aug.	75F	24C	Dec.	37F	3C
	43	6		59	15		30	- 1

Information Sources   For current weather conditions for cities in the United States and abroad, plus the local time and helpful travel tips, call the **Weather Channel Connection** (tel. 900/932–8437; 95¢ per minute) from a touch-tone phone.

Festivals and Seasonal Events

Jan. 1   The **New Year** opens in Vienna with the world-famous concert by the Vienna Philharmonic Orchestra, this year under the direction of Lauren Maazel (Vienna Philharmonic, Musikverein, Bösendorferstr. 12, A–1010 Vienna, tel. 0222/505–6525; write a year—or more—in advance). Those who can't get into the Philharmonic concert try for one of the performances of the Johann Strauss operetta *Die Fledermaus* in the State Opera and Volksoper (Bundestheaterverband, Goethegasse 1, A–1010 Vienna, tel. 0222/513–1513) or for Beethoven's Ninth (Choral) Symphony by the Vienna Symphony Orchestra (Konzerthaus, Lothringerstr. 20, A–1030 Vienna, tel. 0222/712–1211). Those who want to dance their way into the new year can do so at the Kaiserball in the elegant rooms of the Hofburg (WKV, Hofburg, Heldenplatz, A–1014 Vienna, tel. 0222/587–3666–14).

June 2   The religious holiday **Corpus Christi** is celebrated throughout Austria with colorful processions and parades.

Mid-May–mid-June   The **Wiener Festwochen** (Lehargasse 11, A–1060 Vienna, tel. 0222/586–1676) is a festival of theater, music, films, and exhibitions.

July–Aug.   **Musical Summer/Klangbogen** has nightly recitals in one of the city's many palaces or orchestral concerts in the courtyard of the city hall. (Musikalischer Sommer, Friedrich Schmidt-Platz 5, A–1082 Vienna, tel. 0222/4000–8400.)

Sept. 1   This date marks the start of the **theater and music season.** Wiener Fremdenverkehrsverband, Obere Augartenstr. 40, A–1020 Vienna, tel. 0222/211–1400.)

Early Sept.   A series of **trade fairs** packs Vienna during the first weeks of the month; the most interesting is the Hit consumer electronics show, where new products are showcased.

The **International Bruckner Festival** makes Linz come alive: Theater, concerts, fireworks, and art exhibits extend to the St. Florian monastery, where the composer Anton Bruckner worked and is buried (Untere Do naulände 7, A–4010 Linz, tel. 0732/775230).

Mid-Oct.   **Viennale** shows films ranging from the avant-garde to retrospectives (Wiener Filmfestwochen Viennale, Stiftsgasse 8, A–1070 Vienna, tel. 0222/528–5947).

Nov. 11   **St. Martin's Day** is as good as a holiday; restaurants throughout the country serve traditional roast goose and red cabbage in honor of the patron saint of publicans and innkeepers. Called *Martinigansl* or *Ganslessen* ("Martin's goose" or "goose eating"), it's much more than a feast of goose; people celebrate with parties and processions, church services, and village parades.

Dec. 6   On **St. Nicholas's Day** the patron saint of children is honored at *Christkindl* (Christchild) festivals, open-air markets throughout the country selling toys, favors, decorations, and food.

Dec. 24 **Christmas Eve midnight mass** at St. Stephen's cathedral is an impressive, if crowded, event; get an entrance pass at the cathedral in advance.

What to Pack

Clothing Viennese dress conservatively; slacks on women are as rare as loud sport shirts are on men. Jeans are ubiquitous in Vienna as everywhere, but are considered inappropriate at concerts (other than pop) or formal restaurants. For concerts and opera, women may want a skirt or dress, and men a jacket; even in summer, gala performances at small festivals tend to be dressy. And since an evening outside at a *Heuriger* (wine garden) may be on your agenda, be sure to take a sweater or light wrap. Unless you're staying in an expensive hotel or will be in one place for more than a day or two, take hand-washables; laundry service gets complicated. Austria is a walking country. So pack sturdy, comfortable shoes. You'll need flat heels to cope with the cobblestones.

Miscellaneous Bring an extra pair of eyeglasses or contact lenses. Mountainous areas are bright, so bring sunscreen lotion, even in winter. Consider packing a small folding umbrella. If you have a health problem that may require you to purchase a prescription drug, pack enough to last the duration of the trip, or have your doctor write a prescription using the drug's generic name, since brand names vary from country to country. And don't forget to pack a list of the addresses of offices that supply refunds for lost or stolen traveler's checks.

Electricity The electrical current in Austria is 220 volts, 50 cycles alternating current (AC); the United States runs on 110-volt, 60-cycle AC current. Unlike wall outlets in the United States, which accept plugs with two flat prongs, outlets in Austria take continental-type plugs, with two round prongs.

Adapters, To plug in U.S.-made appliances abroad, you'll need an adapter
Converters, plug. To reduce the voltage entering the appliance from 220 to
Transformers 110 volts, you'll also need a converter, unless it is a dual-voltage appliance, made for travel. There are converters for high-wattage appliances (such as hair dryers), low-wattage items (such as electric toothbrushes and razors), and combination models. Hotels sometimes have outlets marked "For Shavers Only" near the sink; these are 110-volt outlets for low-wattage appliances; don't use them for a high-wattage appliance. If you're traveling with a laptop computer, especially an older one, you may need a transformer—a type of converter used with electronic-circuitry products. Newer laptop computers are auto-sensing, operating equally well on 110 and 220 volts (so you need only the appropriate adapter plug). When in doubt, consult your appliance's owner's manual or the manufacturer. Or get a copy of the free brochure "Foreign Electricity Is No Deep Dark Secret," published by adapter-converter manufacturer Franzus (Murtha Industrial Park, Box 142, Beacon Falls, CT 06403, tel. 203/723–6664; send a stamped, self-addressed envelope when ordering).

Luggage Free baggage allowances depend on the airline, the route, and
Regulations the class of your ticket. In general, on domestic flights and on international flights between the United States and foreign destinations, you are entitled to check two bags—neither exceeding 62 inches, or 158 centimeters (length + width +

height), or weighing more than 70 pounds (32 kilograms). A third piece may be brought aboard as a carryon; its total dimensions are generally limited to less than 45 inches (114 centimeters), so it will fit easily under the seat in front of you or in the overhead compartment. There are variations, so ask in advance. The single rule, a Federal Aviation Administration safety regulation that pertains to carry-on baggage on U.S. airlines, requires only that carryons be properly stowed and allows the airline to limit allowances and tailor them to different aircraft and operational conditions. Charges for excess, oversize, or overweight pieces vary, so inquire before you pack.

If you are flying between two foreign destinations, note that baggage allowances may be determined not by piece but by weight, which generally allows 88 pounds (40 kilograms) of luggage in first class, 66 pounds (30 kilograms) in business class, and 44 pounds (20 kilograms) in economy. If your flight between two cities abroad *connects* with your transatlantic or transpacific flight, the piece method still applies.

Safeguarding Your Luggage Before leaving home, itemize your bags' contents and their worth; this list will help you estimate the extent of your loss if your bags go astray. To minimize that risk, tag them inside and out with your name, address, and phone number. (If you use your home address, cover it so that potential thieves can't see it.) At check-in, make sure that the tag attached by baggage handlers bears the correct three-letter code for your destination. If your bags do not arrive with you, or if you detect damage, do not leave the airport until you've filed a written report with the airline.

Taking Money Abroad

Traveler's Checks Although you will want plenty of cash when visiting small cities or rural areas, traveler's checks are usually preferable. The most widely recognized are **American Express, Thomas Cook, Visa,** and those issued by major commercial banks such as **Citibank** and **Bank of America.** American Express also issues *Traveler's Cheques for Two,* which can be counter-signed and used by you or your traveling companion. Some checks are free; usually the issuing company or the bank at which you make your purchase charges 1%–2% of the checks' face value as a fee. Be sure to buy a few checks in small denominations to cash toward the end of your trip, when you don't want to be left with more foreign currency than you can spend. Always record the numbers of checks as you spend them, and keep this list separate from the checks.

Currency Exchange Banks and bank-operated exchange booths at airports and railroad stations are usually the best places to change money. Hotels, stores, and privately run exchange firms typically offer less favorable rates.

Before your trip, pay attention to how the dollar is doing vis-à-vis Austria's currency. If the dollar is losing strength, try to pay as many travel bills as possible in advance, especially the big ones. If it is getting stronger, pay for costly items overseas, and use your credit card whenever possible—you'll come out ahead, whether the exchange rate at which your purchase is calculated is the one in effect the day the vendor's bank abroad processes the charge, or the one prevailing on the day the charge company's service center processes it at home.

To avoid lines at airport currency-exchange booths, arrive in a foreign country with a small amount of the local currency already in your pocket—a so-called tip pack. **Thomas Cook Currency Services** (630 5th Ave., New York, NY 10111, tel. 212/757–6915) supplies foreign currency by mail.

Getting Money from Home

Cash Machines Automated-teller machines (ATMs) are proliferating; many are tied to international networks such as **Cirrus** and **Plus.** You can use your bank card at ATMs away from home to withdraw money from an account and get cash advances on a credit-card account (providing your card has been programmed with a personal identification number, or PIN). Check in advance on limits on withdrawals and cash advances within specified periods. Ask whether your bank-card or credit-card PIN number will need to be reprogrammed for use in the area you'll be visiting—a possibility if the number has more than four digits. Remember that on cash advances you are charged interest from the day you get the money from ATMs as well as from tellers. And note that, although transaction fees for ATM withdrawals abroad will probably be higher than fees for withdrawals at home, Cirrus and Plus exchange rates tend to be good.

Be sure to plan ahead: Obtain ATM locations and the names of affiliated cash-machine networks before departure. For specific foreign Cirrus locations, call 800/424–7787; for foreign Plus locations, consult the Plus directory at your local bank.

American Express Cardholder Services The company's **Express Cash** system lets you withdraw cash and/or traveler's checks from a worldwide network of 57,000 American Express dispensers and participating bank ATMs. You must *enroll first* (call 800/227–4669 for a form and allow two weeks for processing). Withdrawals are charged not to your card but to a designated bank account. You can withdraw up to $1,000 per seven-day period on the basic card, more if your card is gold or platinum. There is a 2% fee (minimum $2.50, maximum $10) for each cash transaction, and a 1% fee for traveler's checks (except for the platinum card), which are available only from American Express dispensers.

At AmEx offices, cardholders can also cash personal checks for up to $1,000 in any seven-day period (21 days abroad); of this $200 can be in cash, more if available, with the balance paid in traveler's checks, for which all but platinum cardholders pay a 1% fee. Higher limits apply to the gold and platinum cards.

Wiring Money You don't have to be a cardholder to send or receive an **American Express MoneyGram** for up to $10,000. To send one, go to an American Express MoneyGram agent, pay up to $1,000 with a credit card and anything over that in cash, and phone a transaction reference number to your intended recipient, who needs only present identification and the reference number to the nearest MoneyGram agent to pick up the cash. There are MoneyGram agents in more than 60 countries (call 800/543–4080 for locations). Fees range from 5% to 10%, depending on the amount and how you pay. You can't use American Express, which is really a convenience card—only Discover, MasterCard, and Visa credit cards.

You can also use **Western Union.** To wire money, take either cash or a check to the nearest office. (Or you can call and use a credit card.) Fees are roughly 5%–10%. Money sent from the United States or Canada will be available for pick up at agent locations in Austria within minutes. (Note that once the money is in the system it can be picked up at *any* location. You don't have to miss your train waiting for it to arrive in City A, because if there's an agent in City B, where you're headed, you can pick it up there, too.) There are approximately 20,000 agents worldwide (call 800/325–6000 for locations).

Austrian Currency

The Austrian unit of currency is the schilling (AS), subdivided into 100 groschen. At this writing, the exchange rate was about AS11.5 to the dollar, AS17 to the pound sterling. These rates can and will vary. The schilling is pegged to the German Deutschemark at a 7-to-1 ratio that remains constant.

There are Austrian coins for 5, 10, and 50 groschen and for 1, 5, 10, and 20 schillings. The paper notes have AS20, AS50, AS100, AS500, AS1,000, and AS5,000 face value. There is little visible difference between the 100- and 500-schilling notes, so be careful, since confusion could be expensive! Legally, foreign exchange is limited to licensed offices (banks and exchange offices); in practice, the rule is universally ignored.

What It Will Cost

Austria continues to offer good value. Indeed, this is the reason behind the annual invasion of Italians, Germans, and Dutch. The Austrians, in turn, are shocked by prices in neighboring countries. Generally, prices for hotels, restaurants, ski lifts, and other costs directly related to tourism have increased less, despite high taxes, than in other major tourist countries.

Taxes Austrian prices include 20% value-added tax (VAT) on most items, 10% on some goods and services. If you buy goods totaling AS1,000 or more in one shop, ask for the appropriate papers *when you make the purchase*, and you can get a refund of the VAT either at the airport when you leave or by mail. You can have the refund credited to your credit card account and not have to worry about the exchange rates. At some resorts, a small local hotel-room tax is added to the bill.

Sample Costs A cup of coffee in a café will cost about AS25; a half-liter of draft beer, AS27–35; a glass of wine, AS32; a Coca-Cola, AS25; an open-face sandwich, AS25; a mid-range theater ticket AS200; a concert ticket AS250; an opera ticket upwards of AS600; a 1-mile taxi ride, AS32. Outside the hotels, laundering a shirt costs about AS30; dry cleaning a suit costs around AS100; a dress, AS70. A shampoo and set for a woman will cost around AS400, a manicure about AS60; a man's haircut (without shampoo) will cost about AS120.

Passports and Visas

If your passport is lost or stolen abroad, report it immediately to the nearest embassy or consulate and to the local police. If you can provide the consular officer with the information contained in the passport, they will usually be able to issue you a new passport. For this reason, it is a good idea to keep a copy of the data page of your passport in a separate place, or to leave the passport number, date, and place of issuance with a relative or friend at home.

U.S. Citizens All U.S. citizens, even infants, need a valid passport to enter Austria for stays of up to three months. You can pick up new and renewal application forms at any of the 13 U.S. Passport Agency offices and at some post offices and courthouses. Although passports are usually mailed within two weeks of your application's receipt, it's best to allow three weeks for delivery in low season, five weeks or more from April through summer. Call the Department of State Office of Passport Services' information line (1425 K St. NW, Washington, DC 20522, tel. 202/647–0518) for fees, documentation requirements, and other details.

Canadian Citizens Canadian citizens need a valid passport to enter Austria for stays of up to three months. Application forms are available at 23 regional passport offices as well as post offices and travel agencies. Whether applying for a first or subsequent passport, you must apply in person. Children under 16 may be included on a parent's passport but must have their own passport to travel alone. Passports are valid for five years and are usually mailed within two weeks of an application's receipt. For fees, documentation requirements, and other information in English or French, call the passport office (tel. 514/283–2152).

U.K. Citizens Citizens of the United Kingdom need a valid passport to enter Austria for stays of up to six months. Applications for new and renewal passports are available from main post offices as well as at the six passport offices, located in Belfast, Glasgow, Liverpool, London, Newport, and Peterborough. You may apply in person at all passport offices, or by mail to all except the London office. Children under 16 may travel on a parent's passport when accompanying them. All passports are valid for 10 years. Allow a month for processing.

A British Visitor's Passport is valid for holidays and some business trips of up to three months to Austria. It can include both partners of a married couple. Valid for one year, it will be issued on the same day that you apply. You must apply in person at a main post office.

Customs and Duties

On Arrival Travelers over 17 *coming from European countries*—regardless of citizenship—may bring in duty-free 200 cigarettes or 50 cigars or 250 grams of tobacco, two liters of wine and one liter of spirits, one bottle of toilet water (approx. 300 ml), and 50 milliliters of perfume. These limits may be liberalized or eliminated under terms of the European Economic Area agreement. Travelers *from all other countries* (such as those coming directly from the United States or Canada) may bring in *twice* these amounts.

Returning Home Provided you've been out of the country for at least 48 hours
U.S. Customs and haven't already used the exemption, or any part of it, in the past 30 days, you may bring home $400 worth of foreign goods duty-free. So can each member of your family, regardless of age; and your exemptions may be pooled, so one of you can bring in more if another brings in less. A flat 10% duty applies to the next $1,000 of goods; above $1,400, the rate varies with the merchandise. (If the 48-hour or 30-day limits apply, your

duty-free allowance drops to $25, which may not be pooled.)
Please note that these are the *general* rules, applicable to most
countries, including Austria.

Travelers 21 or older may bring back 1 liter of alcohol duty-
free, provided the beverage laws of the state through which
they reenter the United States allow it. In addition, 100 non-
Cuban cigars and 200 cigarettes are allowed, regardless of your
age. Antiques and works of art more than 100 years old are
duty-free.

Gifts valued at less than $50 may be mailed duty-free to state-
side friends and relatives, with a limit of one package per day
per addressee (do not send alcohol or tobacco products, nor perfume valued at more than $5). These gifts do not count as part
of your exemption, unless you bring them home with you. Mark
the package "Unsolicited Gift" and include the nature of the
gift and its retail value.

For a copy of "Know Before You Go," a free brochure detailing
what you may and may not bring back to the United States,
rates of duty, and other pointers, contact the **U.S. Customs
Service** (Box 7407, Washington, DC 20044, tel. 202/927–6724).

Canadian Customs Once per calendar year, when you've been out of Canada for at
least seven days, you may bring in $300 worth of goods duty-
free. If you've been away less than seven days but more than 48
hours, the duty-free exemption drops to $100 but can be
claimed any number of times (as can a $20 duty-free exemption
for absences of 24 hours or more). You cannot combine the yearly and 48-hour exemptions, use the $300 exemption only par-
tially (to save the balance for a later trip), or pool exemptions
with family members. Goods claimed under the $300 exemption
may follow you by mail; those claimed under the lesser exemptions must accompany you on your return.

Alcohol and tobacco products may be included in the yearly and
48-hour exemptions but not in the 24-hour exemption. If you
meet the age requirements of the province through which you
reenter Canada, you may bring in, duty-free, 1.14 liters (40 imperial ounces) of wine or liquor *or* two dozen 12-ounce cans or
bottles of beer or ale. If you are 16 or older, you may bring in,
duty-free, 200 cigarettes, 50 cigars or cigarillos, and 400 tobacco sticks or 400 grams of manufactured tobacco. Alcohol and tobacco must accompany you on your return.

Gifts may be mailed to friends in Canada duty-free. These do
not count as part of your exemption. Each gift may be worth up
to of $60—label the package "Unsolicited Gift—Value under
$60." There are no limits on the number of gifts that may be
sent per day or per addressee, but you can't mail alcohol or tobacco.

For more information, including details of duties on items that
exceed your duty-free limit, ask the Revenue Canada Customs
and Excise Department (Connaught Bldg., MacKenzie Ave.,
Ottawa, Ont., K1A OL5, tel. 613/957–0275) for a copy of the
free brochure "I Declare/Je Déclare."

U.K. Customs If your journey was wholly within EC countries, you no longer
need to pass through customs when you return to the United
Kingdom. According to EC guidelines, you may bring in 800
cigarettes, 400 cigarillos, 200 cigars, and 1 kilogram of smoking
tobacco, plus 10 liters of spirits, 20 liters of fortified wine, 90

liters of wine, and 110 liters of beer. If you exceed these limits, you may be required to prove that the goods are for your personal use or are gifts.

For further information or a copy of "A Guide for Travellers," which details standard customs procedures as well as what you may bring into the United Kingdom from abroad, contact HM Customs and Excise (New King's Beam House, 22 Upper Ground, London SE1 9PJ, tel. 071/620–1313).

Traveling with Cameras, Camcorders, and Laptops

About Film and Cameras If your camera is new or if you haven't used it for a while, shoot and develop a few rolls of film before leaving home. Pack some lens tissue and an extra battery for your built-in light meter, and invest in an inexpensive skylight filter, to both protect your lens and provide some definition in hazy shots. Store film in a cool, dry place—never in the car's glove compartment or on the shelf under the rear window.

Films above ISO 400 are more sensitive to damage from airport security X-rays than others; very high speed films, ISO 1,000 and above, are exceedingly vulnerable. To protect your film, don't put it in checked luggage; carry it with you in a plastic bag and ask for a hand inspection. Such requests are honored at American airports, up to the inspector abroad. Don't depend on a lead-lined bag to protect film in checked luggage—the airline may very well turn up the dosage of radiation to see what you've got in there. Airport metal detectors do not harm film, although you'll set off the alarm if you walk through one with a roll in your pocket. Call the Kodak Information Center (tel. 800/242–2424) for details.

About Camcorders Before your trip, put new or long-unused camcorders through their paces, and practice panning and zooming. Invest in a skylight filter to protect the lens, and check the lithium battery that lights up the LCD (liquid crystal display) modes. As for the rechargeable nickel-cadmium batteries that are the camera's power source, take along an extra pair, so while you're using your camcorder you'll have one battery ready and another recharging. Most newer camcorders are equipped with the battery (which generally slides or clicks onto the camera body) and, to recharge it, with what's known as a universal or worldwide AC adapter charger (or multivoltage converter) that can be used whether the voltage is 110 or 220. All that's needed is the appropriate plug.

About Videotape Unlike still-camera film, videotape is not damaged by X-rays. However, it may well be harmed by the magnetic field of a walk-through metal detector. Airport security personnel may want you to turn the camcorder on to prove that that's what it is, so make sure the battery is charged when you get to the airport. Note that although the United States, Canada, Japan, Korea, Taiwan, and other countries operate on the National Television System Committee video standard (NTSC), Austria uses PAL technology. So you will not be able to view your tapes through the local TV set or view movies bought there in your home VCR. Blank tapes bought in Austria can be used for NTSC camcorder taping, however—although you'll probably find they cost more in Austria and wish you'd brought an adequate supply along.

About Laptops Security X-rays do not harm hard-disk or floppy-disk storage. Most airlines allow you to use your laptop aloft but request that you turn it off during takeoff and landing so as not to interfere with navigation equipment. Make sure the battery is charged when you arrive at the airport, because you may be asked to turn on the computer at security checkpoints to prove that it is what it appears to be. If you're a heavy computer user, consider traveling with a backup battery. For international travel, register your laptop with U.S. Customs as you leave the country, providing it's manufactured abroad (U.S.-origin items cannot be registered at U.S. Customs); when you do so, you'll get a certificate, good for as long as you own the item, containing your name and address, a description of the laptop, and its serial number, that will quash any questions that may arise on your return. If your laptop is U.S.-made, call the consulate of the country you'll be visiting to find out whether it should be registered with customs in that country upon arrival. Some travelers do this as a matter of course and ask customs officers to sign a document that specifies the total configuration of the system, computer and peripherals, and its value. In addition, before leaving home, find out about repair facilities at your destination, and don't forget any transformer or adapter plug you may need (*see* Electricity, *above*).

Language

German is the official national language in Austria. In Vienna and in most resort areas, you will have no problem finding people who speak English; hotel and restaurant staffs in particular speak it reasonably well, and most young Austrians speak it at least passably.

Staying Healthy

Shots and Medications No special shots are required before visiting Austria, but if you will be cycling or hiking through the eastern or southeastern parts of the country, get inoculated against encephalitis; it can be carried by ticks.

Finding a Doctor The **International Association for Medical Assistance to Travelers** (IAMAT, 417 Center St., Lewiston, NY 14092, tel. 716/754–4883; 40 Regal Rd., Guelph, Ontario N1K 1B5; 57 Voirets, 1212 Grand-Lancy, Geneva, Switzerland) publishes a worldwide directory of English-speaking physicians whose qualifications meet IAMAT standards and who have agreed to treat members for a set fee. Membership is free.

Assistance Companies Pretrip medical referrals, emergency evacuation or repatriation, 24-hour telephone hot lines for medical consultation, dispatch of medical personnel, relay of medical records, up-front cash for emergencies, and other personal and legal assistance are among the services provided by several membership organizations specializing in medical assistance to travelers. Among them are **International SOS Assistance** (Box 11568, Philadelphia, PA 19116, tel. 215/244–1500 or 800/523–8930; Box 466, Pl. Bonaventure, Montréal, Qué. H5A 1C1, tel. 514/874–7674 or 800/363–0263), **Near Services** (450 Prairie Ave., Suite 101, Calumet City, IL 60409, tel. 708/868–6700 or 800/654–6700), and **Travel Assistance International** (1133 15th St. NW, Suite 400, Washington, DC 20005, tel. 202/331–1609 or 800/821–2828), part of Europ Assistance Worldwide Services, Inc.

Because these companies will also sell you death-and-dismemberment, trip-cancellation, and other insurance coverage, there is some overlap with the travel-insurance policies discussed below, which may include the services of an assistance company among the insurance options or reimburse travelers for such services without providing them.

Insurance

For U.S. Residents Most tour operators, travel agents, and insurance agents sell specialized health-and-accident, flight, trip-cancellation, and luggage insurance as well as comprehensive policies with some or all of these features. But before you make any purchase, review your existing health and homeowner policies to find out whether they cover expenses incurred while traveling.

Health-and-Accident Insurance Supplemental health-and-accident insurance for travelers is usually a part of comprehensive policies. Specific policy provisions vary, but they tend to address three general areas, beginning with reimbursement for medical expenses caused by illness or an accident during a trip. Such policies may reimburse anywhere from $1,000 to $150,000 worth of medical expenses; dental benefits may also be included. A second common feature is the personal-accident, or death-and-dismemberment, provision, which pays a lump sum to your beneficiaries if you die or to you if you lose one or both limbs or your eyesight. This is similar to the flight insurance described below, although it is not necessarily limited to accidents involving airplanes or even other "common carriers" (buses, trains, and ships) and can be in effect 24 hours a day. The lump sum awarded can range from $15,000 to $500,000. A third area generally addressed by these policies is medical assistance (referrals, evacuation, or repatriation and other services). Some policies reimburse travelers for the cost of such services; others may automatically enroll you as a member of a particular medical-assistance company.

Flight Insurance This insurance, often bought as a last-minute impulse at the airport, pays a lump sum to a beneficiary when a plane crashes and the insured dies (and sometimes to a surviving passenger who loses eyesight or a limb); thus it supplements the airlines' own coverage as described in the limits-of-liability paragraphs on your ticket (up to $75,000 on international flights, $20,000 on domestic ones—and that is generally subject to litigation). Charging an airline ticket to a major credit card often automatically signs you up for flight insurance; in this case, the coverage may also embrace travel by bus, train, and ship.

Baggage Insurance In the event of loss, damage, or theft on international flights, airlines limit their liability to $20 per kilogram for checked baggage (roughly about $640 per 70-pound bag) and $400 per passenger for unchecked baggage. On domestic flights, the ceiling is $1,250 per passenger. Excess-valuation insurance can be bought directly from the airline at check-in but leaves your bags vulnerable on the ground.

Trip Insurance There are two sides to this coin. **Trip-cancellation-and-interruption insurance** protects you in the event you are unable to undertake or finish your trip. **Default** or **bankruptcy insurance** protects you against a supplier's failure to deliver. Consider the former if your airline ticket, cruise, or package tour does not allow changes or cancellations. The amount of coverage to buy should equal the cost of your trip should you, a traveling companion, or a family member get sick, forcing you to stay home, plus the nondiscounted one-way airline ticket you would need to buy if you had to return home early. Read the fine print carefully; pay attention to sections defining "family member" and "preexisting medical conditions." A characteristic quirk of default policies is that they often do not cover default by travel agencies or default by a tour operator, airline, or cruise line if you bought your tour and the coverage directly from the firm in question. To reduce your need for default insurance, give preference to tours packaged by members of the United States Tour Operators Association (USTOA), which maintains a fund to reimburse clients in the event of member defaults. Even better, pay for travel arrangements with a major credit card, so that you can refuse to pay the bill if services have not been rendered—and let the card company fight your battles.

Comprehensive Policies Companies supplying comprehensive policies with some or all of the above features include **Access America, Inc.,** underwritten by BCS Insurance Company (Box 11188, Richmond, VA 23230, tel. 800/284–8300); **Carefree Travel Insurance,** underwritten by The Hartford (Box 310, 120 Mineola Blvd., Mineola, NY 11501, tel. 516/294–0220 or 800/323–3149); **Tele-Trip** (Mutual of Omaha Plaza, Box 31762, Omaha, NE 68131, tel. 800/228–9792), a subsidiary of Mutual of Omaha; **The Travelers Companies** (1 Tower Sq., Hartford, CT 06183, tel. 203/277–0111 or 800/243–3174); **Travel Guard International,** underwritten by Transamerica Occidental Life Companies (1145 Clark St., Stevens Point, WI 54481, tel. 715/345–0505 or 800/782–5151); and **Wallach and Company, Inc.** (107 W. Federal St., Box 480, Middleburg, VA 22117, tel. 703/687–3166 or 800/237–6615), underwritten by Lloyds, London. These companies may also offer the above types of insurance separately.

U.K. Residents Most tour operators, travel agents, and insurance agents sell specialized policies covering accident, medical expenses, personal liability, trip cancellation, and loss or theft of personal property. Some policies include coverage for delayed departure and legal expenses, winter sports, accidents, or motoring abroad. You can also purchase an annual travel-insurance policy valid for every trip you make during the year in which it's purchased (usually only trips of less than 90 days). Before you leave, make sure you will be covered if you have a preexisting medical condition or are pregnant; your insurers may not pay for routine or continuing treatment, or may require a note from your doctor certifying your fitness to travel.

For advice by phone or a free booklet, "Holiday Insurance," that sets out what to expect from a holiday-insurance policy and gives price guidelines, contact the **Association of British Insurers** (51 Gresham St., London EC2V 7HQ, tel. 071/600–3333; 30 Gordon St., Glasgow G1 3PU, tel. 041/226–3905; Scottish Provincial Bldg., Donegall Sq. W, Belfast BT1 6JE, tel. 0232/249176; call for other locations).

Car Rentals

Most major car-rental companies are represented in Austria, including **Avis** (tel. 800/331–1084, 800/879–2847 in Canada); **Budget** (tel. 800/527–0700); **Dollar** (tel. 800/800–6000); **Hertz** (tel. 800/654–3001, 800/263-0600 in Canada); **National** (tel. 800/

227–3876), known internationally as InterRent and Europcar. Among the cheapest local rental firms is **Autoverleih Buchbinder** (Schlachthausgasse 38, A–1030 Vienna, tel. 0222/71750, 0222/717–5021, fax 0222/717–5022, with offices throughout Austria). In cities, unlimited-mileage rates range from about $30 per day for an economy car to about $50 for a large car; weekly unlimited-mileage rates range from $181 to $356. This does not include VAT tax, which in Austria is 21.2% on car rentals.

Requirements Your own U.S., Canadian, or U.K. driver's license is acceptable. An International Driver's Permit, available from the American or Canadian Automobile Association, is a good idea.

Extra Charges Picking up the car in one city or country and leaving it in another may entail drop-off charges or one-way service fees, which can be substantial. The cost of a collision or loss-damage waiver (*see below*) can be high, also. Automatic transmissions and air-conditioning are not universally available abroad; ask for them when you book if you want them, and check the cost before you commit yourself to the rental.

Cutting Costs If you know you will want a car for more than a day or two, you can save by planning ahead. Major international companies have programs that discount their standard rates by 15%–30% if you make the reservation before departure (anywhere from two to 14 days), rent for a minimum number of days (typically three or four), and prepay the rental. Ask about these advance-purchase schemes when you call for information. More economical rentals are those that come as part of fly/drive or other packages, even those as bare-bones as the rental plus an airline ticket (*see* Tours and Packages, *above*).

Other sources of savings are the companies that operate as wholesalers—companies that do not own their own fleets but rent in bulk from those that do and offer advantageous rates to their customers. Rentals through such companies must be arranged and paid for before you leave the United States. Among them are **Auto Europe** (Box 1097, Camden, ME 04843, tel. 207/236–8235 or 800/223–5555, 800/458–9503 in Canada), **Connex International** (23 N. Division St., Peekskill, NY 10566, tel. 914/739–0066, 800/333–3949, 800/843–5416 in Canada), **Europe by Car** (mailing address, 1 Rockefeller Plaza, New York, NY 10020; walk-in address, 14 W. 49th St., New York, NY 10020, tel. 212/581–3040 or 212/245–1713; 9000 Sunset Blvd., Los Angeles, CA 90069, tel. 213/252–9401 or 800/223–1516 in CA), **Foremost Euro-Car** (5430 Van Nuys Blvd., Suite 306, Van Nuys, CA 91401, tel. 818/786–1960 or 800/272–3299), and **Kemwel** (106 Calvert St., Harrison, NY 10528, tel. 914/835–5555 or 800/678–0678). These wholesalers' deals are even better in summer, when business travel is down. Always ask whether the prices are guaranteed in U.S. dollars or foreign currency and if unlimited mileage is available. Find out about any required deposits, cancellation penalties, and drop-off charges, and confirm the cost of the CDW.

One last tip: Remember to fill the tank when you turn in the vehicle, to avoid being charged for refueling at what you'll swear is the most expensive pump in town.

Insurance and Collision Damage Waiver The standard rental contract includes liability coverage (for damage to public property, injury to pedestrians, etc.) and coverage for the car against fire, theft (not included in certain countries), and collision damage with a deductible—most commonly $2,000–$3,000, occasionally more. In the case of an accident, you are responsible for the deductible amount unless you've purchased the collision damage waiver (CDW), which costs an average $12 a day, although this varies depending on what you've rented, where, and from whom.

Because this adds up quickly, you may be inclined to say "no thanks"—and that's certainly your option, although the rental agent may not tell you so. Note before you decline that deductibles are occasionally high enough that totaling a car would make you responsible for its full value. Planning ahead will help you make the right decision. By all means, find out if your own insurance covers damage to a rental car while traveling (not simply a car to drive when yours is in for repairs). And check whether charging car rentals to any of your credit cards will get you a CDW at no charge.

Rail Passes

Austria is one of 17 countries in which you can use **EurailPasses,** which provide unlimited first-class rail travel during their period of validity. If you plan to rack up the miles, they can be an excellent value. Standard passes are available for 15 days ($460), 21 days ($598), one month ($728), two months ($998), and three months ($1,260). **Eurail Saverpasses,** valid for 15 days, cost $390 per person; you must do all your traveling with at least one companion (two companions from April through September). **Eurail Youthpasses,** which cover second-class travel, cost $508 for one month, $698 for two; you must be under 26 on the first day you travel. Flexipasses allow you to travel for five, 10, or 15 days within any two-month period. You pay $298, $496, and $676 for the **Eurail Flexipass,** sold for first-class travel; and $220, $348, $474 for the **Eurail Youth Flexipass,** available to those under 26 on their first travel day, sold for second-class travel. Apply through your travel agent, or **Rail Europe** (226–230 Westchester Ave., White Plains, NY 10604, tel. 914/682–5172 or 800/848–7245 from the East and 800/438–7245 from the West).

Don't make the mistake of assuming that your rail pass guarantees you seats on the trains you want to ride. Seat reservations are required on some trains, particularly high-speed trains, and are a good idea on trains that may be crowded. You will also need reservations for overnight sleeping accommodations. Rail Europe can help you determine if you need reservations and can make them for you (about $10 each, less if you purchase them in Europe at the time of travel). *See also* Staying in Austria: Getting Around by Train, *below.*

Student and Youth Travel

ÖKISTA-Reisen (Türkenstr. 6, A–1090 Vienna, tel. 0222/410–480, and at Karlsgasse 3, A–1040, tel. 022/505–0128) organizes student travel and cheap charters in Austria. It arranges standby and other inexpensive flights and weekend excursions to Budapest, Prague, and other Eastern European cities.

Travel Agencies The foremost U.S. student travel agency is **Council Travel,** a subsidiary of the nonprofit Council on International Educational Exchange. It specializes in low-cost travel arrangements, is the exclusive U.S. agent for several discount cards, and, with its sister CIEE subsidiary, **Council Charter,** is a source of airfare bargains. The Council Charter brochure and CIEE's twice-yearly *Student Travels* magazine, which details its programs, are available at the Council Travel office at CIEE headquarters (205 E. 42nd St., New York, NY 10017, tel. 212/661–1450) and at 37 branches in college towns nationwide (free in person, $1 by mail). The **Educational Travel Center** (ETC, 438 N. Francis St., Madison, WI 53703, tel. 608/256–5551) also offers low-cost rail passes, domestic and international airline tickets (mostly for flights departing from Chicago), and other budgetwise travel arrangements. Other travel agencies catering to students include **Travel Management International** (TMI, 18 Prescott St., Suite 4, Cambridge, MA 02138, tel. 617/661–8187) and **Travel Cuts** (187 College St., Toronto, Ont. M5T 1P7, tel. 416/979–2406).

Discount Cards For discounts on transportation and on museum and attractions admissions, buy the **International Student Identity Card** (ISIC) if you're a bona fide student, or the **International Youth Card** (IYC) if you're under 26. In the United States the ISIC and IYC cards cost $15 each and include basic travel accident and sickness coverage. Apply to **CIEE** (*see* address *above*, tel. 212/661–1414; the application is in *Student Travels*). In Canada the cards are available for $15 each from **Travel Cuts** (*see above*). In the United Kingdom they cost £5 and £4 respectively at student unions and student travel companies, including Council Travel's London office (28A Poland St., London W1V 3DB, tel. 071/437–7767).

Hosteling In Austria, youth hostels are coordinated through the Österreichische **Jugendherbergverband** (Gonzagagasse 22, A–1010 Vienna, tel. 0222/533–5353), which can help you plan a hostel holiday of hiking, cycling, or camping.

An **International Youth Hostel Federation** (IYHF) membership card is the key to more than 5,300 hostel locations in 59 countries; the sex-segregated, dormitory-style sleeping quarters, including some for families, go for $7–$20 a night per person. Membership is available in the United States through **American Youth Hostels** (AYH, 733 15th St. NW, Washington, DC 20005, tel. 202/783–6161), the American link in the worldwide chain, and costs $25 for adults 18–54, $10 for those under 18, $15 for those 55 and over, and $35 for families. Volume 1 of the two-volume *Guide to Budget Accommodation* lists hostels in Europe and the Mediterranean ($13.95, including postage). IYHF membership is available in Canada through the **Canadian Hostelling Association** (1600 James Naismith Dr., Suite 608, Gloucester, Ont. K1B 5N4, tel. 613/748–5638) for $26.75, and in the United Kingdom through the **Youth Hostel Association of England and Wales** (8 St. Stephen's Hill, St. Albans, Herts. AL1 2DY, tel. 0727/55215) for £9.

Traveling with Children

Publications *Family Travel Times,* published 10 times a year by **Travel With**
Newsletter **Your Children** (TWYCH, 45 W. 18th St., 7th Floor Tower, New York, NY 10011, tel. 212/206–0688; annual subscription $55), covers destinations, types of vacations, and modes of travel.

Books *Traveling with Children—And Enjoying It,* by Arlene K. Butler ($11.95 plus $3 shipping per book; Globe Pequot Press, Box

833, Old Saybrook, CT 06475, tel. 800/243–0495, or 800/962–0973 in CT), helps plan your trip with children, from toddlers to teens. *Innocents Abroad: Traveling with Kids in Europe,* by Valerie Wolf Deutsch and Laura Sutherland ($15.95 or $4.95 paperback, Penguin USA, *see above*), covers child- and teen-friendly activities, food, and transportation.

Tour Operators   **GrandTravel** (6900 Wisconsin Ave., Suite 706, Chevy Chase, MD 20815, tel. 301/986–0790 or 800/247–7651) offers international and domestic tours for grandparents traveling with their grandchildren. The catalogue, as charmingly written and illustrated as a children's book, positively invites armchair traveling with lap-sitters aboard. **Families Welcome!** (21 W. Colony Pl., Suite 140, Durham, NC 27705, tel. 919/489–2555 or 800/326–0724) packages and sells family tours to Europe. **Rascals in Paradise** (650 5th St., Suite 505, San Francisco, CA 94107, tel. 415/978–9800, or 800/872–7225) specializes in programs for families.

Getting There
Airfares   On international flights, the fare for infants under 2 not occupying a seat is generally 10% of the accompanying adult's fare; children ages 2–11 usually pay half to two-thirds of the adult fare. On domestic flights, children under 2 not occupying a seat travel free, and older children currently travel on the "lowest applicable" adult fare.

Baggage   In general, infants paying 10% of the adult fare are allowed one carry-on bag, not to exceed 70 pounds or 45 inches (length + width + height). The adult baggage allowance applies for children paying half or more of the adult fare. Check with the airline for particulars, especially regarding flights between two foreign destinations, where allowances for infants may be less generous than those above.

Safety Seats   The FAA recommends the use of safety seats aloft and details approved models in the free leaflet "**Child/Infant Safety Seats Recommended for Use in Aircraft**" (available from the Federal Aviation Administration, APA–200, 800 Independence Ave. SW, Washington, DC 20591, tel. 202/267–3479). Airline policy varies. U.S. carriers must allow FAA-approved models, but because these seats are strapped into a regular passenger seat, they may require that parents buy a ticket even for an infant under 2 who would otherwise ride free. Foreign carriers may not allow infant seats, may charge the child's rather than the infant's fare for their use, or may require you to hold your baby during takeoff and landing, thus defeating the seat's purpose.

Facilities Aloft   Airlines do provide other facilities and services for children, such as children's meals and freestanding bassinets (to those sitting in seats on the bulkhead, where there's enough legroom to accommodate them). Make your request when reserving. The annual February/March issue of *Family Travel Times* gives details of the children's services of dozens of airlines ($10; *see above*). "Kids and Teens in Flight" (free from the U.S. Department of Transportation, tel. 202/366–2220) offers tips for children flying alone.

Lodging   Most hotels in Austria welcome children and will arrange special beds and baby-sitters. There's even a hotel in Carinthia named **Austria's First Baby Hotel** (Trebesing Bad 1, A–9852 Trebesing, tel. 04732/2350) where parents accompany the babies instead of the other way around; services for the babies are incredible! Ask for the brochure on hotels with special facilities for children at any Austrian National Tourist Offices. Many of the smaller holiday hotels are family-run and have special programs for younger guests that leave parents free.

Baby-sitting Concierges can arrange reliable baby-sitting, but make your
Services request a day in advance; don't expect baby-sitters at a moment's notice. In Vienna, you can call on the **Babysitter** of the Austrian Academic Guest Service (Mühlgasse 20, A–1040, tel. 0222/587–3525). Since the organization draws mainly on students for their sitters, you can arrange for someone who speaks English.

Hints for Travelers with Disabilities

The Austrian National Tourist Office can provide a guide to accessible Austrian hotels. The tourist office in New York City also has a guide to Vienna for the disabled, a special map of the city's accessible sights, and a booklet on Vienna with facilities for travelers with disabilities. The Hilton, InterContinental, and Marriott chain hotels plus a number of smaller ones are accessible. The railroads are both understanding and helpful. If prior arrangements have been made, taxis and private vehicles are allowed to drive right to the train platform; railway personnel will help with boarding and leaving trains; and with three days' notice, a special wheelchair can be provided for getting around train corridors.

Once in Austria, check with the **Österreichischer Zivilinvalidenverband** (Lange Gasse 60, A–1080 Vienna, tel. 0222/408–5505) for more information. The **Sozialamt der Stadt Wien** (Gonzagagasse 23, A–1010, tel. 0222/531140) and the **Vienna Tourist Office** (Obere Augartenstr. 40, A–1020, tel. 0222/211140) also have the booklet on Vienna hotels and the city guide for the disabled. A number of stations in the Vienna subway system have only stairs or escalators, no elevators.

Organizations Several organizations provide travel information for people with disabilities, usually for a membership fee, and some publish newsletters and bulletins. Among them are the **Information Center for Individuals with Disabilities** (Fort Point Pl., 27–43 Wormwood St., Boston, MA 02210, tel. 617/727–5540 or 800/462–5015 in MA between 11 and 4, or leave message; TDD/TTY tel. 617/345–9743); **Mobility International USA** (Box 3551, Eugene, OR 97403, voice and TDD tel. 503/343–1284), the U.S. branch of an international organization based in Britain (*see below*) and present in 30 countries; **MossRehab Hospital Travel Information Service** (1200 W. Tabor Rd., Philadelphia, PA 19141, tel. 215/456–9603, TDD tel. 215/456–9602); the **Society for the Advancement of Travel for the Handicapped** (SATH, 347 5th Ave., Suite 610, New York, NY 10016, tel. 212/447–7284, fax 212/725–8253); the **Travel Industry and Disabled Exchange** (TIDE, 5435 Donna Ave., Tarzana, CA 91356, tel. 818/368–5648); and **Travelin' Talk** (Box 3534, Clarksville, TN 37043, tel. 615/552–6670).

In the United Main information sources include the **Royal Association for Dis-**
Kingdom **ability and Rehabilitation** (RADAR, 25 Mortimer St., London W1N 8AB, tel. 071/637–5400), which publishes travel information for the disabled in Britain, and **Mobility International** (228 Borough High St., London SE1 1JX, tel. 071/403–5688), the headquarters of an international membership organization

Hints for Older Travelers   **21**

that serves as a clearinghouse of travel information for people with disabilities.

Travel Agencies and Tour Operators   **Directions Unlimited** (720 N. Bedford Rd., Bedford Hills, NY 10507, tel. 914/241–1700), a travel agency, has expertise in tours and cruises for the disabled. **Evergreen Travel Service** (4114 198th St. SW, Suite 13, Lynnwood, WA 98036, tel. 206/776–1184 or 800/435–2288) operates Wings on Wheels Tours for those in wheelchairs, White Cane Tours for the blind, and tours for the deaf and makes group and independent arrangements for travelers with any disability. **Flying Wheels Travel** (143 W. Bridge St., Box 382, Owatonna, MN 55060, tel. 800/535–6790 or 800/722–9351 in MN), a tour operator and travel agency, arranges international tours, cruises, and independent travel itineraries for people with mobility disabilities. **Nautilus,** at the same address as TIDE (_see above_), packages tours for the disabled internationally.

Publications   In addition to the fact sheets, newsletters, and books mentioned above are several free publications available from the Consumer Information Center (Pueblo, CO 81009): "New Horizons for the Air Traveler with a Disability," a U.S. Department of Transportation booklet describing changes resulting from the 1986 Air Carrier Access Act and those still to come from the 1990 Americans with Disabilities Act (include Department 608Y in the address), and the Airport Operators Council's _Access Travel: Airports_ (Dept. 5804), which describes facilities and services for the disabled at more than 500 airports worldwide.

Twin Peaks Press (Box 129, Vancouver, WA 98666, tel. 206/694–2462 or 800/637–2256) publishes the _Directory of Travel Agencies for the Disabled_ ($19.95), listing more than 370 agencies worldwide; _Travel for the Disabled_ ($19.95), listing some 500 access guides and accessible places worldwide; the _Directory of Accessible Van Rentals_ ($9.95) for campers and RV travelers worldwide; and _Wheelchair Vagabond_ ($14.95), a collection of personal travel tips. Add $2 per book for shipping.

Hints for Older Travelers

Austria has so many senior citizens that facilities almost everywhere cater to the needs of older travelers, with discounts for rail travel and museum entry. Check with the Austrian National Tourist Office to find what form of identification is required.

Organizations   The **American Association of Retired Persons** (AARP, 601 E St. NW, Washington, DC 20049, tel. 202/434–2277) provides independent travelers the Purchase Privilege Program, which offers discounts on hotels, car rentals, and sightseeing, and arranges group tours, cruises, and apartment living through AARP Travel Experience from American Express (400 Pinnacle Way, Suite 450, Norcross, GA 30071, tel. 800/927–0111); these can be booked through travel agents, except for the cruises, which must be booked directly (tel. 800/745–4567). AARP membership is open to those 50 and over; annual dues are $8 per person or couple.

Two other membership organizations offer discounts on lodgings, car rentals, and other travel products, along with such nontravel perks as magazines and newsletters. The **National Council of Senior Citizens** (1331 F St. NW, Washington, DC

20004, tel. 202/347–8800) is a nonprofit advocacy group with some 5,000 local clubs across the United States; membership costs $12 per person or couple annually. **Mature Outlook** (6001 N. Clark St., Chicago, IL 60660, tel. 800/336–6330), a Sears Roebuck & Co. subsidiary with 800,000 members, charges $9.95 for an annual membership.

Note: When using any senior-citizen identification card for reduced hotel rates, mention it when booking, not when checking out. At restaurants, show your card before you're seated; discounts may be limited to certain menus, days, or hours. If you are renting a car, ask about promotional rates that might improve on your senior-citizen discount.

Educational Travel **Elderhostel** (75 Federal St., 3rd floor, Boston, MA 02110, tel. 617/426–7788) is a nonprofit organization that has offered inexpensive study programs for people 60 and older since 1975. Programs take place at more than 1,800 educational institutions in the United States, Canada, and 45 countries; and courses cover everything from marine science to Greek myths and cowboy poetry. Participants generally attend lectures in the morning and spend the afternoon sightseeing or on field trips; they live in dorms on the host campuses. Fees for two- to three-week international trips—including room, board, and transportation from the United States—range from $1,800 to $4,500.

Interhostel (University of New Hampshire, 6 Garrison Ave., Durham, NH 03824, tel. 800/733–9753), a slightly younger enterprise than Elderhostel, caters to a slightly younger clientele—that is, 50 and over—and runs programs in some 25 countries. But the idea is similar: Lectures and field trips mix with sightseeing, and participants stay in dormitories at cooperating educational institutions or in modest hotels. Programs are usually two weeks in length and cost $1,500–$2,100, not including airfare from the United States.

Tour Operators **Saga International Holidays** (222 Berkeley St., Boston, MA 02116, tel. 800/343–0273), which specializes in group travel for people over 60, offers a selection of variously priced tours and cruises covering five continents. If you want to take your grandchildren, look into **GrandTravel** (*see* Traveling with Children, *above*).

Further Reading

Richard Rickett's *A Brief Survey of Austrian History* (Heinemann, 1983) is a good overview, and Edward Crankshaw's *The Habsburgs* (Weidenfeld & Nicolson, 1972) is a good and brief history of the royal house that ruled Austria from 1278 to 1918. Sarah Gainham's *Night Falls on the City* (Collins, 1967) is an extraordinary novel about the struggle of an actress to hide her Jewish husband from the Nazis in wartime Vienna. *Music and Musicians in Vienna* (Heinemann, 1973), also by Richard Rickett, is a compact guide to those musicians who helped make Vienna the musical capital of the world.

For Vienna coverage, see Henriette Mandl, *Vienna Downtown Walking Tours* (Ueberreuter, 1987), an excellent guide to seeing Vienna on foot, and Christian Nebehay, *Vienna 1900* (Brandstätter, 1984), a set of profusely illustrated guides to architecture, painting, music, and literature in turn-of-the-century Vienna. Carl E. Schorske's concise, readable, and well-illustrated *Fin-de-Siècle Vienna: Politics and Culture* (Vintage/Random House, 1981) helps unravel today's Vienna and Austria.

Arriving and Departing

From North America by Plane

Flights are either nonstop, direct, or connecting. A **nonstop** flight requires no change of plane and makes no stops. A **direct** flight stops at least once and can involve a change of plane, although the flight number remains the same; if the first leg is late, the second waits. This is not the case with a **connecting** flight, which involves a different plane and a different flight number.

Airports and Airlines Scheduled international flights from North America all fly into Vienna's Schwechat airport, about 12 miles southeast of the city. Airlines serving Austria from major U.S. cities (usually New York) include **Austrian Airlines** (tel. 800/843–0002), **Delta** (tel. 800/221–1212), **Lauda Air** (tel. 800/325–2832), **TWA** (tel. 800/221–2000), and **Air Canada** (tel. 416/925–2311 or 800/268–7240).

Flying Time From New York, a nonstop flight to Vienna takes just over eight hours. From Toronto, a direct flight takes about 11 hours.

Cutting Flight Costs The Sunday travel section of most newspapers is a good source of deals. When booking, particularly through an unfamiliar company, call the Better Business Bureau to find out whether any complaints have been registered against the company, pay with a credit card if you can, and consider trip-cancellation and default insurance (*see* Insurance, *above*).

Promotional Airfares All the less expensive fares, called promotional or discount fares, are round-trip and involve restrictions. The exact nature of the restrictions depends on the airline, the route, and the season and on whether travel is domestic or international, but you must usually buy the ticket—commonly called an APEX (advance purchase excursion) when it's for international travel—in advance (seven, 14, or 21 days are usual). You must also respect certain minimum- and maximum-stay requirements (for instance, over a Saturday night or at least seven and no more than 30, 45, or 90 days), and you must be willing to pay penalties for changes. Airlines generally allow some changes for a fee. But the cheaper the fare, the more likely the ticket is nonrefundable; it would take a death in the family for the airline to give you any of your money back if you had to cancel. The cheapest fares are also subject to availability; because only a certain percentage of the plane's total seats will be sold at that price, they may go quickly.

Consolidators Consolidators or bulk-fare operators—also known as bucket shops—buy blocks of seats on scheduled flights that airlines anticipate they won't be able to sell. They pay wholesale prices, add a markup, and resell the seats to travel agents or directly to the public at prices that still undercut the airline's promotional or discount fares. You pay more than on a charter but ordinarily less than for an APEX ticket, and, even when there is not much of a price difference, the ticket usually comes without the advance-purchase restriction. Moreover, although tickets are marked nonrefundable so you can't turn them in to the airline for a full-fare refund, some consolidators sometimes give you your money back. Carefully read the fine print detailing penalties for changes and cancellations. If you doubt the reliability of a company, call the airline once you've made your booking and confirm that you do, indeed, have a reservation on the flight.

The biggest U.S. consolidator, C.L. Thomson Express, sells only to travel agents. Well-established consolidators selling to the public include **UniTravel** (Box 12485, St. Louis, MO 63132, tel. 314/569–0900 or 800/325–2222); **Council Charter** (205 E. 42nd St., New York, NY 10017, tel. 212/661–0311 or 800/800–8222), a division of the Council on International Educational Exchange and a longtime charter operator now functioning more as a consolidator; and **Travac** (989 6th Ave., New York, NY 10018, tel. 212/563–3303 or 800/872–8800), also a former charterer.

Charter Flights Charters usually have the lowest fares and the most restrictions. Departures are limited and seldom on time, and you can lose all or most of your money if you cancel. (Generally, the closer to departure you cancel, the more you lose, although sometimes you will be charged only a small fee if you supply a substitute passenger.) The charterer, on the other hand, may legally cancel the flight for any reason up to 10 days before departure; within 10 days of departure, the flight may be canceled only if it becomes physically impossible to operate it. The charterer may also revise the itinerary or increase the price after you have bought the ticket, but if the new arrangement constitutes a "major change," you have the right to a refund. Before buying a charter ticket, read the fine print for the company's refund policy and details on major changes. Money for charter flights is usually paid into a bank escrow account, the name of which should be on the contract. If you don't pay by credit card, make your check payable to the escrow account (unless you're dealing with a travel agent, in which case, his or her check should be payable to the escrow account). The Department of Transportation's Consumer Affairs Office (I–25, Washington, DC 20590, tel. 202/366–2220) can answer questions on charters and send you its "Plane Talk: Public Charter Flights" information sheet.

Charter operators may offer flights alone or with ground arrangements that constitute a charter package. Well-established charter operators include **Council Charter** (205 E. 42nd St., New York, NY 10017, tel. 212/661–0311 or 800/800–8222), now largely a consolidator, despite its name, and **Travel Charter** (1120 E. Long Lake Rd., Troy, MI 48098, tel. 313/528–3570 or 800/521–5267), with midwestern departures. **DER Tours** (Box 1606, Des Plains, IL 60017, tel. 800/782–2424), a charterer and consolidator, sells through travel agents.

Discount Travel Clubs Travel clubs offer their members unsold space on airplanes, cruise ships, and package tours at nearly the last minute and at well below the original cost. Suppliers thus receive some revenue for their "leftovers," and members get a bargain. Membership generally includes a regular bulletin or access to a toll-free telephone hot line giving details of available trips departing anywhere from three or four days to several months in the future. Packages tend to be more common than flights alone, so if airfares are your only interest, read the literature before joining. Reductions on hotels are also available. Clubs include **Discount Travel International** (114 Forrest Ave., Suite 203, Narberth, PA 19072, tel. 215/668–7184; $45 annually, single or family), **Moment's Notice** (425 Madison Ave., New York, NY 10017, tel. 212/486–0503; $45 annually, single or family), **Travelers Advantage** (CUC Travel Service, 49 Music Sq. W, Nashville, TN 37203, tel. 800/548–1116; $49 annually, single or family), and **Worldwide Discount Travel Club** (1674 Meridian Ave., Miami Beach, FL 33139, tel. 305/534–2082; $50 annually for family, $40 single).

Enjoying the Flight Fly at night if you're able to sleep on a plane. Because the air aloft is dry, drink plenty of beverages while on board; remember that drinking alcohol contributes to jet lag, as do heavy meals. Sleepers usually prefer window seats to curl up against; restless passengers ask to be on the aisle. Bulkhead seats, in the front row of each cabin, have more legroom, but since there's no seat ahead, trays attach awkwardly to the arms of your seat, and you must stow all possessions overhead. Bulkhead seats are usually reserved for the disabled, the elderly, and people traveling with babies.

Smoking Since February 1990, smoking has been banned on all domestic flights of less than six hours duration; the ban also applies to domestic segments of international flights aboard U.S. and foreign carriers. On U.S. carriers flying to Austria and other destinations abroad, a seat in a no-smoking section must be provided for every passenger who requests one, and the section must be enlarged to accommodate such passengers if necessary as long as they have complied with the airline's deadline for check-in and seat assignment. If smoking bothers you, request a seat far from the smoking section.

Foreign airlines are exempt from these rules but do provide no-smoking sections, and some nations have gone as far as to ban smoking on all domestic flights; other countries may ban smoking on flights of less than a specified duration. The International Civil Aviation Organization has set July 1, 1996, as the date to ban smoking aboard airlines worldwide, but the body has no power to enforce its decisions.

From the United Kingdom by Plane, Car, and Train

By Plane **British Airways** (tel. 071/897–4000), **Austrian Airlines** (tel. 071/439–0741), **Dan Air** (tel. 0293/567955), and **Lauda Air** (tel. 071/494–0702) have nonstop service from London to Vienna. There are at least six flights daily to Vienna from London Heathrow, a trip of a little more than two hours.

By Car The best way to reach Austria by car from England is to take a North Sea/Cross Channel ferries to Oostende or Zeebrugge in Belgium or Dunkirk in northern France. Then take the toll-free Belgian motorway (E5) to Aachen, and head via Stuttgart to Innsbruck and the Tirol (A61, A67, A5, E11, A7) or east by way of Nürnberg and Munich, crossing into Austria at Walserberg and then on to Salzburg and Vienna. Total distance to Vienna is about 1,600 km (1,000 mi). The most direct way to Vienna is virtually all on the autobahn via Nürnberg, Regensburg, and Passau, entering Austria at Schärding. In summer, border delays are much shorter at Schärding than at Salzburg.

By Train There's a choice of rail routes to Austria, but check services first; long-distance passenger service across the Continent is undergoing considerable reduction. You can take the direct London-Vienna *Austria Nachtexpress*, leaving London's Victoria Station at 11:15 AM or 1:30 PM and arriving via Oostende in Vienna at 10:58 the next morning. Check other services such as the *Orient Express*. If you don't mind changing trains, you can travel via Paris, where you change stations to board the overnight *Arlberg Express* via Innsbruck and Salzburg to Vienna. First- and second-class sleepers and second-class couchettes are available as far as Innsbruck.

When you have the time, a strikingly scenic route to Austria is via Cologne and Munich; after an overnight stop in Cologne, you take the EuroCity Express *Johann Strauss* to Vienna. Make reservations with **Eurotrain** (52 Grosvenor Gardens, London SW1W OAG, tel. 071/730–3402), which offers excellent deals for those under 26. Otherwise, book through **British Rail Travel Centers** (tel. 071/834–2345). For additional information, call **DER Travel Service** (071/408–0111) or the Austrian National Tourist Office.

Staying in Vienna

Getting Around

By Plane Austria has domestic air service, but fares are high. The train is much cheaper and, in most cases, about as convenient. **Austrian Airlines** and its subsidiary, **Austrian Air Services,** have flights connecting Vienna with Linz, Salzburg, Graz, and Klagenfurt. **Tyrolean** flies between Vienna and Innsbruck, and it has a fly/drive combination with Avis that can save you money. Tyrolean also connects to points outside Austria, and **Rheintalflug** flies between Vienna and Altenhausen, in Switzerland. Winter schedules on all domestic lines depend on snow conditions.

By Train Austrian train service is excellent: It's fast and, for Western Europe, relatively inexpensive, particularly if you take advantage of the discount fares. Trains on the mountainous routes are slow, but driving is no faster, and the scenery is gorgeous! Many of the remote rail routes will give you a look at traditional Austria, complete with Alpine cabins tacked onto mountainsides and a backdrop of snowcapped peaks.

For train schedules, ask at your hotel or stop in at the train station and look for large posters labeled *Abfahrt* (departures) and *Ankunft* (arrivals). In the Abfahrt listing you'll find the departure time in the main left-hand block of the listing and, under the train name, details of where it stops en route and the time of each arrival. There is also information about connecting trains and buses, with departure details.

Austrian Federal Railways trains are identifiable by the letters that precede the train number on the timetables and posters. The *Ex* and *D* trains are fastest, but a supplement of AS30 is included in the price of the ticket. All tickets are valid without supplement on *Eilzug* (fast) and local trains. Seat reservations are required on some trains; on most others you can reserve for a small charge up until a few hours before departure. Be sure to do this on the major trains at peak holiday times.

The difference between first and second class on Austrian trains is mainly a matter of space. First- and second-class sleepers, and couchettes (six to a compartment), are available on international runs, as well as on long trips within Austria. If you're driving and would rather watch the scenery than the traffic, you can put your car on a train in Vienna and take it to Salzburg, Innsbruck, Feldkirch, or Villach. You relax in a compartment or sleeper for the trip, and the car is unloaded when you arrive.

Railroad enthusiasts and those with plenty of time can treat themselves to a ride on narrow-gauge lines found all over Austria that amble through Alpine meadows; some even make flower-picking stops in season. A few lines still run under steam power, and summertime steam excursions are increasingly easy to find. Local stations have descriptive brochures with dates, points of origin, and fares.

Discount Fares Even if you'll be in Austria for only a short time, you can save money on one of the discount rail fares. For AS240 and a passport photo, women over 60 and men over 65 can obtain a *Seniorenpass*, which carries discounts up to 50% on rail tickets. The pass also has a host of other benefits, including reduced-price entry into museums. Most rail stations can give you information.

Travelers under 26 should inquire about discount fares under the Billet International Jeune (BIJ). The special one-trip tickets are sold by **Eurotrain International** by travel agents and youth-travel specialists and at rail stations.

The **Rabbit Card** permits four days of travel within a 10-day period on any rail route, including the private lines and cog railways. The card also allows free travel on ships on the Wolfgangsee and a 50% reduction on some steamer travel within the country. The Rabbit Card costs AS1,700 first class, AS1,130 second class; AS1,050 first class, AS700 second, for travelers under 26. Rail Europe issues the card, which may also be purchased from any rail station in Europe. Unless you'll be confining your rail travel to Austria, the Eurailpass (*see* Rail Passes, *above*) will probably be cheaper.

A *Bundesnetzkarte* (full-network pass) gives you unlimited travel for a month (AS5,400 for first class, AS3,600 second class) and will allow you a 50% reduction on Austrian intercity buses and private rail lines. The ticket is also good on the suburban rail system (*S-Bahn*) around Vienna and ships on the Wolfgangsee. Apply at any large rail station, and expect the cost to be higher in 1994. You will need a passport photo.

By Bus Where Austrian trains don't go, buses do, and you will find the yellow railroad and post-office buses in the remotest regions carrying passengers as well as the mail. You can get tickets on the bus, and in the off-season there is no problem getting a seat, but on routes to favored ski areas and during holiday periods reservations are essential. Bookings can be handled at the ticket office (there's one in most towns with bus service) or by travel agents. In most communities, bus routes begin and end at or near the railroad station, making transfers easy. Increasingly, coordination of bus service with railroads means that many of the discounts and special tickets available for trains apply to buses as well.

By Car
Road Conditions The Austrian highway network is excellent, and roads are well maintained and well marked. Secondary roads may be narrow and winding. The main through routes (autobahns) are packed during both Austrian and German school holidays, as well as on weekends in summer. As a nod to the environment, less salt is being used on highways in winter, but few drivers seem to take heed of the greater hazard. In winter you will need snow tires and often chains, even on well-traveled roads. Austrians are aggressive drivers and are inclined to take chances; drive defensively.

Rules of the Road Tourists from European Community countries may bring their cars to Austria with no documentation other than the normal registration papers and their regular driver's license. A Green Card, the international certificate of insurance, is recommended for EC drivers and compulsory for others. All cars must carry a first-aid kit and a red warning triangle (obtainable at border crossings or from the Automobile Club—*see below*) to use in case of accident or breakdown.

The minimum driving age in Austria is 18, and children under 12 years must ride in the back seat. Passengers in the front seats must use seat belts. Vehicles coming from the right have the right of way, except that at unregulated intersections streetcars coming from either direction have the right of way. No turns are allowed on red.

Unless otherwise marked, the speed limit on autobahns is 130 kph (80 mph), although this is not strictly enforced. On other highways and roads, the limit is 100 kph (62 mph), 80 kph (49 mph) for RVs or cars pulling a trailer weighing more than 750 kilos (about 1,650 lbs). In built-up areas, a 50 kph (31 mph) limit applies and is likely to be taken seriously.

Maps A set of eight excellent detailed road maps is available from the **Austrian Automobile Club/ÖAMTC** (Schubertring 1–3, A–1010 Vienna, tel. 0222/711–9955), at most service stations, and at many bookstores. The maps supplied without charge by the Austrian National Tourist Office are adequate for most needs, but if you will be covering much territory, the better ÖAMTC maps are a worthwhile investment.

Gasoline Gasoline is readily available, but on Sunday, rural stations may be closed. Stations carry only unleaded (*bleifrei*) gas, both regular and premium (*super*). Diesel fuel may not be easy to find off the beaten path. Gasoline prices are the same throughout the country, slightly lower at discount filling stations and self-service stations. Expect to pay about AS10 per liter for regular, AS11.50 for premium. Oil in Austria is expensive, retailing at AS50–AS80 per liter.

Breakdown Assistance Austria has two automobile clubs, ÖAMTC and ARBÖ, both of which operate motorist service patrols. You'll find emergency phones along all the key highways. Otherwise, if you have problems, call ARBÖ (tel. 123) or ÖAMTC (tel. 120) anywhere in the country. No area or other code is needed for either number. Both clubs charge nonmembers for emergency service.

By Boat For leisurely travel between Vienna and Linz or eastward across the border into Slovakia or Hungary, consider taking a Danube boat. More than 300 km (187 mi) of Austria's most beautiful scenery awaits you, as you glide past castles and ruins, medieval monasteries and abbeys, and lush vineyards.

One of the lovelier spots, particularly in spring, is the Wachau valley near Vienna. For current fares contact your travel agent or, in Austria, the **DDSG/Danube Steamship Company** (Handelskai 265, A–1020 Vienna, tel. 0222/217100). Fares vary according to the type of accommodation. The river cruiser *Mozart*—complete with swimming pool—and the *Donauprinzessen*, which runs from Passau to Linz, are in the luxury category.

Day trips are also possible on the Danube, and in the Wachau you can use the boats to move from one riverside community to the next. The Eurailpass includes the DDSG network.

Hydrofoils run daily from Vienna to Bratislava in Slovakia and to Budapest in Hungary. You can travel via the Danube to the Black Sea and back on river passenger ships.

Telephones

Local Calls Austria's telephone service is in a state of change as the country converts to a digital system. We make every effort to keep numbers up to date, but do recheck the number if you have problems getting the connection you want. All numbers given here include the city or town area code; if you are calling within that city or town, dial the local number only.

Basic telephone numbers in Austria are three to seven digits; longer numbers are the basic number plus a direct-dial extension of two to four digits.

Pay Phones Coin-operated pay telephones are numerous and take a one-schilling piece for local calls. Drop in the coin, pick up the receiver and dial; when the party answers, push the indicated button and the connection will be made. If there is no response, your coin will be returned into the bin to the lower left.

If you plan to make many calls from pay phones, a *Wertkarte* is a convenience. You can buy this electronic credit card at any post office for AS95 or AS48 that allows AS100 or AS50 worth of calls from any *Wertkartentelephon*. You simply insert the card and dial; the cost of the call is automatically deducted from the card.

Long-distance Calls Calls within Austria are one-third cheaper between 6 PM and 8 AM on weekdays and from 1 PM on Saturday to 8 AM on Monday.

International Calls You can dial direct to almost any point on the globe from Austria. The international access code for the United States and Canada is 001, followed by the area code and number. For Great Britain, first dial 0044, then the city code *without the usual "0"* (71 or 81 for London), and the number. Other country and many city codes are given in the front of telephone books (in Vienna, in the *A–H* book).

Don't make long-distance calls from your hotel room without first checking carefully on the cost of the call. Hotels in Austria, as in many countries, frequently add several hundred percent to such calls. AT&T's **USADirect** plan enables you to charge the call to your calling card or call collect. The access number, 022–903011, is a local call all over Austria. For information, tel. 412/553–7458, ext. 314 (collect from outside the United States), or 800/874–4000. All post offices in Austria have public telephone facilities, and you can get assistance in placing a long-distance call. In large cities, these centers are open around the clock.

Operators and Information For information on local calls, dial 1611; for assistance with long-distance service, dial 09; and for information on direct dialing out of Austria, call 08.

Mail

Postal Rates Within Europe, all mail goes by air, so there's no supplement on letters or postcards. A letter of up to 20 grams (about ¾ ounce) takes AS7, a postcard AS6. To the United States or Canada, a letter of up to 20 grams takes AS10 minimum, plus AS1.50 per 5 grams for airmail. If in doubt, mail your letters from a post office and have the weight checked. The Austrian post office also adheres strictly to a size standard; if your letter or card is outside the norm, you'll have to pay a surcharge. Postcards via airmail to the United States or Canada need AS8.50. Post offices have air-letter (aerogram) forms for AS12 to any overseas destination.

Receiving Mail When you don't know where you'll be staying, **American Express** mail service is a great convenience, with no charge to anyone either holding an American Express credit card or carrying American Express traveler's checks. Offices are at Kärntner Str. 21–23, A–1015 **Vienna,** tel. 0222/515400; Mozartplatz 5, A–5020 **Salzburg,** tel. 0662/842501; Brixner Str. 3, A–6020 **Innsbruck,** tel. 0512/582491; and Bürgerstr. 14, A–4021 **Linz,** tel. 0732/669013. You can also have mail held at any Austrian post office; letters should be marked *Poste Restante* or *Postlagernd*. You will be asked for identification when you collect mail. In Vienna, this service is handled through the main post office (Fleischmarkt 19, A–1010 Vienna, tel. 0222/512–76810), located at Postgasse/Barbaragasse 2 until renovations on the Fleischmarkt building are completed.

Tipping

Although virtually all hotels and restaurants include service charges in their rates, tipping is still customary, but at a level lower than in the United States. Tip the hotel doorman AS10 per bag, and the porter who brings your bags to the room another AS10 per bag. In very small country inns, such tips are not expected but are appreciated. Tip the hotel concierge only for special services or in response to special requests. Room service gets AS10 for snacks or ice, AS20 for full meals. Maids normally get no tip unless your stay is a week or more or service has been special.

In restaurants, round up the bill by AS5 to AS50, depending on the size of the check and the class of the restaurant. Big tips are not usual in Austrian restaurants, since 10% has already been included in the prices. Hat-check attendants get AS7–AS15, depending on the locale. Washroom attendants get about AS2–AS5. Wandering musicians and the piano player get AS20, AS50 if they've filled a number of requests.

Round up taxi fares to the next AS5 or AS10; a minimum AS5 tip is customary. If the driver offers (or you ask for) special assistance, such as carrying your bags beyond the curb, an added tip of AS5–AS10 is in order.

Opening and Closing Times

Banks Banks are open weekdays from 8 to 3, on Thursday until 5:30 PM. Smaller bank offices close from 12:30 to 1:30. All are closed on Saturday, but you can change money at various locations (such as American Express offices on Saturday morning and major railroad stations around the clock).

Museums Museum hours vary from city to city and museum to museum; if there's a closing day, it will usually be Monday. Few museums are open at night.

Shops In general, you'll find shops open weekdays from 8:30 or 9 AM until 6 PM, with a lunchtime closing from noon to 1 or 1:30. In smaller villages, the midday break may run until 3 PM. Many food stores, bakeries, and small grocery shops open at 7 or 7:30 AM and, aside from the noontime break, stay open until 6 or 6:30 PM. Shops in large city centers take no noon break. On Saturday, shops stay open until noon or 1 PM, except on the first Saturday of the month, when (except for food stores) they stay open until 5, a few until 6 PM. Barbers and hairdressers traditionally take Monday off, but there are exceptions.

National Holidays All banks and shops are closed on national holidays: Jan. 1, New Year's Day; Jan. 6, Epiphany; Apr. 3–4, Easter Sunday and Monday; May 1, May Day; May 12, Ascension Day; May 22, 23, Pentecost Sunday and Monday; June 2, Corpus Christi; Aug. 15, Assumption; Oct. 26, National Holiday; Nov. 1, All Saints' Day; Dec. 8, Immaculate Conception; Dec. 25–26, Christmas. Museums are open on most holidays and closed on Good Friday and Dec. 24.

Shopping

You'll find specific shopping tips in the individual chapters. In general, such locally produced goods as textiles, crystal, porcelain figurines, leather goods, wood carvings, and other handicrafts are good value. Prices are similar throughout the country, but higher, of course, in the major tourist centers. Shops will ship your purchases, but if you can, take them with you. If you do ship goods, be sure you know the terms in advance, how the items will be sent, and when you can expect to receive them, *and get all these details in writing.*

Sports and the Outdoors

Austria is one of the most participant-sports-minded countries anywhere. At a snowflake's notice, half the population will take to their skis; in summer, water sports are just as popular. But new attractions are appearing; golf, for example, is becoming more common. National Tourist Offices have information on many specific sports.

Ballooning Contact the **Austrian Ballooning Club** (Endresstr. 79/4, A–1230 Vienna, tel. 0222/889–8222); **Austrian Aero-Club** (Prinz Eugen-Str. 12, A–1040 Vienna, tel. 0222/505–1028, fax 0222/505–7923) or the **Vienna Ballooning Club** (tel. 0222/587–8139–20).

Bicycling Cyclists couldn't ask for much more than the new cycle track that runs the length of the Danube or the many cycling routes that crisscross the country, major cities included. You can rent a bicycle for AS90 per day (AS45, if you've a rail ticket in your hand) at any of about 100 railroad stations throughout the country and return it to another. Brochures available from National Tourist Offices have details, including maps and hints for trip planning and mealtime and overnight stops. Ask for the booklet *Radfahren in Österreich*, or contact **Austria Radreisen** (A–4780 Schärding, tel. 07712/2409, fax 07712/4811), which organizes cycling tours. There's also a brochure in English: *Biking Austria—On the Trail of Mozart.*

Boating and Sailing You can rent a rowboat on almost all of Austria's lakes and on the side arms of the Danube (Alte Donau and the Donauinsel) in Vienna. Information is available from the **Österreichischer Segel-Verband,** the Austrian Yachting Club (Grosse Neugasse 8, A–1040 Vienna, tel. 0222/587–8688, fax 0222/566171).

Windsurfing (*Windsegeln*) is extremely popular, particularly on the side arms of the Danube in Vienna. There are schools at all these locations with lessons and rentals.

Camping Most campsites have full facilities, often including swimming pools and snack bars or grocery shops. Charges range from about AS40 to AS70 per person per day (depending on the location, range, and quality of services offered), plus AS30–AS40 for car parking. Many campsites have a fixed basic fee for three adults and one child, parking included. For details, check with the **Österreichischer Camping Club** (Schubertring 1–3, A–1010 Vienna, tel. 0222/71199–1272, fax 0222/71199–1498). Camping is not restricted to the summer season; some sites are open year-round, with about 155 specifically set up for winter camping.

Fishing Ask the Austrian National Tourist Office for the guidebook "Fishing in Austria"; it includes licensing details. Unfortunately, the rights along many of the best streams have been given, meaning that no additional licenses will be issued, but ask at the local tourist office.

Gliding From May to September you can glide solo or learn to glide at one of Austria's schools. In Zell am See and at Wien-Donauwiese (Vienna) there are two-seater gliders, for instructor and passenger. For details, contact the **Austrian Aero Club** (Prinz Eugen-Str. 12, A–1040 Vienna, tel. 0222/505–1028, fax 0222/505–7923).

Golf Austria now has more than 50 courses. Most are private, but for a greens fee you can arrange a temporary membership. Several courses are associated with hotels, so package arrangements can be made. Austrian National Tourist Offices have golfing brochures, or you can write **Golf Green Austria** (Panzaunweg 1g, A–5071 Wals, tel. 0662/850805–67, fax 0662/853190).

Hiking and Climbing With more than 50,000 kilometers (about 35,000 miles) of well-maintained mountain paths through Europe's largest reserve of unspoiled landscape, the country is a hiker's paradise. Three long-distance routes traverse Austria: E-4, the Pyrenees–Jura–Neusiedler See route, ending in Burgenland on the Hungarian border; E-5 from Lake Constance in Vorarlberg to the Adriatic; and E-6 from the Baltic, cutting across mid-Austria via the Wachau valley region of the Danube and on to the Adriatic. Wherever you are in Austria, you will find shorter hiking trails requiring varying degrees of ability. Routes are well marked, and maps are readily available.

Horseback Riding Whether you want to head off cross-country or just canter around a paddock, Austria offers many kinds of equestrian holidays, and some hotels have their own riding schools. Ask for the booklet "Equestrian Sports in Austria" from the tourist office. The provinces of Styria, Burgenland, and Upper and Lower Austria are particularly popular with riders.

Skiing Skiing is the Austrian national sport, so you'll have plenty of company wherever there's a slope and a snowflake. Here babies barely out of diapers practically learn to walk and ski at the same time. The season runs from late November to April, depending on snow conditions. But there are enough year-round skiing regions on glaciers at 3,300 meters (11,000 ft) or more to satisfy even the wildest enthusiast.

Water Sports and Swimming In the Vienna area, the Alte Donau and Donauinsel arms of the Danube are accessible by public transportation and are suitable for families. It's best to go early to avoid the crowds on hot summer weekends. The Alte Donau beaches have changing rooms and checkrooms. Swimming in the Neusiedler See in Burgenland is an experience; you can touch bottom at virtually any place in this vast brackish lake.

Spectator Sports Soccer is a national favorite. Every town has at least one team, and rivalries are fierce; matches are held regularly in Vienna. There's horse racing with pari-mutuel betting at the track in the Prater in Vienna. Tennis matches are held in Vienna and Linz.

Dining

Restaurant food in Austria ranges from fine (and expensive) offerings at elegant restaurants to simple, inexpensive, and wholesome meals in small country inns. Wherever you go, you will find traditional restaurants, with all the atmosphere typical of such places—good value included. If you crave a Big Mac you can find it, and you can even get a bad meal in Austria, but it will be the exception; the simplest *Gasthaus* takes pride in its cooking, no matter how standard it may be.

Austrian cuisine is heavily influenced by that of its neighbors. This accounts for the cross-fertilization of tastes and flavors, with Hungarian, Czechoslovak, Polish, Yugoslav, and Italian cooking all in the mix. The delicious, thick Serbian bean soup came from an area of the former Yugoslavia; the bread dumpling (*Knödel*) that accompanies many standard dishes has its parentage in the former Czechoslovakia; the exquisitely rich (more butter than sugar) *Dobostorte* comes straight from Hungary.

All too often justice is not done to the relatively few Austrian national dishes. You're likely to get a soggy Wiener schnitzel as often as a supreme example, lightly pan-fried in a dry, crisp breading. Austrian cooking on the whole is more solid than delicate. Try *Tafelspitz* (boiled beef); when well done it is outstanding in flavor and texture. Reflecting the Italian influence, Austrian cooking also leans heavily on pastas and rice. *Schinkenfleckerl* is a good example: a casserole of confettilike flecks of ham baked with pasta. A standard roast of pork (*Schweinsbraten*) served hot or cold can be exquisite.

When dining out, you'll get best value at the simpler restaurants. Most post menus with prices outside. If you begin with the *Würstelstand* (sausage vendor) on the street, the next category would be the *Imbissstube*, for simple, quick snacks. You'll find many of them at city markets, serving soups and a daily special at noon. Many cafés also are open for lunch, but watch the prices; some can turn out to be more expensive than restaurants. *Gasthäuser* are simple restaurants or country inns. Austrian hotels have some of the best restaurants in the country, often with outstanding chefs.

Wine cellars and wine gardens, or *Heuriger* (for new wine), are a special category among Austrian eateries. They serve everything from a limited selection of cold cuts and cheeses to full meals. Some urban wine cellars are known as much for their food as for the wines.

Austrian vintage wines range from good to outstanding. Don't hesitate to ask waiters for advice, even in the simpler restaurants. The best whites come from the Wachau and Kamptal, Weinviertel (Lower Austria), Styria, and the area around Vienna. Grüner Veltliner, a light dry-to-medium-dry wine that goes well with many foods, is the most popular. The Welschriesling is a slightly heavier, fruitier wine. The favored Austrian reds are those of Burgenland. Blauer Portugieser and Zweigelt tend to be lighter. For a slightly heavier red, select a Blaufränkisch, Blauer Burgunder, or St. Laurent. These are all good value, and there is little difference among the years. Most of these wines can be bought by the glass. Look for labels from vintners Beck in Gols, Bründlmayer in Langenlois, Hirtzberger in Spitz/Donau, Jamek in Joching, Sonnhof in Langenlois, Dolle in Strass, Wieninger in Vienna, and Freie Weingärtner Wachau in Dürnstein.

For Grüner Veltliner, Blaufränkisch, and St. Laurent, the recommended vintages are '81, '83, '85, '86, '89 and '90. Mainly these same years go for Rheinriesling and Welschriesling, as well. In every case '85 and '86 were exceptional for both whites and reds; '90 was generally outstanding.

Lunch in Austria is usually served between noon and 2 PM, dinner between 6 and 9 PM, tending toward the later hour. Many restaurant kitchens close in the afternoon, but some post a notice saying *Durchgehend warme Küche*, meaning that hot food is available even between regular mealtimes.

Restaurants in our listings are divided by price into four categories: Very Expensive, Expensive, Moderate, and Inexpensive. *See* Dining in individual chapters for specific prices, which vary from region to region. Prices quoted are for a three-course meal with house wine, including all service and taxes.

Lodging

You can live like a king in a real castle in Austria or get by on a modest budget. Starting at the lower end, you can find a room in a private house or on a farm, or dormitory space in a youth hostel. Next up the line come the simpler pensions, many of them identified as *Frühstückspension*, meaning bed-and-breakfast. Then come the *Gasthäuser*, the simpler country inns. The fancier pensions in the cities can often cost as much as hotels; the difference lies in the services they offer. Most pensions, for example, do not staff the front desk around the clock. Among the hotels, you can find accommodations ranging from the most modest, with a shower and toilet down the hall, to the most elegant, with every possible amenity.

We divide hotels into four price categories: Very Expensive, Expensive, Moderate, and Inexpensive, giving rates for a standard double room with private bath in peak season (where applicable).

All hotel prices include service charges (usually 10% but occasionally higher) and federal and local taxes—and in a few places, a small local tourism tax is added later. Some country hotels may add a heating supplement in winter.

Breakfast is included at virtually all hotels *except* those in the Very Expensive category, where it is extra—and expensive. It may range from rolls, marmalade, and coffee to an expansive buffet with eggs and meat dishes. You can usually get juice or an egg, but in some cases you'll be asked to pay extra. Some of the top resort hotels insist on half or full board in season; at other times, you can set your own terms.

Home Exchange This is obviously an inexpensive solution to the lodging problem, because house-swapping means living rent-free. You find a house, apartment, or other vacation property to exchange for your own by becoming a member of a home-exchange organization, which then sends you its annual directories listing available exchanges and includes your own listing in at least one of them. Arrangements for the actual exchange are made by the two parties to it, not by the organization. Principal clearinghouses include **Intervac U.S./International Home Exchange** (Box 590504, San Francisco, CA 94159, tel. 415/435–3497), the oldest, with thousands of foreign and domestic homes for exchange in its three annual directories; membership is $62, or $72 if you want to receive the directories but remain unlisted. The **Vacation Exchange Club** (Box 650, Key West, FL 33041, tel. 800/638–3841), also with thousands of foreign and domestic listings, publishes four annual directories plus updates; the $50 membership includes your listing in one book. **Loan-a-Home** (2 Park La., Apt. 6E, Mount Vernon, NY 10552, tel. 914/664–7640) specializes in long-term exchanges; there is no charge to list your home, but the directories cost $35 or $45 depending on the number you receive.

Apartment and Villa Rentals If you want a home base that's roomy enough for a family and comes with cooking facilities, a furnished rental may be the solution. It's generally cost-wise, too, although not always—some rentals are luxury properties (economical only when your party is large). Home-exchange directories do list rentals—often second homes owned by prospective house swappers—and there are services that can not only look for a house or apartment for you (even a castle if that's your fancy) but also handle the paperwork. Some send an illustrated catalogue and others send photographs of specific properties, sometimes at a charge; up-front registration fees may apply.

Among the companies are **Interhome Inc.** (124 Little Falls Rd., Fairfield, NJ 07004, tel. 201/882–6864), **Overseas Connection** (31 North Harbor Dr., Sag Harbor, NY 11963, tel. 516/725–9308), **Rent a Home International** (7200 34th Ave. NW, Seattle, WA 98117, tel. 206/789–9377 or 800/488–7368), and **Villas International** (605 Market St., Suite 510, San Francisco, CA 94105,

tel. 415/281–0910 or 800/221–2260). **Hideaways International**
(767 Islington St., Box 4433, Portsmouth, NH 03802, tel. 603/
430–4433 or 800/843–4433) functions as a travel club. Membership ($79 yearly per person or family at the same address) in-
cludes two annual guides plus quarterly newsletters; rentals
are arranged directly between members, not by the club staff.

Credit Cards

The following credit card abbreviations are used: AE, American Express; DC, Diner's Club; MC, MasterCard/Access/
Barclays; V, Visa.

2 Portraits of Austria

The Land of the Waltz

By Hans Fantel

A native of Austria and longtime resident of the United States, Hans Fantel is currently a syndicated columnist for the New York Times.

The Viennese traditionally live in two countries. One is on the map. The other is the imaginary region where wine flows, love triumphs, and everything is silk-lined. This is the land of the waltz.

A century ago, during the sunset years of Austria's 1,000-year-old empire, there was no clear demarcation between the real world and that mythical land of the waltz. The two realms merged along the hazy boundary that never quite separates fact from fancy in Vienna.

This region of the Viennese mind is not just a shallow, sybaritic fantasy. Like Viennese music itself, it embodies a substantial premise. If melody could be translated, a Viennese waltz would add up to 100 ways of saying that, all considered, and with due allowance for everything, simply being alive is a cause for celebration.

At its surprising best—in such creations as *The Blue Danube*, the *Emperor Waltz*, or *Tales from the Vienna Woods*—the waltz is perhaps the closest description of happiness ever attained in any art.

Paradoxically, the music is not merry. A haze of wistfulness lies over the sunniest tunes, and their sweetness sometimes touches on melancholy. Though the dance is a swirling embrace, the music countermands sensual abandonment. It insists on grace; it remains pensive in the midst of pleasure. And in this blending of the sensual with the reflective, the Viennese waltz expresses and creates a condition of durable bliss—a measured joy.

For almost 100 years, while the last Habsburg emperors ruled the real Austria, the land of the waltz had its own dynasty—the Waltz Kings. Both were named Johann Strauss.

Johann Strauss I ruled over this mythical realm of music during the first part of the 19th century. A generation later, his son, Johann Strauss II, extended the scope of the waltz to symphonic proportions, writing dance music in the form of orchestral tone poems that transformed the ballroom into a concert stage.

These two men welded their city and their music into a single identity, making Vienna and the waltz almost a single thought. Viennese historians are fond of florid metaphors suggesting that Johann Strauss—father and son—did not so much compose their waltzes as ineffably transmute their city into music. Such notions seem altogether plausible to the romantic Viennese, including the younger Strauss himself. "If it is true that I have talent," he wrote during the latter part of his life, "I owe it, above everything else, to my beloved city of Vienna . . . in whose soil is rooted my whole strength, in whose air float the melodies which my ear has caught, my heart has drunk in, and my hand has written down."

Sentimental, yes. Unrealistic, no. Strauss's own assessment of his creative act is probably accurate. *Zeitgeist* and *genius loci*—the spirits of time and place—have always whispered to the creative imagination, and Strauss, being a musician, surely had a fine ear for such promptings.

I t is impossible to weigh such ephemeral influences, but one can hardly dispute the perceptive comment made by Marcel Brion on Vienna's matchless array of musicians: "They would not have been what they were, what they had to be, if chance had forced them to live anywhere but in Vienna."

Music, like wine, takes its flavor from the soil and the season in which it grows, and the roots of the waltz were nourished by a moment of history in which an aging civilization had reached the peak of mellowness. No other city has ever been so suffused by an art as Vienna was by music. Painting, perhaps, was of similarly intense concern to the Florentines of the Renaissance. But this enthusiasm was confined to a relatively small circle of aristocratic sponsors centering around the Medicis, and it seems unlikely that painting played a major part in the life of the ordinary Florentine.

By contrast, Vienna's involvement with music was shared by its shopkeepers and janitors. The barriers between serious and popular music had not yet become impassable. There was no "music business" in the modern sense, for commercial pressures had not yet debased and polarized public taste. In the crowds who thronged to hear performances of Beethoven symphonies, Haydn oratorios, or Mozart operas, burghers and artisans easily joined princes of the realm. Conversely, in the little rustic inns tucked among the hillsides of the Vienna Woods, members of the nobility mixed quite casually with lesser folk to dance to the sweet and giddy folk tunes of the region. Here lay the tree-shaded courtyards of the *Heurigen*, the vintners' houses where the Viennese sampled the new wine. And if the white wines that grow along the Danube lack the finesse of more famous vintages from the Rhine or the Moselle, they have a tart freshness and a light headiness that make them all the more inviting for casual tippling.

During the long spring and fall seasons, and during the mild summers, these spacious gardens and courtyards were filled daily from about four in the afternoon until the early hours, and their mood of easy conviviality shaped the pattern of Viennese leisure. Drunkenness was not tolerated; the typical Viennese was a thoughtful drinker who made a glass last a long time by puffing, between sips, on a pencil-thin, foot-long cigar that he smoked through a straw. Groups of strolling musicians would pass from one to another of these inns, entertaining the patrons with tunes of the Austrian countryside—the lilting *Ländler*, which was the rural precursor of the not yet invented waltz, and the *Schnadahüpfl*, a jaunty country hop. Here, too, the sound of music created an instant democracy of manners, and class barriers melted in the balmy atmosphere of relaxed hedonism.

This aspect of Vienna's life invariably amazed foreign visitors, particularly those from France, where such casual friendliness between people of widely different social standing was unthinkable either before or after the revolution. "Ancestors and rank seem to be forgotten," reports one traveler, "and aristocratic pride laid aside. Here we see artisans, artists, merchants, councillors, barons, counts and excellencies dancing together with waitresses, women of the middle class, and ladies."

At private concerts, too, there was congenial mingling of persons from different social strata. Tradespeople with sincere musical interests often found access to the musical soirées which were the chief entertainment in the Baroque town houses of the high bourgeoisie.

In an ancient monarchy whose minutely graded class structure might otherwise have calcified into social arthritis, music thus served a vital limbering function. In an order where status—being mostly fixed by birth—could rarely be achieved, music provided the safety valve that kept the pressure of social unrest from building up and enabled absolutism to maintain its sway over Austria long after the American and French revolutions had shaken other thrones.

For centuries, the Habsburg rulers maintained a tradition of fostering the arts. The theater, as long as it confined itself to entertainment and did not become a platform for ideas, received royal encouragement, as did the pictorial arts; sculpture; and, above all, music, architecture, and landscaping.

The implicit tenet was that beauty begets pleasure, and pleasure begets contentment. The great cities of imperial Austria—Vienna, Prague, Salzburg, and Budapest—owe their splendor to the endearing assumption that civic beauty is the key to civic tranquillity.

To accuse the Habsburgs of prostituting art for political aims would be unjust. Its furtherance was no cynically contrived policy. In fact, it was no policy at all, never having been consciously formulated. The state of the arts in Austria sprang quite naturally from a naïvely mystic faith—not uncommon in Catholic countries—that aesthetic grace was akin to divine grace and that to invest a country with outward beauty would somehow bestow civic virtues that would hold it together inwardly. This sort of intuition is legitimate to statecraft. What, after all, is a nation but an agreement on style and a cohesive sharing of myths?

Under these conditions, the whole country seemed pervaded by a certain musicality—an innate, casual feeling for form and harmony. It was evident in the visual charm of the Austrian Baroque that left its mark not alone on the great cities but also on many of the smaller towns and villages.

A feeling for the Baroque and its later, lighter variants, with their graceful, almost melodic lines, was by no means confined to the leading architects employed in the design of palaces and manors. It filtered down to the humblest mason molding garlanded cherubs above the gate of an ordinary house. It shaped the vision of the local builder who quite matter-of-factly bestowed an exquisite harmony of proportions. It guided the hand of the cabinetmaker who filled the house with the playful curves of Rococo and Biedermeier furniture. It influenced the gardener and blacksmith alike, one arranging flowerbeds like calligraphy, the other echoing the scrolls in wrought iron. The tailor and the pastry cook shared a concern for graceful shape, and even the gestures of ordinary citizens reflected a certain elegance as they went about their business.

Industrial manufacture had not yet cast its equalizing pall on the design of objects that fill the household and pass through hands in daily use. Far longer than the more industrialized countries to the west, Austria retained the practice and attitudes of individual craftsmanship. The decorative merit of a product ranked at least as high as its utility. Beauty had market value, and the combination of commercial worth and aesthetic joy bestowed on tradesmen and their customers alike a measure of dignity and satisfaction.

In such an ambience, the ear, too, became attuned to the refinements and delights of form. Music derived from the surroundings. It was inescapable. It lay before the eyes.

Vienna, and much of Austria, thus became a natural breeding ground for musicians. A contemporary chronicler, Eduard Bauernfeld, observes that "every hole is full of musicians who play for the people. Nobody wants to eat his *Bratl* at the inn if he can't have table music to go with it." No feast or celebration was complete without a special overture composed for the occasion. Virtually every bourgeois family could muster a passable string quartet among its members, creating a constant demand for new scores. More than 60 piano factories flourished in the city, which numbered a mere 250,000 inhabitants, and next to good looks and a dowry, musical talent was considered a girl's chief asset.

Every Sunday, the churches resounded with musical settings of the Mass—"operas for the angels," as Mozart called them. Performed by choirs and orchestras of remarkable proficiency, these compositions by Mozart, Haydn, and Schubert were splendidly melodic, and the occasion, despite its ecclesiastical setting, was often more of a public concert than a divine service. The clergy never objected to mixing devotion and enjoyment. In fact, the monasteries owned some of the best vineyards and maintained some of the coziest inns to dispense their wine. Austrian Catholicism had been spared the more Puritan notions of sin that had shaped the restrictive attitudes of northern Europe. It had also escaped much of the cruel virulence of the Counter Reformation. Austria's faith, touchingly expressed in countless sculptures of smiling, childlike Madonnas, never really clashed against that other trinity in Vienna's heaven—wine, women, and song.

Perhaps the most significant aspect of Vienna's musical life was the attitude of the typical listener. In Paris or London, for example, music was regarded as an entertainment. Not so in Vienna. Here it was a personal necessity, an indispensable part of everyday life. In its lighter forms, music was a needed refreshment; in its more demanding forms, an exercise of the spirit in search of illumination.

It is hardly surprising that such a society left considerable room for individuality. The forces of regimentation and efficiency were traditionally resisted, thus preparing the ground for Vienna's famed *Gemütlichkeit*, the characteristic attitude of unhurried bonhomie.

No doubt the most benign economic influence on the social climate was the virtual absence of extreme poverty. To be sure, Vienna had its share of improvidents and people suffering ill fortune. But the causes of their plight were personal rather than built into an exploitive system. Hence their number was small and they did not constitute an embittered group endangering the balance of the community. Where in Paris a Jacobin majority marshaled the envy and fear of the deprived into an orgy of class hatred, the Viennese joined all classes in self-indulgent epicureanism.

Even lowly citizens ate well in Vienna. A surviving restaurant menu lists a complete meal for 13 *Kreuzer*—the equivalent of about 25¢. For this modest sum one could regale oneself on soup, smothered liver, roast beef, vegetables, bread, and a quarter-liter of wine. A remarkable document survives in the City Archives showing that during one typical year (1786) some 200,000 Viennese managed to do away with 42,197 oxen, 1,511 cows, 66,353 calves, 43,925 sheep, 164,700 lambs, 96,949 pigs, 12,967 suckling pigs, 454,063 buckets of local wine, 19,276 buckets of Hungarian and Tirolean wine, and 382,478 buckets of beer. No one seems to have made per-capita comparisons, but this document is generally taken as historic proof of an ample appetite.

Such statistics are not irrelevant to music, for they bespeak a love of life and a general greediness for good things, be they products of art or of the kitchen.

With comforts of mind and body abundant and readily available, economic incentive never was honed to an irritant edge. Material possessions alone could not change one's social standing in a fixed-status society, and since the public environment was generally delightful, there was less need for private luxury. Consequently, acquisitive drive, the dominant motivating force in open and industrial societies, rarely inspired the Viennese. Their motivation was not so much material success but satisfaction with the task at hand, or, quite often, simply the leisurely enjoyment of the day. To the Viennese, this was the utmost practicality and realism.

As long as external conditions supported this mode of existence, remarkably little cruelty or vulgarity crept to the surface of Austrian life. The feral substrate at the bottom of any society remained nicely covered. And those who, by dark intuition, knew it was there said nothing of it.

Of course, not even an unfailing surfeit of music and Wiener schnitzel could remove all challenges from life, but in an age of indulgent epicureanism, these challenges could usually be surmounted by not trying too hard. That, too, lies in the music. The cardinal rule for playing a waltz is the same as for mastering other phases of life in Vienna: Don't push it—and keep the tempo loose.

Its cushioned resilience made Vienna relatively crisis-proof—at least until the final, cataclysmic collapse of the empire. Nonchalant self-irony lent Vienna, and all Austria, the buoyancy to clear minor hurdles. For example, during a government scandal involving payoffs at the ministerial level, the noted Viennese journalist Karl Kraus soothed tempers by explaining that the accused civil servant "took such small bribes as to border on incorruptibility."

Scanning 1,000 years of Austrian history, John Gunther observed that the country "in its own inimitable, slippery way wriggled out of any difficulty. Something of the very softness of the Austrian character had been a factor of strength, because the horns of a crisis were apt to disappear through absorption—the crisis lost its point, melted in the prevailing solvent of easygoing compromise."

This is hardly a country to be admired by moralists. Philosophers may not find it much to their liking, either. But poets and musicians have always felt at home there, for the land pulses with the heartbeat of humanity.

Johann Strauss felt that pulse and shaped it into a special music that lifted Vienna from its moorings on the map, wafting the city across that misty line between reality and dream into the land of the waltz.

The Law of the Heuriger

By Alan Levy

Maria Theresa's son, Emperor Joseph II (1741–90), who wanders in and out of the play and movie *Amadeus* muttering, "Well, there you are," uttered far more enduring words on August 17, 1784, when he proclaimed to the Austrian people that "we give every man the freedom to sell or dispense—year-round, in any form, at any time, and at whatever price he wants—food, wine, or fruit juice that he has produced himself."

Handed this entrepreneurial key by royalty, the farmers of the Vienna Woods unlatched the *Heuriger:* a unique wine tavern that proliferates in the capital and eastern Austria. Heuriger is a noun derived from an adjective meaning "this year's," which applies not only to young wines, but also to such crops as cabbage and potatoes. To the thirsty, however, the only real heuriger is the farmhouse facade adorned by a sprig of pine, a branch of fir, or a wreath of holly and a plaque on the door signifying that the new wine is in and has been pressed on the premises. Open that door in summer and you'll feast your eyes upon an inviting courtyard lined with picnic tables and crowded with Austrians making merry (which, often as not, means intense intellectual conversations about trivia), frequently hoisting glasses for toasting or refilling, and occasionally lifting voices, too, in song.

Inside the house you'll usually find a buffet from which you can buy hot or cold food and, in those that stay open year-round, a cozy hearth around which you can also eat, drink, and revel. In the larger heurige (plural) or posher ones that cater to tourists and businesspeople, you'll find live music—usually *Schrammelmusik*, named after a 19th-century family who composed, played, sang, and ordained the wistful sound of music still heard in the heuriger.

Rendered by violins, guitar, and clarinet or accordion and sung in an impenetrable Austrian dialect, the songs counterpoint the conversation by treating such earthy themes as a lover's lane in the Vienna Woods that's too small for one person but big enough for two, or lamenting that "the old cog-wheel railway is scrap iron now," or wrestling with the dilemma of a would-be lover who's making headway but watching the clock in the knowledge that the last streetcar leaves soon and he doesn't have money for the taxi ride that would clinch his case. This song is called "The Little Blue Light," and, while the last No. 38 streetcar from the wine suburb of Grinzing no longer wears a blue lamp on its tail, its illuminated destination signs bear equally ominous blue squares of cardboard.

In Grinzing, in particular, one must be wary of places where the Vienna-by-night tour buses draw up every half hour and the schrammel musicians drop everything to play "Deep in the Heart of Texas" or "If I Were a Rich Man." Stick around there and you won't be rich for long. Far better to follow a Viennese drinking song with lyrics that list virtually every wine village within easy reach, starting with "a little Grinzing, a little Sievering, a little Neuwaldegg, Nussdorf, Ottakring and Petersdorf." Or play it safe at the elegantly rustic Grinzinger Hauermandl, where the music, chicken, and wine are consistently first-rate.

Today, within the city limits of Vienna, there are some 800 families growing wine on more than 1,800 acres to produce about 12 million quarter-liter glasses of wine per year. Heuriger wine is mostly white: clear, sparkling, dry, and, thanks to its high acidity, possessed of a fresh bite that can bite back the morning after. It is wise to switch, after a couple of glasses, from new wine to old *(alt)*. The price may be a dime more tonight, but tomorrow's pain will be less.

The Vienna Tourist Board once published a brochure, "Heurige in Wien," listing 150 of them by neighborhood. There are at least five times that many, and one of the charms of a summer night is to discover your own. Even the farsighted Joseph II, "the People's Emperor" who encouraged Mozart and tried to democratize the Habsburg monarchy, might be astonished at how the cottage industry he envisioned has become a backbone of both Austrian tourism and Viennese life.

"During the warm season, from May to September, people go early, around six o'clock in the evening," says Traudl Lessing, a Viennese chronicler and connoisseur of heuriger living. "They take their children and dogs along, as both provide excellent starting points for conversation and friendly relations. As soon as the benches around the rough wooden tables have filled, people sit down with strangers and begin to confide in each other. They tell their unknown friends about the wife's illness, the cranky boss, and how they avoid the burdens of taxation."

Frau Lessing and her husband, Erich, gave their daughter Hannah's wedding party indoors last January at the spacious and lively Heuriger Schübel-Auer in the Heiligenstadt neighborhood. Beethoven once lived in this district and cursed the church bells he could see tolling but not hear. In fact, just around the corner, a 17th-century house where the peripatetic composer resided for part of 1817 is now one of Vienna's most famous heurige: Mayer am Pfarrplatz.

After Joseph II's 1784 proclamation, known in Vienna as "the law of the heuriger," farmers started selling pork, poultry, and sometimes beef from their own livestock in the front rooms where their customers used to sample their wines. Farmers' daughters found work at home as cooks and waitresses instead of migrating to the city or marrying for survival. Soon, whole families were making cheese and peddling their produce to a market that came to them.

Early in the 20th century, this laissez-faire law of the heuriger was modified for the only time in its 207-year history. Its provisions had spawned too many child alcoholics and adult workaholics—the former souring on not-always-unfermented grape juice; the latter missing church—so certain soft drinks were sanctioned (usually Almdudler Limonade, which tastes like ginger ale), and farmers were forbidden to sell their wines on more than 300 days a year. The amendment also permitted ham and cheese and fowl to be sold by wine farmers who didn't have their own pigs and cows and chickens. Even today, though, a wine tavern peddling beer, coffee, or Coca-Cola isn't an authentic heuriger and shouldn't be displaying the symbolic green bush outside.

During and after two devastating world wars, the heuriger assumed a new social role in Viennese lives. Rather than entertain in cramped, shabby, or bomb-damaged quarters, hosts invited their guests to meet them at "our heuriger," where they would buy drinks and sometimes dinner—though it is still good form in many heurige to bring your own picnic and buy just wine. If the coffeehouse, a tradition a century older than the heuriger, remains the living room of the Viennese—"neither at home nor in the fresh air," they like to say—the heuriger is their summer garden and year-round retreat.

How the heuriger has kept pace with modern times, trends, and thinking can be experienced most happily on a visit to Gumpoldskirchen, a wine village some seven miles outside the city. On the dividing line between the slopes of the *Wienerwald* (Vienna Woods, the northeastern foothills of the Alps) and the *Puszta* (the flat Hungarian plain that begins in Austria), Gumpoldskirchen is a more early-to-sing, early-to-bed place than Grinzing—and the prices are better. If you arrive around 3 or 4 PM, there is ample light to explore some of the 100 charming courtyards behind welcoming green laurels and tarry perhaps in the Renaissance sobriety of the Benedictine monks' heuriger or the cozy nook carved out of a wine barrel in Schabl's Pressehaus (both on the main street) before bearing left at the onion-domed church around which the town was built several centuries ago.

This will put you on a *Weinwanderweg* through the vineyards: a 30- to 45-minute circle walk designed and decorated in 1975 by the vintners of Gumpoldskirchen. An ancient wine press looms up on a hillside like a gallows. A modern metal sculpture of an insect magnifies and gentrifies the *Reblaus* (phylloxera), a plant pest that came over from California in the 1870s and destroyed most of

Europe's wines; the vines were restored only when reblaus-resistant strains were also imported from California.

Along its way, the Weinwanderweg relates the history of Austrian wines from the third century, when the Roman Emperor Probus first allowed grapes to be grown outside Italy, up through Joseph II to the present day, when Gumpoldskirchen leads all of Austria in the production of Zierfandler, another white wine deceptively called Rotgipfler, and Blauer Portugieser, which is red and Austrian.

Somehow, one develops a thirst along the Weinwanderweg, and in gathering darkness, dozens of pine bushes of Gumpoldskirchen are already illuminated and beckoning below. Safely down, you should head for one of the twin heurige of the Bruckberger family at Wienerstrasse 1 and Kirchenplatz 1, where the music has already started and the partying has been going on for hours.

The Bruckbergers have been in the wine business for more than three centuries. They slaughter their homefed livestock once a week. Apple-cheeked young Hans Bruckberger presides over the noisy, happy, 800-seat heuriger that bears the family name on the main street. A couple of blocks away, right where the Weinwanderweg begins and ends, his sister Elisabeth runs a more intimate cellar heuriger for romantic dining by candlelight and softer music. The wine, music, and strudel in both places are just right—and so are the duck at Elisabeth's and the crisp bread and spicy Liptauer cheese, roast chicken, and steamy pigs' knuckles at Hans's.

Hans's and Elisabeth's sister, Hansi, runs a *Heuriger-proviant*, a food-supply store adjacent to the larger heuriger. Here you can buy cold cuts and bread for snacking along the Weinwanderweg or on a Wienerwald hike or if you just don't feel like hacking the buffet in the heuriger. At the end of an evening, when a Bruckberger patron expresses the need for a cup of coffee before heading back to the real world, particularly by car, the dirndled wine waitress will respond demurely with: "That would be against the law of the heuriger. But we can send out. Give me the money and I'll go next door and buy you one."

Taking your schillings and accepting a small tip, she strides through Hans's kitchen into Hansi's store. As a shopkeeper, Hansi is allowed to brew and sell coffee. The law of the heuriger has been circumvented, but if it helps a drinker to arrive home safely, well, as Joseph II might say, there you are.

3 Vienna

Introduction

By George H. Sullivan

Vienna is a city that deeply loves its past. For many centuries it was one of the great capitals of Europe, home to the Habsburg rulers of the Austro-Hungarian Empire. Today the empire is long gone, but many reminders of the city's imperial heyday remain, carefully preserved by the tradition-loving Viennese. Most of Vienna's renowned 18th- and 19th-century buildings have been preserved as well, attesting to a brilliant architectural past that few cities can match.

From the late 18th century until World War I, Vienna's culture—particularly its musical culture—was famous throughout Europe. Haydn, Mozart, Beethoven, Schubert, Brahms, Strauss, Mahler, and Bruckner all lived in the city, producing music that is still played in concert halls all over the world. And at the tail end of the 19th century the city's artists and architects—Gustav Klimt, Egon Schiele, Oskar Kokoschka, Josef Hoffmann, Otto Wagner, and Adolf Loos among them—brought about an unprecedented artistic revolution, a revolution that swept away the past and set the stage for the radically experimental art of the 20th century.

At the close of World War I the Austro-Hungarian Empire was dismembered, and Vienna lost its cherished status as the seat of imperial power. Its influence was much reduced, and (unlike most of Europe's other great cities) its population began to decline, from around 2 million to the current 1.5 million. Today, however, the city's future looks bright, for with the collapse of the Iron Curtain, Vienna may at long last regain its traditional status as the hub of central Europe.

For many first-time visitors, the city's one major disappointment is the Danube River. The inner city, it turns out, lies not on the river's main stream but on one of its narrow offshoots, known as the Danube Canal. As a result, the sweeping river views expected by most newcomers fail to materialize.

The Romans are to blame, for when Vienna was founded as a Roman military encampment around AD 100, the walled garrison was built not on the Danube's main stream but rather on the largest of the river's eastern branches, where it could be bordered by water on three sides. (To this day the outline of the Roman walls, a lopsided square, can be seen in the street plan of the inner city: Naglergasse and the Graben to the southwest, Kramergasse and Rotgasse to the southeast, Salzgasse to the northeast, and Tiefer Graben to the northwest.) The wide present-day Danube did not take shape until the late 19th century, when its various branches were rerouted and merged to prevent flooding.

The Romans maintained their camp for some 300 years (the emperor Marcus Aurelius is thought to have died there in AD 180) and finally abandoned it around AD 400. The settlement survived, however, and by the 13th century growth was sufficient to require new city walls to the south. According to legend, the walls were financed by the English: In 1192 the local duke kidnapped King Richard I, who was on his way home from the Third Crusade, and held him prisoner for two years until he was expensively ransomed.

Vienna's third set of walls dates from 1544, when the existing walls were improved and extended. The new fortifications were built by the Habsburg dynasty, who ruled the Austro-Hungarian Empire for an astonishing 640 years, beginning with Rudolf I in 1273 and ending with Karl I in 1918. The walls stood until 1857, when Emperor Franz Josef finally decreed that they be demolished and replaced by the famous Ringstrasse ("Ring Street").

During medieval times the city's growth was relatively slow, and its heyday as a European capital did not begin until 1683, after a huge force of invading Turks laid siege to the city for two months and were finally routed by an army of Habsburg allies. Among the supplies that the fleeing Turks left behind were sacks filled with coffee beans. It was these beans, so the story goes, that gave a local entrepreneur the idea of opening the first public coffeehouse. Cafés remain a Viennese institution to this day.

The passing of the Turkish threat produced a Viennese building boom, and the Baroque style was the architectural order of the day. The style had originated in Italy around 1600, when a group of brilliantly inventive Italian architects began to embroider and transform the classical motifs that the High Renaissance had copied from ancient Rome. Architects in other countries throughout Europe followed suit, and during the 17th century England, France, and Austria all developed Baroque styles that were very much their own. Austrian Baroque possessed a special grace, described in detail in the walking tours to follow, and it is this grace that gives Vienna the distinctive architectural character that sets the city so memorably apart from its great rivals London, Paris, and Rome.

Essential Information

Important Addresses and Numbers

By George W. Hamilton

Tourist Information

The main point for information is the **Vienna City Tourist Office** *(Fremdenverkehrsstelle der Stadt Wien)*, around the corner from the Hotel Sacher, at Kärntner Strasse 38 (tel. 0222/513–8892) open from 9 to 7 daily. The **Österreichisches Verkehrsbüro** (in Opernpassage, underground in front of the Opera, tel. 0222/586–2352) offers similar services and can provide theater tickets, Monday–Saturday 9–6, Sunday 9–2.

If you need a room, go to **Information-Zimmernachweis** operated by the Verkehrsbüro in the Westbahnhof (tel. 0222/892–3392, open daily 6:15 AM–11 PM) and in the Südbahnhof (tel. 0222/505–3132, open daily 6:30 AM–9 PM). At the airport, the information and room-reservation office (tel. 0222/71110–2617) is open Mon.–Thurs. 9–4:30 and Fri. 9–3 for reservations, for information daily 8:30 AM–10 PM. The information office at the DDSG dock on the Danube (tel. 0222/21750–454) is open when ships are docking and embarking. None of these offices can arrange room bookings by telephone.

If you're driving into Vienna, get information or book rooms at **Information-Zimmernachweis** at the end of the Westautobahn at Wientalstrasse/Auhof (tel. 0222/971271) or at the end of the Südautobahn at Triesterstrasse 149 (tel. 0222/674151 or 0222/677100).

Embassies The U.S. embassy is at Boltzmanngasse 16, tel. 0222/31339; the consulate is at Gartenbaupromenade, Parkring 12A, in the Marriott building, tel. 0222/31339. The **Canadian embassy** is at Dr. Karl Lueger-Ring 10, tel. 0222/533-3691. The **U.K. embassy and consulate** are at Jauresgasse 10; embassy tel. 0222/713-1575, consulate tel. 0222/714-6117.

Emergencies The emergency numbers are 133 for the **police,** 144 for an **ambulance,** 122 for the **fire department.** If you need a doctor and speak no German, ask your hotel, or in an emergency, phone your consulate.

English-language Bookstores **Big Ben Bookstore** (Porzellangasse 24, tel. 0222/319-6412), **British Bookstore** (Weihburggasse 8, tel. 0222/512-1945), **Pickwick's** (Marc-Aurel-Str. 10-12, tel. 0222/533-0182), **Shakespeare & Co.** (Sterngasse 2, tel. 0222/535-5053).

English-language Radio "Blue Danube Radio" on FM at 103.8 and 93.9 MHz carries news, music, and information in English (and some in French) throughout the day and evening.

Late-night Pharmacies In each area of the city one pharmacy stays open 24 hours; if a pharmacy is closed, a sign on the door will tell you the address of the nearest one that is open. Call 0222/1550 for names and addresses (in German) of the pharmacies open that night.

Lost and Found Check with the police at the **Fundamt** (Wasagasse 22, tel. 0222/313440 or 0222/31344-9211). If your loss occurred on a train, check the **Bundesbahn Fundamt** (railway lost property office, tel. 5800 for information). If you were coming in from Salzburg, call the office at the **Westbahnhof** (tel. 0222/5800-32996). Losses on the subway system or streetcars can be checked by calling the **Zentrale Fundstelle** (tel. 0222/50130-3500).

Travel Agencies **American Express** (Kärntner Str. 21-23, tel. 0222/51540, fax 0222/51540-70), **Thomas Cook/Wagon-Lits** (Kärntner Ring 2, tel. 0222/50160, fax 0222/50160-65), **Cosmos** (Kärntner Ring 15, tel. 0222/515330, fax 0222/513-4147), **Ruefa Reisen** (Fleischmarkt 1, tel. 0222/53404, fax 0222/53404-394), **Österreichisches Verkehrsbüro** (Friedrichstr. 7, opposite Sezession, tel. 0222/588000, fax 0222/568533).

Arriving and Departing by Plane

Vienna's airport is at Schwechat, about 19 km (12 mi) southeast of the city. For flight information, call 0222/71110-2233. **Austrian Airlines, Air Canada, Delta, Lauda Air,** and **TWA** fly into Schwechat from North America.

Between the Airport and City Center *By Bus* A bus leaves the airport every 20 minutes for the city air terminal beside the Hilton Hotel. The trip takes about 25 minutes and costs AS60; you buy your ticket on the bus, so be sure to have Austrian money handy. A bus also runs every half hour to the Westbahnhof (West rail station) via the Südbahnhof (South station); this bus might land you closer to your hotel, and taxis are available at the station.

By Taxi Taxis will take about 30 minutes to most downtown locations, longer when traffic is heavy (7-8:30 AM and 4:30-6:30 PM on weekdays). Taxis from Vienna are not allowed to pick up passengers at the airport unless they've been ordered; only those from Lower Austria (where the airport is located, beyond the city limits) can take passengers into town. This means that taxis travel one way empty, so the meter fare is doubled; you'll end up with a bill of about AS350. You can cut the charge in half by phoning one of the Vienna cab companies from the airport (tel. 0222/31300, 0222/60160, or 0222/40100) and asking for a taxi to take you into town. They'll give you the last couple of digits of the taxi license, and you wait until it arrives. Be sure to arrange where the taxi will meet you. The same scheme applies when you leave: Not all Vienna cabs have permits for airport service, so call in advance to get one that can take you out for about AS250–AS270.

By Limousine **Mazur** limos provide door-to-door transportation that's cheaper than a taxi. Look for the Mazur stand at the airport, or call 0222/ 604–9191 or 0222/604–2233.

By Train Fast trains run from the airport to the **Wien Mitte** station across the street from the Hilton Hotel and to the **Wien Nord** station, Praterstern, but the rail service is less frequent than the bus (about one train an hour), and both land you in virtually the same spot. Fare: AS30, or a Vienna streetcar ticket plus AS15.

Arriving and Departing by Car, Train, Boat, and Bus

By Car On the road from the airport and on highways from points south or west, **Zentrum** signs clearly mark the route to the center of Vienna. From there, however, finding your way to your hotel can be no mean trick, for traffic planners have installed a devious scheme prohibiting through traffic in the city core (the First District) and scooting them out again via a network of exasperating one-way streets. In the city itself a car is a burden, though very useful for trips outside town. Overnight street parking in the First District is restricted to residents with special permits.

By Train Trains from Germany, Switzerland, and western Austria arrive at the **Westbahnhof** (West Station), on Europaplatz, where the Mariahilfer Strasse crosses the Gürtel. If you're coming from Italy or Hungary, you'll generally arrive at the **Südbahnhof** (South station, Wiedner Gürtel 1). The current stations for trains to and from Prague and Warsaw are **Wien Nord** (North Station, Praterstern) and **Franz-Josef Bahnhof** (Julius-Tandler-Platz). Central train information will have details (tel. 0222/1717, or tel. 0222/1552 for taped schedule information).

By Boat If you arrive in Vienna via the Danube, the DDSG ship will leave you at **Praterlände** near Mexikoplatz (Handelskai 265, tel. 0222/217100), although some downstream ships also make a stop at **Nussdorf** (Heiligenstädter Str. 180, tel. 0222/371257). The Praterlände stop is a short taxi ride from the Vorgartenstrasse subway station, or you can take a taxi directly into town.

By Bus International long-distance bus service (Bratislava, Brno) and most postal and railroad buses arrive at the **Wien Mitte** central bus station (Landstrasser Hauptstr. 1B, tel. 0222/711070 or 0222/71101), across from the Hilton Hotel.

Getting Around

Vienna is divided into 23 numbered districts. Taxi drivers may need to know which district you seek, as well as the street address. The district number is coded into the postal code with the second and third digits; thus A–1010 (the "01") is the First District, A-1030 is the Third, A-1110 is the 11th, and so on. Some sources and maps still give the district numbers, either in Roman or Arabic numerals, as Vienna X or Vienna 10.

Vienna is a city to tackle on foot. With the exception of the Schönbrunn and Belvedere palaces and the Prater amusement park, most sights are concentrated in the center, the First District (A–1010), much of which is a pedestrian zone anyway.

Get public-transport maps at a tourist office or at the transport-information offices *(Wiener Verkehrsbetriebe),* underground at Karlsplatz, Stephansplatz, and Praterstern. Vienna's public transportation system is fast, clean, safe, and easy to use. You can transfer on the same ticket between subway, streetcar, bus, and long stretches of the fast suburban railway, *Schnellbahn (S–Bahn).* Buy single tickets for AS20 from dispensers on the streetcar or bus or at one of the subway stations, you'll need exact change. At *Tabak-Trafik* (cigarette shops/newsstands) or the underground *Wiener Verkehrsbetriebe* offices you can get a block of five tickets for AS75, each ticket good for one uninterrupted trip in more or less the same general direction with unlimited transfers. Or you can get a three-day ticket for AS115, good on all lines for 72 hours from the time you validate the ticket; there's also a 24-hour ticket for AS45. If you're staying longer, get an eight-day (AS235) ticket, which can be used on eight separate days or by any number of persons (up to eight) at any one time. A useful address is Tabak-Trafik Almassy (Stephansplatz 4, to the right behind the cathedral, tel. 0222/512–5909); it is open every day from 8 AM to 7 PM and has tickets as well as film and other items.

By Rental Car **Avis** (at airport, tel. 0222/71110–2700), Opernring 1, tel. 0222/587–6241.

Budget (at airport, tel. 0222/71110–2711), Hilton Hotel, Am Stadtpark, tel. 0222/714–6565.

EuroDollar (at airport, tel. 0222/71110–2699), Schubertring 9, tel. 0222/714–6717.

Hertz (at airport, tel. 0222/71110–2661), Kärntner Ring 17, tel. 0222/512–8677; international reservations, tel. 0222/713–1596.

National (Europcar/interRent at airport, tel. 0222/71110–3316), Denzel Autovermietung, Kärntner Ring 14, tel. 0222/505–4166.

By Subway Five subway lines *(U-bahn),* whose stations are prominently marked with blue *U* signs, crisscross the city. Karlsplatz and Stephansplatz are the main transfer points between lines. The last subway (U4) runs at about 12:20 AM. The U3 line is now extended to the Westbahnhof.

By Streetcar and Bus The first streetcars run about 5:15 AM, for those Viennese who start work at 8. From then on, service (barring gridlock on the streets) is regular and reliable, and most lines operate until about midnight. Where streetcars don't run, buses do; route maps and schedules are posted at each bus or subway stop.

Should you miss the last streetcar or bus, special night buses with an *N* designation operate at half-hour intervals on Saturday nights and nights before a holiday over several key routes; the starting (and transfer) point is Schwedenplatz. The night-owl buses take a special fare of AS25, tickets available on the bus; normal tickets are not valid.

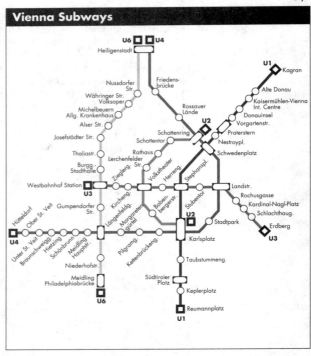

Vienna Subways

Within the heart of the city, bus lines 1A, 2A and 3A are useful crosstown routes. These carry a reduced fare of AS7.50 per trip if you have bought the *Kurzstrecke* ticket (AS30), good for four trips or up to four people on one trip (with no transfer). The *Kurzstrecke* tickets are also valid for two stops on the subway or shorter distances on the streetcar lines.

By Taxi Taxis in Vienna are relatively inexpensive. The initial charge is AS24 for as many as four people weekdays from 6 AM to 11 PM, AS25 for weekdays between 11 PM and 6 AM and on Saturdays, Sundays and holidays. AS12 is added for radio cabs ordered by phone and for each piece of luggage that must go into the trunk, and a charge is added for waiting beyond a reasonable limit. It's customary to round up the fare to cover the tip. Taxis can be flagged on the street (when the roof light is on), taken from regular stands, or ordered by phone. To get a radio cab, call 0222/31300, 0222/40100, or 0222/60160. Service is usually prompt, but at rush hour, when weather is bad, or if you need to keep to an exact schedule, call ahead and order a taxi for a specific time. If your destination is the airport, ask for a reduced-rate taxi.

By Limousine For a chauffeured limousine call **Avis-Adler** (tel. 0222/216–0990), **Göth** (tel. 0222/713–7196), **Mazur** (tel. 0222/604–2233), **Mietwagen Sidlo** (tel. 0222/314244), or **Peter Urban** (tel. 0222/713–5255 or 713–3781).

Guided Tours

Orientation When you're pressed for time, a good way to see the highlights of Vienna is via a sightseeing-bus tour, which gives you a once-over-lightly of the heart of the city and allows a closer look at Schönbrunn and Belvedere palaces. **Vienna Sightseeing Tours** (Stelzhammergasse 4/11, tel. 0222/712–4683, fax 0222/712–4683–77; a booking office is downstairs in the Opernpassage) runs a 1¼-hour "get acquainted" tour daily, leaving from in front of the Opera at 10:30 and 11:45 AM and 3 PM (adults AS190, children AS100). **Vienna Line** (Johannesgasse 14, tel. 0222/512–8091, fax 0222/513–9397) runs a similar tour at 9:30 AM and 2:30 PM in summer, 10:30 AM in winter, for AS200, leaving from the Kursalon at Johannesgasse 33, close to the U4 subway station. You can cover almost the same territory on your own by taking either the No. 1 or No. 2 streetcar around the Ring, and then walking through the heart of the city (*see* Self-guided, *below*). **Vienna Sightseeing, Vienna Line,** and **Cityrama/Gray Line** (Börsegasse 1, tel. 0222/534–130, fax 0222/534–1322) all have tours of about three hours (adults AS320–340, children AS100), including visits to Schönbrunn and Belvedere palace grounds. If you want to see the Schönbrunn interior, you'll have to pay a separate entrance fee and find your way back to the center of town yourself (*see* Tour 7, *below*). The Vienna Line trip includes the 150-meter (488-foot) Donauturm tower. Cityrama and Vienna Sightseeing tours start daily at 9:30 and 10:30 AM, and 2:30 PM; the Vienna Line tours at 10 AM and 2 PM, plus one at 11 AM in summer. All three firms offer a number of other tours as well (your hotel will have detailed programs), and provide hotel pickup for most tours. For other than the "get acquainted" tours, the Vienna Sightseeing buses leave the central loading point in front of the Opera 10 minutes before scheduled tour departures to make the hotel pickups. Cityrama and Vienna Line tours start from Johannesgasse at the Stadtpark station on the U4 subway line, across from the InterContinental hotel.

Streetcar Tours From early May through mid-October, a 1929 vintage streetcar leaves each Saturday at 1:30 PM and Sundays and holidays at 10 AM and 1:30 PM from the Otto Wagner Pavilion at Karlsplatz for a guided tour. For AS200 (children AS70), you'll go around the Ring, out past the big Ferris wheel in the Prater and past Schönbrunn and Belvedere palaces in the course of the two-hour trip. Get tickets in advance at the transport-information office underground at Karlsplatz, weekdays 7–6, weekends and holidays 8:30–4 (tel. 0222/587–3186).

Boat Tours The **Donau-Dampfschiffahrts-Gesellschaft** (DDSG; tel. 0222/217100) runs a three-hour boat tour up the Danube Canal and down the Danube, from Schwedenbrücke, by Schwedenplatz, May through September, daily at 10:30 AM, 1, 2:30, and 4:30 PM. From early to late April and late September to October 26, tours run daily at 1 PM. There are "golden oldies" disco-dancing cruises, from mid-May to late September every Friday and Saturday, from mid-June to late September on Thursdays as well, departing at 8:30 PM. Reservations are essential (tel. 0222/21750–451).

Personal Guides Guided walking tours (in English) are a great way to see the city highlights. Tour topics range from "Unknown Underground Vienna" to "1,000 Years of Jewish Tradition" and "Vienna Around Sigmund Freud." Tours take about 1½ hours, are held in any weather provided at least three persons turn up, and cost AS105 (ages 15–18, AS50) plus any entry fees. No reservations are needed. Get a list of the guided-tour possibilities at the city information office at Kärntner Strasse 38 (tel. 0222/513–8892). Ask for the monthly brochure "Walks in Vienna," which details the tours, days, times, and starting points. You can also arrange to have your own privately guided tour for AS1,085 for a half day.

Self-guided Get a copy of *Vienna: Downtown Walking Tours* by Henriette Mandl (Ueberreuter, 1987; AS198) from any bookshop. The six tours take you through the highlights of central Vienna with excellent commentary and some entertaining anecdotes, which most of your Viennese acquaintances won't know. The booklet "Vienna from A–Z" (in English, AS40; available at bookshops) explains the numbered plaques attached to all major buildings.

Horse Cab A *Fiaker*, or horse cab, will trot you around to whatever destination you specify, but this is an expensive way to see the city. A short tour of the inner city takes about 20 minutes and costs AS400; a longer one including the Ringstrasse takes 40–45 minutes and costs AS800, for the whole Fiaker. The carriages accommodate four (five if someone sits next to the coachman). Starting points are Heldenplatz in front of the Hofburg, Stephansplatz beside the cathedral, and across from the Albertina, all in the First District. For longer trips, or any variation of the regular route, agree on the price first.

Exploring Vienna

Orientation

By George H. Sullivan

To the Viennese, the most prestigious address of Vienna's 23 *Bezirke*, or districts, is the First District (the inner city, bounded by the Ringstrasse and the Danube Canal). The Second through the Ninth districts surround the inner city (starting with the Second District across the Danube Canal and running clockwise); the 10th through the 23rd districts form a second concentric ring of suburbs. The vast majority of sightseeing attractions are to be found in the First District. For hard-core sightseers who wish to supplement the walking tours that follow, the tourist office (*see* Important Addresses and Numbers in Essential Information, *above*) has a booklet "Vienna from A–Z" (AS40) that gives short descriptions of some 250 sights around the city, all numbered and keyed to a fold-out map at the back, as well as to wall plaques on the buildings themselves. The more important churches possess coin-operated (AS10) tape machines that give an excellent commentary in English on the history and architecture of the church.

The description of the city on the following pages is divided into seven tours: six walks that explore the architectural riches of central Vienna, and a seventh tour that describes Schönbrunn Palace and its gardens. If you arrive in the city in the early afternoon and do not want to plunge into inner-city sightseeing, a visit to Schönbrunn is highly recommended, since the half-day sightseeing trips no longer include a tour inside Schönbrunn. In any case, it's far cheaper and more flexible to tackle the palace on your own.

Highlights for First-time Visitors

St. Stephen's Cathedral (*see* Tour 1: The City's Ancient Core)

The Hofburg (*see* Tour 4: The Hofburg and the Ringstrasse)

Schönbrunn Palace (*see* Tour 7: Schönbrunn Palace)

Belvedere Palace (*see* Tour 6: South of the Ring to the Belvedere)

Kunsthistorisches Museum (Museum of Art History; *see* Tour 4: The Hofburg and the Ringstrasse)

Tour 1: The City's Ancient Core

Numbers in the margin correspond to points of interest on the Vienna map.

The citizens of Vienna, it has often been said, waltz only from the waist down, whirling around the crowded dance floor while holding their upper bodies motionless and ramrod straight. The sight can be breathtaking in its sweep and splendor, and its elegant coupling of freewheeling exuberance and rigid formality—of license and constraint—is quintessentially Viennese.

Architecture is frozen music, said the German poet Goethe, and the closest that European architecture ever came to embodying the Viennese waltz, appropriately enough, is the Viennese town palace. Built mostly during the 18th century, these Baroque mansions can be found all over the inner city, and they present in stone and stucco the same artful synthesis of license and constraint as the dance that was so often performed inside them. They make Vienna a Baroque city that is, at its best, an architectural waltz.

The inner city is by no means exclusively Baroque, however. Occasional survivors from medieval times as well as many additions from the 19th and 20th centuries dot the cityscape, and sometimes they present startling alternatives to the city's prevailing architectural style.

❶ Tour 1 begins with the most prominent of these anomalies: **St. Stephen's Cathedral** (in German, *Stephansdom*), at the heart of the inner city. Consecrated in 1147, St. Stephen's is the hub of the city's wheel; for more than eight centuries its enormous bulk has served as the nucleus around which the city has grown. The top of its tall south tower is the city's preeminent lookout point, offering fine views in all directions. Be warned, however, that the 345-step ascent is long and arduous; you may want to postpone it until the last day of your visit, when the city's landmarks will be familiar and the views will serve to fix them in your memory. An easier alternative is to take the elevator from inside the church up the north tower to the level of the great "Pummerin" bell. *Admission (south tower, open daily 9–5:30): AS20 adults, AS15 children; (elevator, open daily 9–6): AS40 adults, AS15 children.*

As architecture, St. Stephen's possesses a fierce presence that is blatantly un-Viennese, a stylistic jumble, ranging from 13th-century Romanesque to 15th-century Gothic. Like the exterior, St. Stephen's interior lacks the soaring unity of Europe's greatest Gothic cathedrals, with much of its decoration dating from the later Baroque era.

The wealth of decorative sculpture in St. Stephen's can be demoralizing to the nonspecialist, so if you wish to explore the cathedral in detail, you may want to buy the admirably complete English-language description sold in the small room marked *Schriften und Opferkerzen* (Pamphlets and Votive Candles).

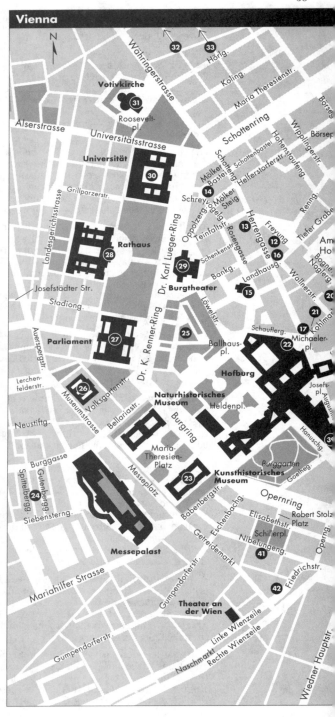

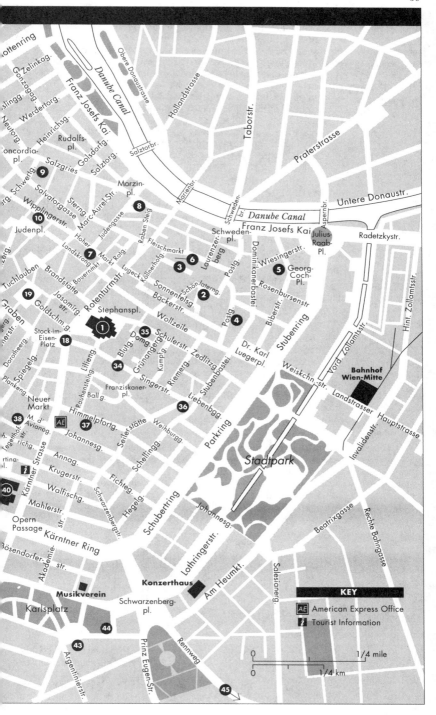

One particularly masterly work, however, should be seen by everyone: the stone pulpit attached to the second freestanding pier on the left of the central nave, carved by Anton Pilgram around 1510. The spun-sugar delicacy of its decoration would in itself set the pulpit apart, but even more intriguing are its five sculpted figures. Carved around the outside of the pulpit proper are the four Latin Fathers of the Church (from left to right: Saint Augustine, Saint Gregory, Saint Jerome, and Saint Ambrose), and each is given an individual personality so sharply carved as to suggest satire, perhaps of living models. (The four figures may also have been meant to represent the Four Temperaments of ancient lore: melancholic, phlegmatic, choleric, and sanguine.) There is no satire suggested by the fifth figure, however; below the pulpit's stairs Pilgram sculpted a fine self-portrait, showing himself peering out a half-open window.

St. Stephen's was devastated by bombing during World War II, and the extent of the damage may be seen by leaving the cathedral through the south porch, where a set of prereconstruction photographs commemorates the disaster. Restoration was protracted and difficult, but today the cathedral once again dominates the center of the city.

Walk up to the Wollzeile and cut through one of the narrow passageways, turning right down Bäckerstrasse. Café Alt Wien at Bäckerstrasse 9 is a true original and a hangout for artists and students young and old. Other cafés, bars, and small restaurants along the street are equally worth a visit. Don't overlook the amusing, 18th-century cow playing checkers painted on the facade of the house at No. 12. Bäckerstrasse brings you to Dr.-Ignaz-Siepel-Platz, named for the theology professor who was chancellor of Austria during the 1920s. On the north side is the **Universitätskirche,** or **Jesuitenkirche,** built around 1630. Its flamboyant Baroque interior contains a fine trompe l'oeil ceiling fresco by that master of visual trickery, Andrea Pozzo, who was imported from Rome in 1702 for the job.

The exterior of the church provides an illuminating contrast to the **Academy of Science** (Old University) on the west side of the square. While the church's facade exhibits a rudimentary classicism—the decorative pediments above the windows and the double-story pilasters are plain and rather awkwardly arranged—there is nothing awkward about the Academy of Science, built more than a century later, in 1753. Here the Baroque style is in full flower. The classical elements no longer look pasted on; instead, the columns and pediments act both to frame the building's windows and to organize the facade into a carefully balanced composition of considerable complexity. Like so many of Vienna's great Baroque buildings, the Academy of Science looks as if it is about to set out for the Opera Ball. Josef Haydn's last public appearance took place here in 1808 at a performance of his monumental oratorio *The Creation*, with the 38-year-old Beethoven in attendance.

In their own small way, the Academy of Science and the Hildebrandthaus mark the extremes of Viennese Baroque architecture—the one urbane and patrician, the other frivolous and frothy. Most famous Viennese Baroque facades fall somewhere in between these extremes, but the fundamental architectural dialogue—the interplay between classical dignity and decorative vivacity—remains a constant, and it can be found all over the inner city.

Turn north from Sonnenfelsgasse (the street on the north side of the academy) on Köllnerhofgasse, then immediately right onto the short Grashofgasse. The door at the far end leads into
❸ **Heiligenkreuzerhof** (Holy Cross Court), one of the city's most peaceful backwaters. This complex of buildings, owned by the Holy Cross Abbey, 32 km (20 mi) south of the city, dates from the 17th century but got an 18th-century face-lift. Appropriately, the restraint of the architecture—with only here and there a small outburst of Baroque spirit—gives the courtyard a distinct feeling of retreat. If you're lucky, you might catch a wedding here; the chapel is a favorite spot for nuptial masses.

Through the far gate of Heiligenkreuzerhof is Schönlaterngasse (Beautiful Lantern Street), named for the wall lantern at No. 6. The house known as the **Basiliskenhaus**, at No. 7, was according to legend first built for a baker; on June 26, 1212, a foul-smelling basilisk (half rooster, half toad, with a glance that could kill) took up residence in the courtyard well, poisoning the water. An enterprising apprentice dealt with the problem by climbing down the well armed with a mirror; when the basilisk saw its own reflection it turned to stone. The petrified creature can still be seen in a niche on the building's facade. Today, modern science accounts for the contamination with a more prosaic explanation: natural-gas seepage.

To the east of Schönlaterngasse, on Postgasse, is an unex-
❹ pected visitor from Rome: the **Dominikanerkirche.** Built in the 1630s, some 50 years before the Viennese Baroque building boom, its facade is modeled after any number of Roman churches of the 16th century. The interior illustrates why the Baroque style came to be considered the height of bad taste during the 19th century and still has many detractors today. "Sculpt 'til you drop" seems to have been the motto here, and the viewer's eye is given no respite. This sort of Roman architectural orgy never really gained a foothold in Vienna, and when the great Viennese architects did pull out all the decorative stops—Hildebrandt's interior at the Belvedere Palace, for instance (*see* Tour 6, *below*)—they did it in a very different style and with far greater success.

Two blocks northeast of the Dominikanerkirche is the **Georg-Coch-Platz,** a small square bounded on the west by the
❺ **Post Office Savings Bank.** The former **War Ministry,** to the east across the Ring, was constructed in 1909 at the tail end of the 19th-century Viennese building boom. Its Baroque Revival facade derives from the Academy of Science, but here the small scale of the academy is blown up to ponderous proportions, and the earlier building's delicate decoration has been transformed into bellicose piles of carved weaponry meant to symbolize imperial might.

The Post Office Savings Bank is one of Modern architecture's greatest curiosities. It was designed in 1904 by Otto Wagner, whom many consider the father of 20th-century architecture. In his famous manifesto, *Modern Architecture*, Wagner condemned 19th-century revivalist architecture and pleaded for a modern style that honestly expressed modern building methods. Accordingly, the exterior walls of the Post Office Savings Bank are mostly flat and undecorated; visual interest is supplied merely by varying the pattern of the bolts that were used to hold the marble slabs in place on the wall surface during construction. Later architects were to embrace Wagner's beliefs wholeheartedly, although they used different, truly modern building materials: glass and concrete rather than marble. As a result the oddly metallic look Wagner created here has today the air of a failed futuristic fantasy, akin to the clunky spaceships in an old Buck Rogers movie serial. The Post Office Savings Bank was indeed a bold leap into the future, but unfortunately the future took a different path. Go inside for a look at the restored *Kassa Saal*, or central cashier's hall, to see how Wagner carried his concepts over to interior design.

Next go to Fleischmarkt, where between Nos. 9 and 11 the picturesque Griechengasse forks off to the right, just beyond the glittering 19th-century Greek Orthodox church. This corner of the inner city has a medieval feel that is quite genuine; there has been a tavern at **No. 11 Fleischmarkt** for some 500 years. The wooden carving on the facade of the current Griechenbeisl restaurant commemorates Max Augustin—best known today from the song "Ach du lieber Augustin"—an itinerant musician who sang here during the plague of 1679. Augustin survived being thrown alive into a pit filled with dead plague victims; he had been thought dead by the body collectors, when in fact he had only been dead drunk.

Time Out   Take a break for coffee at the corner of Fleischmarkt and Wolfengasse, at the **Café Vienne,** famous for baking the biggest cakes in the city.

From Fleischmarkt, a turn left onto Rotenturmstrasse and a right turn onto Lichtensteg leads into **Hoher Markt.** The square was badly damaged during World War II, but the famous Anker Clock at the east end survived the bombing. The huge mechanical timepiece took six years (1911–17) to build and still attracts crowds at noon when the full panoply of mechanical figures representing Austrian historical personages parades by. The figures are identified on a plaque to the bottom left of the clock. The graceless buildings erected around the square since 1945 are not aging well and do little to show off the square's lovely Baroque centerpiece, the St. Joseph Fountain (portraying the marriage of Joseph and Mary), designed in 1729 by Joseph Emanuel Fischer von Erlach, son of the great Johann Bernhard Fischer von Erlach. The Hoher Markt does harbor one wholly unexpected attraction, however: **underground Roman ruins.** This was once the main east–west axis of the Roman encampment of Vindobona, and the foundations of several officers' houses built in the 2nd century have been uncovered. The excavations are entered through the snack bar in the passageway at No. 3; a short descriptive pamphlet in English is available at the ticket table. *Hoher Markt 3, tel. 0222/ 535–5606. Admission: AS15 adults, AS5 children. Open Tues.–Sun. 9–12:15 and 1–4:30.*

Beginning beneath the Anker Clock, follow Bauernmarkt back to Fleischmarkt. To the left, next to the steps leading up to Ruprechtsplatz, is one of the city's most eccentric buildings: the **Kornhäusel Tower,** built around 1825. Joseph Kornhäusel was the most puritanical of Vienna's great architects; his restrained classicism rejected all but the plainest decoration and ran distinctly counter to the Viennese love of architectural finery. Apparently he had a misanthropic personality to match, for the starkly unornamented tower here, which was attached to his home, was reportedly built so he could get away from his wife (the studio at the top could be reached only by climbing up a ladder and through a trap door). Whatever the truth may be, the Kornhäusel Tower remains a profoundly antisocial building and a startling contrast to the highly active "Bermuda Triangle" at the top of the steps, with its lively bars, restaurants, and galleries.

Several of Kornhäusel's more conventional buildings can be seen up the steps and around the corner to the right, at Seitenstettengasse at **Nos. 2–4** and at **No. 5**. The building at Nos. 2-4 houses the only synagogue in Vienna to survive the Nazi holocaust; its lack of an appropriate facade results from the 19th-century Viennese law that required all synagogues to be hidden from street view.

To the north of the Kornhäusel Tower lies Ruprechtsplatz, another of Vienna's time-warp backwaters. The church in the middle, **Ruprechtskirche** (St. Rupert's), is the city's oldest. According to legend it was founded in 740; the oldest part of the present structure (the lower half of the tower) dates from the 11th century. Set on the ancient ramparts overlooking the Danube Canal, it is serene and unpretentious.

To the west of the Ruprechtsplatz entrance, steps on Sterngasse lead down to Marc-Aurel-Strasse. The lump of stone set into a wall niche at Sterngasse 3, at the top of the stairs, is a cannonball fired into the city during the unsuccessful Turkish siege of 1683; the larger lump of stone near the bottom of the stairs is a section of wall from the ancient Roman baths.

Continue west; at the end of Sterngasse a left turn and a short flight of steps lead to Salvatorgasse, with a timeworn Renaissance doorway at No. 5 (circa 1525). As you walk west, Salvatorgasse curves slightly, skirting the edge of the Gothic church of **Maria am Gestade** (St. Mary on the Banks). Built around 1400 (but much restored in the 17th and 19th centuries), the church incorporated part of the Roman city walls into its foundation; the north wall, as a result, takes a slight but noticeable dogleg to the right halfway down the nave. Like St. Stephen's, Maria am Gestade is rough-hewn Gothic, with a simple but forceful facade. The church is especially beloved, however, because of its unusual details—the pinnacled and saint-bedecked gable that tops the front facade, the stone canopy that hovers protectively over the front door, and (most appealing of all) the intricate openwork lantern atop the south-side bell tower. Appropriately enough in a city famous for its pastry, the lantern lends its tower an engaging suggestion of sugar caster.

The small square in front of Maria am Gestade overlooks Tiefer Graben, which until the 15th century was a tributary of the Danube that served as a moat just outside the city walls. The view is worth noting, for on clear days the famed Vienna Woods can be seen to the west, down the line of Börsegasse.

Tour 2: Baroque Gems

From Maria am Gestade, walk south on Schwertgasse and turn
10 left onto Wipplingerstrasse. At No. 7 is the former **Bohemian
Court Chancery,** built between 1708 and 1714 by Johann Bernhard Fischer von Erlach. Fischer von Erlach and his contemporary Johann Lukas von Hildebrandt were the reigning
architectural geniuses of Baroque Vienna; they designed their
churches and palaces during the building boom that followed
the defeat of the Turks in 1683. Both had studied architecture
in Rome, and both were deeply impressed by the work of the
great Italian architect Francesco Borromini, who had brought
to his designs a wealth and freedom of invention that was
looked upon with horror by most contemporary Romans. But
for Fischer von Erlach and Hildebrandt, Borromini's ideas
were a source of triumphant architectural inspiration, and
when they returned to Vienna they between them produced
many of the city's most beautiful buildings.

Across the street from the Bohemian Chancery is the **Altes Rathaus** (Old City Hall), dating from the 14th century but sporting
18th-century Baroque motifs on its facade. The interior passageways and courtyards, which are open during the day,
house a Gothic chapel (open at odd hours), a much-loved Baroque wall fountain (Georg Raphael Donner's **Andromeda
Fountain** of 1741), and display cases exhibiting maps and photos illustrating the city's history.

From Wipplingerstrasse, follow the short Fütterergasse south
to **Judenplatz,** from the 13th century onward the center of
Vienna's ghetto. Today the square's centerpiece is a statue of
the 18th-century Jewish playwright Gotthold Ephraim Lessing, erected after World War II; disconcertingly, the statue
suggests the underground comics of the American artist R.
Crumb.

Kurrentgasse leads south from the square's east end; the beautifully restored 18th-century houses on its east side make this
one of the most unpretentiously appealing streets in the city.
And at the far end of the street is one of Vienna's most appealing museums: the **Uhrenmuseum,** or Clock Museum (enter to
the right on the Schulhof side of the building). The museum's
three floors display a splendid array of clocks and watches—
more than 3,000 timepieces—dating from the 15th century to
the present. *Schulhof 2, tel. 0222/533–2265. Admission: AS30
adults, AS10 children. Open Tues.–Sun. 9–4:30.*

Equally appealing is the **Doll and Toy Museum** next door, with
its collections of dolls and dollhouses, teddies and trains.
*Schulhof 4, tel. 0222/535–6860. Admission: AS60 adults, AS30
children. Open Tues.–Sun. 10–6.*

Time Out A number of restaurants in the Kurrentgasse area serve good
traditional Viennese food at moderate prices, among them
Ofenloch (Kurrentgasse 8), **Gösser Bierklinik** (Steindlgasse 4),
and **Stadtbeisl** (Naglergasse 21). All three will supply English
menus on request.

From the Clock Museum, Schulhof leads into Am Hof, one of
the city's oldest squares. In the Middle Ages, the ruling
Babenberg family built their castle on the site of No. 2; hence
the name of the square, which means simply "at court." The Ba-

roque **Column of Our Lady** in the center dates from 1667; the **Civic Armory** at the northwest corner has been used as a fire station since 1685 (the high-spirited facade, with its Habsburg eagle, dates from 1731) and today houses the headquarters of Vienna's fire department.

⓫ The **Kirche Am Hof,** on the east side of the square, is identified by its sprawling Baroque facade. Bognergasse leaves the square to the right of the church. At No. 9 is the **Engel Pharmacy,** with a Jugendstil mosaic depicting winged women collecting the elixir of life in outstretched chalices. At the turn of the century the inner city was dotted with storefronts decorated in a similar manner; today this is the sole survivor.

From Bognergasse, the tiny Irisgasse—only a few yards long—leads to Naglergasse, another of Vienna's beautifully restored Baroque streets. The curve at the street's west end is due to the much earlier curve of the Roman city wall, which turned north here to run along Tiefer Graben to the Danube.

Naglergasse leads, at its curved end, into Heidenschuss, which in turn leads down a slight incline to Freyung, meaning "freeing." The square was so named because for many centuries the monks at the adjacent Schottenkirche (Scottish Church, though in fact the original monks were probably Irish) possessed the privilege of offering sanctuary. In the center of the square stands the allegorical **Austria Fountain** (1845), notable because its Bavarian designer, one Ludwig Schwanthaler, had the statues cast in Munich and then supposedly filled them with cigars to be smuggled into Vienna for black-market sale.

⓬ At Freyung 2 stands the recently restored **Palais Ferstel,** which is not a palace at all but a commercial shop-and-office complex designed in 1856 and named for its architect, Heinrich Ferstel. The facade is Italianate in style, harking back, in its 19th-century way, to the Florentine palazzi of the early Renaissance. The interior is unashamedly eclectic: vaguely Romanesque in feel and Gothic in decoration, with here and there a bit of Renaissance or Baroque sculpted detail thrown in for good measure. Such eclecticism is sometimes dismissed as mindlessly derivative, but here the architectural details (recently restored) are so respectfully and inventively combined that the interior becomes a pleasure to explore.

Returning to Freyung, proceed to its west end, dominated by the hulking and haphazardly decorated Schottenkirche. The square's best-known palace, one of the most sophisticated pieces of Baroque architecture in the city, is across the street at ⓭ No. 4: the **Kinsky Palace,** built between 1713 and 1716 by Hildebrandt. Its only real competition comes a few yards farther on: the Greek temple facade of **Schottenhof,** attached at right angles to the church. Designed by Joseph Kornhäusel in a very different style from his antisocial tower seen earlier, the Schottenhof facade typifies the change that came over Viennese architecture during the Biedermeier era (1815–48). The Viennese, according to the traditional view, were at the time so relieved to be rid of the upheavals of the Napoleonic Wars that they accepted without protest the ironhanded repression of Prince Metternich, chancellor of Austria, and retreated into a cozy and complacent domesticity. Restraint also ruled in architecture, with Baroque license rejected in favor of a new and his-

torically "correct" style that was far more controlled and reserved. Kornhäusel led the way in Vienna; his Schottenhof facade is all sober organization and frank repetition. But in its
marriage of strong and delicate forces it still pulls off the great
Viennese-waltz trick of successfully merging seemingly anti-
thetical characteristics.

Time Out   In summer, **Café Haag** and **Wienerwald** restaurant share the
tree-shaded courtyard of the Schottenhof, ideal for a relaxed
coffee or a full meal.

Follow Teinfaltstrasse (just opposite the Schottenkirche facade) one block west to Schreyvogelgasse on the right. The
doorway at No. 8 (up the incline) was made famous in 1949 by
the film *The Third Man;* it was here that Orson Welles, as the
malevolently knowing Harry Lime, stood hiding in the dark,
only to have his smiling face illuminated by a sudden light from
the upper-story windows of the house across the alley.

🄮 Around the corner at No. 8 Mölker Bastei is the **Pasqualatihaus,** where Beethoven lived while he was composing his only
opera, *Fidelio,* as well as his Seventh Symphony and Fourth Piano Concerto. Today his apartment houses a small commemorative museum. *Tel. 0222/637-0665. Admission: AS15 adults,
AS5 children. Open Tues.–Sun. 9–12:15 and 1–4:30.*

Four blocks south of Schreyvogelgasse is the Minoritenplatz,
🄯 named after its centerpiece, the **Minoritenkirche** (Church of
the Minorite Order), a Gothic stump of a church built mostly in
the 14th century. The front is brutally ugly, but the back is a
wonderful (if predominantly 19th-century) surprise. The interior contains the city's most imposing piece of kitsch: a large
mosaic reproduction of Leonardo da Vinci's *Last Supper,* com-
missioned by Napoleon in 1806 and later purchased by the Emperor Franz I.

From the east end of Minoritenplatz, follow Landhausgasse
one block east to Herrengasse. Across the street to the left is
🄰 the entrance to the **Café Central,** part of the Ferstel Palace
complex and one of Vienna's most famous cafés, recently restored. No matter how crowded the café may become, you can
linger as long as you like over a single cup of coffee and a newspaper from the huge international selection provided.

In its prime (before World War I), the Café Central was home to
some of the most famous literary figures of the day—home in
the literal as well as the figurative sense. In those days, housing was one of the city's most intractable problems. The large
apartment houses that had gone up to accommodate the surge
in Vienna's population were often (despite their imposing facades) no better than tenements, and overcrowding was so extreme that many apartment dwellers sublet space by the
square foot—just enough room for a spare bed. As a result,
many of Vienna's artists and writers spent as little time as possible in their "homes" and instead ensconced themselves at a
favorite café, where they ate, socialized, worked, and even received mail. The denizens of the Central favored political argu-
ment; indeed, their heated and sometimes violent discussions
became so well known that in October 1917, when Austria's foreign secretary was informed of the outbreak of the Russian
Revolution, he dismissed the report with a facetious reference
to a well-known local Marxist, the chess-loving (and presum-

ably harmless) "Herr Bronstein from the Café Central." The remark was to become famous all over Austria, for Herr Bronstein had disappeared and was about to resurface in Russia bearing a new name: Leon Trotsky.

Herrengasse is lined with Baroque town houses and is also home to the inner city's first "skyscraper," on the corner of Herrengasse and Fahnengasse. This 20th-century addition to the cityscape (called *Hochhaus*, or high house) is much decried by the Viennese, although it will seem innocuous enough to visitors from New York or London. At No. 13 is the Palace of the Lower Austrian Diet, more familiarly known as the **Landhaus.** In front of this building on March 13, 1848, Imperial troops fired into a crowd of demonstrators, killing four men and one woman and signaling the beginning of the abortive Revolution of 1848.

Tour 3: From Michaelerplatz to the Graben

At the south end of Herrengasse, in **Michaelerplatz,** one of Vienna's most evocative squares, the feel of the medieval city remains very strong; the buildings seem to crowd in toward the center of the small plaza as if the city were bursting at its seams, desperate to break out of its protective walls. The buildings around the perimeter present a synopsis of the city's entire architectural history: medieval church spire, Renaissance church facade, Baroque palace facade, 19th-century apartment house, and 20th-century bank. In the center, recent excavations have turned up extensive traces of the old Roman city and relics of the 18th and 19th centuries. **Michaelerkirche** (the Church of St. Michael's), with its unpretentious spire, dates from the 13th and 14th centuries, although the ground-floor entrance porch and upper-story decoration were not added until several hundred years later.

The **Palais Herberstein,** across Herrengasse, was built in 1903, and its recognizably Viennese decoration is typical of the neo-Baroque style of the day. Eight years later Adolf Loos, one of the founding fathers of 20th-century Modern architecture, ⓱ built the **Looshaus** next door, facing the Imperial Palace entrance. It was anything but typical—it was more like an architectural declaration of war. After two hundred years of Baroque and neo-Baroque exuberance, the first generation of 20th-century architects had had enough. Loos led the revolt against architectural tradition; *Ornament and Crime* was the title of his famous manifesto, in which he inveighed against the conventional architectural wisdom of the 19th century— against the style of the Palais Herberstein—and denounced Vienna's decorative vivacity. Instead, he advocated buildings that were plain, honest, and functional. When he built the Looshaus for Goldman and Salatsch (men's clothiers) in 1911 the city was scandalized. Archduke Franz Ferdinand, heir to the throne, was so offended that he vowed never again to use the Michaelerplatz entrance to the Imperial Palace. Everyone in the city took sides, and the debate over the merits of Modern architecture began. Today the Looshaus has lost its power to shock, and the facade seems quite innocuous. The recently restored interior, however, remains a breathtaking suprise. Loos's plain surfaces allow his carefully selected materials, particularly the richly grained wood he so loved, to shine with a luster that positively dazzles.

The passageway just to the right of St. Michael's, with its large 15th-century relief depicting Christ on the Mount of Olives, leads into the Stallburggasse, named after the Imperial Stables on the right. The area is dotted with antiques stores, attracted by the presence of the **Dorotheum,** the famous Viennese auction house that began as a state-controlled pawnshop in 1707 (known as "Aunt Dorothy" to its patrons). Merchandise coming up for auction is on display at Dorotheergasse 17. The showrooms—packed with everything from carpets and pianos to cameras and jewelry—are well worth a visit. Some wares are not for auction but for immediate sale.

The city's long-discussed Jewish Museum has now found its definite home in the former Eskeles Palace at Dorotheergasse 11.

At No. 6 Dorotheergasse, hidden behind an unprepossessing doorway, the **Café Hawelka** is one of the few famous inner-city cafés that has survived without major restoration. The Hawelka's air of romantic shabbiness—the product of Viennese *Fortwursteln,* or "muddling through"—is especially evocative.

The Dorotheergasse leads out into the Graben, a pedestrian mall lined with luxury shops and open-air cafés. Turn right into Stock-im-Eisen-Platz, where opposite the southwest corner of St. Stephen's, set into the corner of the building on the west side of Kärntner Strasse, is one of the city's most revered relics: the **Stock-im-Eisen,** or iron tree stump. Chronicles first mention the Stock-im-Eisen in 1533, but it is probably far older, and for hundreds of years any apprentice metalsmith who came to Vienna to learn his trade hammered a nail into the tree trunk for good luck. During World War II, when there was talk of moving the relic to a museum in Munich, it mysteriously disappeared; it reappeared, perfectly preserved, after the threat of removal had passed.

Across the street from Stock-im-Eisen is Vienna's newest and (for the moment, at least) most controversial piece of architecture: **Neues Haas Haus.** It was designed by Hans Hollein, Austria's best-known living architect. Detractors consider its aggressively contemporary style out of place opposite St. Stephen's, while advocates consider the contrast enlivening; whatever the verdict, the new building has been a notable commercial failure.

Set into the paving stones between Stock-im-Eisen Platz and the cathedral you'll find the outline of a chapel; this is the medieval **Virgilkapelle,** which you can see below ground by going into the subway station. It was discovered in the 1970s during excavations for the subway system.

The **Graben,** leading west from Stock-im-Eisen-Platz, is a street whose unusual width gives it the presence and weight of a city square. Its shape is due to the Romans, who dug the city's southwestern moat here, adjacent to the original city walls. The Graben's centerpiece is the **Pestsäule,** or Plague Column, erected by Emperor Leopold I between 1687 and 1693, in thanks to God for delivering the city from a particularly virulent plague.

The real glory of the Graben, however, is not the Plague Column but the architecture that surrounds it, creating the city's finest ensemble of buildings. Most of the buildings date from the late 19th century, but a few of them are earlier or later, and the contrast is illuminating. Be sure to look upward to catch the many fascinating details. You'll find a full-size statue of a mounted Turk at the corner of the Kohlmarkt.

⑲ Just north of the Graben is Petersplatz, site of **Peterskirche** (St. Peter's Church), constructed between 1702 and 1708 by Hilde-brandt, using an earlier plan by the Italian Gabriele Montani. The facade possesses angled towers, graceful towertops (said to have been inspired by the tents of the Turks during the siege of 1683), and an unusually fine entrance porch. Inside the church, the Baroque decoration is elaborate, with some fine touches (particularly the glass-crowned galleries high on the walls to either side of the altar), but the lack of light and years of accumulated dirt create a prevailing gloom, and the much-praised ceiling frescoes by J. M. Rottmayr are impossible to make out.

Proceed west on Milchgasse and turn left onto Tuchlauben. Tuchlauben leads back to the west end of the Graben and then **⑳** continues on as **Kohlmarkt.** None of the buildings here is re-markable, although they do include an entertainingly ironic odd-couple pairing: **No. 11** (early 18th century) and **No. 9** (early 20th century). The mixture of architectural styles is similar to the Graben, but the general feel is low-key, as if the street were consciously deferring to its splendid view stopper, the dome over the Michaelerplatz entrance to the Imperial Palace (*see* Tour 4). Still, Kohlmarkt lingers in the memory when flashier streets have faded. This is, after all, Vienna's most elegant shopping street.

Time Out **Demel's** (Kohlmarkt 14), Vienna's best-known (and priciest) **㉑** pastry shop, offers a dizzying selection, and if you possess a sweet tooth, a visit will be worth every penny of the extra cost. Chocolate lovers will want to participate in the famous Vien-nese Sachertorte debate by sampling Demel's version and then comparing it with its rival at the Hotel Sacher (*see* Tour 5). For considerably less elegance but excellent value, go instead to the **Arabia** café at Kohlmarkt 5.

Tour 4: The Hofburg and the Ringstrasse

㉒ The Imperial Palace, known as the **Hofburg,** faces Kohlmarkt on the opposite side of Michaelerplatz. Until 1918 the Hofburg was the home of the Habsburgs, rulers of the Austro-Hungari-an Empire. Today it is a vast smorgasbord of sightseeing at-tractions; the Imperial Apartments, two Imperial treasuries, *six* museums, the National Library, and the famous Winter Riding School all vie for attention. The entire complex takes a minimum of a full day to explore in detail; if your time is limited (or if you want to save most of the interior sightseeing for a rainy day), you should omit the Imperial Apartments, the Court Silver and Tableware Treasury, and all the museums mentioned below except the Kunsthistorisches (the Museum of Art History). An excellent multilingual, full-color booklet de-scribing the palace in detail is for sale at most ticket counters within the complex; it gives a complete list of attractions and maps out the palace's complicated ground plan and building history wing by wing.

70

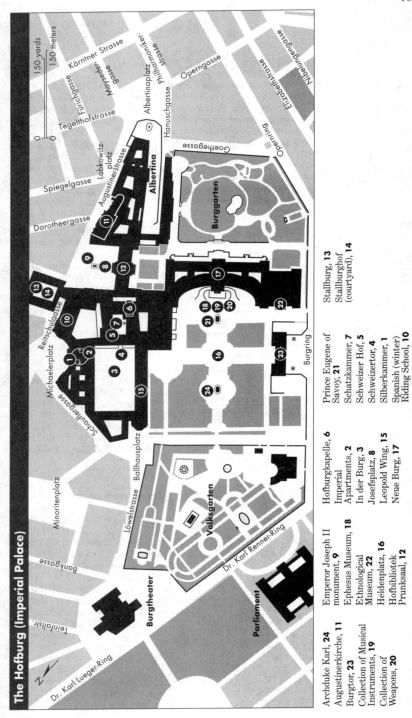

The Hofburg (Imperial Palace)

Archduke Karl, **24**
Augustinerkirche, **11**
Burgtor, **23**
Collection of Musical
Instruments, **19**
Collection of
Weapons, **20**

Emperor Joseph II
monument, **9**
Ephesus Museum, **18**
Ethnological
Museum, **22**
Heldenplatz, **16**
Hofbibliotek
Prunksaal, **12**

Hofburgkapelle, **6**
Imperial
Apartments, **2**
In der Burg, **3**
Josefsplatz, **8**
Leopold Wing, **15**
Neue Burg, **17**

Prince Eugene of
Savoy, **21**
Schatzkammer, **7**
Schweizer Hof, **5**
Schweizertor, **4**
Silberkammer, **1**
Spanish (winter)
Riding School, **10**

Stallburg, **13**
Stallburghof
(courtyard), **14**

Architecturally, the Hofburg is (like St. Stephen's) far from refined. It grew up over a period of 700 years (its earliest mention in court documents is 1279, at the very beginning of Habsburg rule), and its spasmodic, haphazard growth kept it from attaining any sort of unified identity. But many of the bits and pieces are fine, and one interior (the National Library) is a tour de force.

Turn into Reitschulgasse to reach **Josefsplatz,** the most imposing of the Hofburg courtyards, with an equestrian monument (1807) to Emperor Joseph II in the center. To the right is the entrance to the **Spanische Reitschule,** the famous Spanish Riding School. Tickets to performances must be ordered in writing many weeks in advance. Performance schedules for winter 1993/94 will partly depend on renovations of the riding school hall. Information offices have a brochure with the detailed schedule. Generally the 80-minute full shows take place on Sundays at 10:45 AM and selected Wednesday evenings at 7. Check for hour-long morning performances on Saturdays at 10; tickets for Saturday shows are available only from ticket and travel agencies. Morning training sessions Tuesday through Saturday are usually open to the public. Tickets must be bought at the door and the line starts forming between 9 and 9:30 for the opening at 10; most sightseers are unaware that visitors may come and go as they please between 10 and noon. The interior, the work of Fischer von Erlach the younger, is itself an attraction—surely Europe's most elegant sports arena—and if the prancing horses begin to pall, move up to the top balcony and examine the ceiling. *Josefsplatz 6, tel. 0222/533–9031, fax 0222/535–0186. Admission: AS70 adults, AS20 children. Open mid-Feb.–June and Sept.–mid-Dec. (tour weeks excluded), Tues.–Sat. 10–noon.*

Across the square from the Riding School is the entrance to the **Augustinerkirche** (Church of the Augustinian Order), built during the 14th century and possessing the most unified Gothic interior in the city. But the church is something of a fraud; the interior, it turns out, dates from the late 18th century, not the early 14th. During the 1600s the old Gothic interior was completely remodeled in the Baroque style; then, at the beginning of the Gothic Revival in 1784, it was gutted and "restored" by the architect Ferdinand von Hohenberg. A historical fraud the church may be, but a spiritual fraud it is not. The view from the entrance doorway is stunning: a soaring harmony of vertical piers, ribbed vaults, and hanging chandeliers that makes Vienna's other Gothic interiors look earthbound by comparison.

Back out on the square, a left turn from the Augustinerkirche exit leads to the entrance to the **Hofbibliothek Prunksaal** (the Grand Hall of the National Library), and a greater contrast between two interiors would be hard to imagine. The Augustinerkirche is one of the city's most restrained compositions; the National Library is one of its most ornate. Designed by Fischer von Erlach the elder just before his death in 1723 and completed by his son, the Grand Hall is full-blown High Baroque, with trompe-l'oeil ceiling frescoes by Daniel Gran. As usual, the frescoes are elaborately allegorical, the side ceilings are devoted to personifications of the sciences of peace and war, and the dome is devoted to a complicated symbolic glorification of the Emperor Charles VI, pictured in a medallion as supported by Apollo and Hercules.

The library may not be to everyone's taste but in the end it is the books themselves that come to the rescue. They are as lovingly displayed as the gilding and the frescoes, and they give the hall a warmth and humanity that the rest of the palace decidedly lacks. *Josefsplatz 1 (at the top of the stairs inside), tel. 0222/53410-397. Admission: AS15. Open mid-May–Oct., Mon. and Wed.–Sat. 10–4, Sun. and holidays 10–1; Nov.–Apr., Mon.–Sat. 11–noon. Don't overlook the intriguing museum of globes on the third floor. Tel. 53410-297. Admission: AS10. Open Mon.–Wed., Fri. 11–12. Thurs. 2–3.*

Return on Reitschulgasse to the domed rotunda on Michaelerplatz; the **Silberkammer** (the Court Silver and Tableware Treasury) is to the right, while the **Imperial Apartments** are to the left. The former is much as might be expected, an extremely well stocked royal pantry turned royal museum. The latter, however, may come as a shock. The long, repetitive suite of conventionally luxurious rooms has a sad and poignant feel. The decoration (19th-century imitation of 18th-century Rococo) tries to look regal, but much like the Empire itself in its latter days, it is only going through the motions and ends up looking merely official. Among the few signs of genuine life are Emperor Franz Joseph's Spartan iron field bed, on which he slept every night, and the Empress Elizabeth's wooden gymnastics equipment, on which she exercised every morning. Amid all the tired splendor they look decidedly forlorn. *Silberkammer, tel. 0222/523-4240-99. Admission: AS30 adults, AS5 senior citizens and children. Open Tues.–Fri. and Sun. 9–1. Imperial Apartments, tel. 0222/587-5554-515. Admission: AS25 adults, AS10 children. Open Mon.–Sat. 8:30–noon, 12:30–4; Sun. and holidays 8:30–12:30.*

On the far side of the rotunda is a large courtyard (known as In der Burg); set into the far left-hand wall is the **Schweizertor,** or Swiss Gate (dating from 1552 and decorated with some of the earliest classical motifs in the city), which leads through to the oldest section of the palace, a small courtyard known as the **Schweizer Hof.** In the southeast corner (at the top of the steps) is the entrance to the **Hofburgkapelle,** or Imperial Chapel, where the Vienna Boys' Choir sings Mass on Sundays and holidays from September to June (*see* Music in The Arts and Nightlife, *below*). At ground level is the entrance to the **Schatzkammer,** or Imperial Treasury, with its 1,000 years of treasures. The display here is a welcome antidote to the monotony of the Imperial Apartments, for the entire Treasury was completely renovated in 1983–87, and the crowns and relics and vestments fairly glow in their new surroundings. *Schweizer Hof, tel. 0222/52177-365. Admission: AS60 adults, AS30 children. Open Tues.–Sun. 10–6.*

Walking back through the Schweizertor, turn left and walk under the Leopold Wing and out into the vast Heldenplatz. The long wing on the left is the youngest section of the palace, called the **Neue Burg.** It houses no fewer than four specialty museums: the **Ephesus Museum,** containing Roman antiquities unearthed by Austrian archaeologists in Turkey at the turn of the century; the **Collection of Musical Instruments,** including pianos that belonged to Beethoven, Brahms, Schumann, and Mahler (alas, this museum seems to be perpetually closed for renovations, although opening was promised for fall of 1993; be sure to check); the **Collection of Weapons,** one of the most extensive arms-and-armor collections in the world; and the **Ethnological Museum,** devoted to anthropology (Montezuma's feathered headdress is a highlight of its collection). The first three museums are entered at the triumphal arch set into the middle of the curved portion of the facade; the Ethnological Museum is entered farther along, at the end pavilion. *Heldenplatz, tel. 0222/521–770. Admission to Ephesus, Musical Instrument, and Weapons Museums on one ticket: AS45 adults, AS20 children. Open Wed.–Mon. 10–6. Admission to Ethnological Museum: AS30 adults, AS15 senior citizens, children free. Open Wed.–Mon. 10–4.*

The Neue Burg stands today as a symbol of architectural overconfidence. Designed for Emperor Franz Joseph in 1869, it was part of a much larger scheme that was meant to make the Hofburg rival the Louvre, if not Versailles. The German architect Gottfried Semper planned a twin of the present Neue Burg on the opposite side of the Heldenplatz, with arches connecting the Neue Burg and its twin with the other pair of twins on the Ringstrasse, the Kunsthistorisches Museum (Museum of Art History) and the Naturhistorisches Museum (Museum of Natural History). But World War I intervened, and with the Empire's collapse the Neue Burg became merely the last in a long series of failed attempts to bring architectural order to the Hofburg.

The failure to complete the Hofburg building program left the Heldenplatz without a discernible shape, and today it's an amorphous space, with the Burgtor (the old main palace gate) stranded in the middle. On the other side of the Burgtor, across the Ringstrasse, is a much more successfully organized space, the **Maria-Theresien-Platz,** laid out in the 1870s around a matronly centerpiece monument to the matronly Empress Maria Theresa. To the west is the **Naturhistorisches Museum,** or Natural History Museum, home of, among other artifacts, the famous Venus of Willendorf, a tiny statuette thought to be some 20,000 years old. *Maria-Theresien-Platz, tel. 0222/52177–365. Admission: AS30 adults, AS20 children. Open Wed.–Mon. 9–6; in winter, ground floor only, 9–3.*

㉓ To the east is the **Kunsthistorisches Museum,** or Museum of Art History, housing one of the finest art collections in Europe. The collection was assembled by the ruling Habsburgs over several hundred years, and even a cursory description would run on for pages. Most of the great European old masters are represented, although many of the masterpieces are disgracefully dirty. Even the shortest list of highlights must include Rogier van der Weyden's *Crucifixion Triptych,* Raphael's *Madonna in the Meadow,* Holbein's *Portrait of Jane Seymour, Queen of England,* Titian's *Portrait of the Elector Johann Friedrich of Saxony,* the world-famous roomful of masterworks by Brueghel, Caravaggio's *Madonna of the Rosary,* a fine selection of Rembrandt portraits, and Vermeer's peerless *Allegory of the Art of Painting.* Benvenuto Cellini's famous gold saltcellar—certainly one of the most sumptuous pieces of tableware ever created—is on display amid the treasures of the applied-arts wing. *Maria-Theresien-Platz, tel. 0222/52177–365. Admission: AS60 adults, AS30 children. Open Tues.–Sun. 10–6. Picture gallery open Tues. and Fri. evenings 6–9.*

One block northwest of Maria-Theresien-Platz, walk west on Burggasse. The engaging 18th-century survivors at Nos. 11

and 13 are adorned with religious and secular decorative sculpture, the latter with a niche statue of St. Joseph, the former with cherubic work-and-play bas-reliefs. For several blocks around—walk down Gutenberggasse and back up Spittelberggasse—the 18th-century houses of the **Spittelberg quarter** have been beautifully restored (the entire area was scheduled for demolition in the 1970s but was saved by student protest). The sequence from No. 5 to No. 19 Spittelberggasse is an especially fine array of Viennese plain and fancy.

Time Out Stop for a typical Viennese lunch at **Witwe Bolte** (Gutenberggasse 13), where in 1778, as noted on the arch just inside the entrance, the management unknowingly ejected Emperor Joseph II (apparently he was out for an incognito night on the town and was acting a bit strange). Good unpretentious Viennese food can also be found at **Boheme** (Spittelberggasse 19) and downstairs at **Zu ebener Erde und im ersten Stock** (Burggasse 13).

After continuing north from Spittelberggasse, take a right on Neustiftgasse and then cross Museumstrasse to Volksgartenstrasse; Volksgartenstrasse leads to the **Volksgarten,** on the east side of Dr.-Karl-Renner-Ring. The beautifully planted garden contains a little 19th-century Greek temple that offers an appropriate spot to sit for a few minutes and consider Vienna's most ambitious piece of 19th-century city planning: the famous **Ringstrasse.**

On December 20, 1857, Emperor Franz Josef issued a decree announcing the most ambitious piece of urban redevelopment Vienna had ever seen. The inner city's centuries-old walls were to be torn down, and the glacis—the wide expanse of open field that acted as a protective buffer between inner city and outer suburbs—was to be filled in. In their place was to rise a wide, tree-lined boulevard, upon which would stand an imposing collection of new buildings that would reflect Vienna's special status as the political, economic, and cultural heart of the Austro-Hungarian Empire.

During the 50 years of building that followed, many factors combined to produce the Ringstrasse as it now stands, but the most important was the gradual rise of liberalism after the failed Revolution of 1848. By the latter half of the Ringstrasse era, support for constitutional government, democracy, and equality—for all the concepts that liberalism traditionally equates with progress—was steadily increasing. As the turn of the century approached, the emperor's subjects were slowly but surely doing away with the Empire's long-standing tradition of absolute imperial power, and it looked as if the transition from absolute to constitutional monarchy would be peaceful and unchallenged. Liberal Viennese voters could point with pride to a number of important civic improvements: The Danube was controlled and canalized, a comprehensive municipal water-supply system was constructed, a public-health system was established, and the countryside bordering the city (including the Vienna Woods) was protected by new zoning laws. As it went up, the Ringstrasse stood as the definitive symbol of this liberal progress; as Carl E. Schorske put it in his *Fin-de-Siècle Vienna,* it celebrated "the triumph of constitutional *Recht* (right) over Imperial *Macht* (might), of secular culture over religious faith. Not palaces, garrisons, and churches, but

centers of constitutional government and higher culture dominated the Ring."

But what should these centers of culture look like? The answer
was the result of a new passion among the intelligentsia: architectural Historicism. Greek temples, it was argued, reminded
the viewer of the cradle of democracy; what could be more appropriate than a Parliament building designed in Greek Revival style? Gothic architecture, on the other hand, betokened
the rule of the church and the rise of the great medieval city-
states; the new Votive Church and the new City Hall would
therefore be Gothic Revival. And the Renaissance Era, which
produced the unprecedented flowering of learning and creativi-
ty that put an end to the Middle Ages, was most admired of all;
therefore, the new centers of high culture, the museums, the
theaters, and the university—would be Renaissance Revival.
In building after building, architectural style was dictated by
historical association, and gradually the Ringstrasse of today
took shape.

The highest concentration of public building occurred in the
area around the Volksgarten, where are clustered (moving
from south to north, from Burgring to Schottenring) the **Museum of Art History,** the **Museum of Natural History,** the

 Justizpalast (Palace of Justice), the **Parlament** (Parliament),
the **Rathaus** (City Hall), the **Burgtheater** (National Theater),
the **Universität** (University of Vienna), and the **Votivkirche.** As
an ensemble, the collection is astonishing in its architectural
presumption: It is nothing less than an attempt to assimilate
and summarize the entire architectural history of Europe. As
critics were quick to notice, however, the complex suffers from
a serious organizational flaw: Most of the buildings lack effec-
tive context. Rather than being the focal points of an organized
overall plan, they are plunked haphazardly down on an avenue
that is itself too wide to possess a unified, visually comprehen-
sible character.

The individual buildings, too, came in for immediate criticism.
The Gothic Revival design of the City Hall, for instance, produced an interior so dark that large parts of it had to be fully lit
all day long; the National Theater auditorium was so incompe-
tently designed (bad sight lines and worse acoustics) that it had
to be thoroughly reworked a few years later. And the Greek Revival Parliament building emerged looking monolithic and ponderous—traits more characteristic of bad bureaucracy than
good government. The City Hall and the National Theater
present the best face; they, at least, are sensibly placed, nod-
ding soberly to each other across the Rathausplatz. But it is
hard, when exploring the avenue, not to be oppressed by the
overbearing monumentality of it all.

Exploring the Ringstrasse complex requires a considerable
amount of time, but two attractions beyond the Votive Church
at the Schottenring end deserve mention: Sigmund Freud's
apartment (now a museum) and the Museum of Modern Art.

Freud's Apartment at Berggasse 19 (Apt. 6, one flight up; ring
the bell and push the door simultaneously) was his residence
from 1891 to 1938. The three-room collection of memorabilia is
mostly a photographic record of Freud's life, with some documents, publications, and a portion of his collection of antiquities also on display. The waiting-room furniture is authentic,

but the consulting-room and study furniture (including the famous couch) can be seen only in photographs. *Berggasse 19, tel. 0222/319–1596. Admission: AS60 adults, AS40 children. Open daily 9–3.*

㉝ The **Museum Moderner Kunst** (Museum of Modern Art) is at Fürstengasse 1, three blocks north of Freud's apartment. The large 18th-century mansion was originally the Liechtenstein Summer Palace; today it houses the national collection of 20th-century art. Artists from Gustav Klimt to Robert Rauschenberg and Nam June Paik are represented, and a more inappropriate environment for modern art would be hard to imagine. Twentieth-century art and 18th-century architecture here declare war on each other and fight to an uneasy draw. Still, if you can shut out the architecture (or the art, depending on your taste), the museum is well worth a visit. *Fürstengasse 1, tel. 0222/341259. Admission: AS30 adults, AS15 senior citizens, children free. Open Wed.–Mon. 10–6.*

Tour 5: From St. Stephen's to the Opera

From the tall south tower of St. Stephen's Cathedral, the short Churhausgasse leads south to Singerstrasse. Two 18th-century palaces on this street are worth noting: the **Neupauer-Breuner Palace,** at No. 16 (1715, architect unknown), with its monumental entranceway and inventively delicate windows, and the **Rottal Palace,** at No. 17 (1750, attributed to Hildebrandt), with its wealth of classical wall motifs. For a contrast, turn up the narrow Blutgasse, with its simple 18th-century facades. The little building at No. 3 is especially appealing, for it looks as if it's being bullied by the buildings on either side and has buckled under the pressure.

㉟ Blutgasse ends at Domgasse; at No. 5 is the **Figarohaus,** one of Mozart's 11 rented Viennese residences. It was here that he wrote *The Marriage of Figaro* and the six quartets dedicated to Joseph Haydn; the apartment he occupied now contains a small commemorative museum. *Domgasse 5, tel. 0222/513–6294. Admission: AS15. Open Tues.–Sun. 10–12:15 and 1–4:30.*

At the east end of Singerstrasse the 19th century takes over, and the 18th-century interplay between strength and delicacy disappears. Monumentality has won out, as can be seen at the **㊱** **Coburg Palace** (1843) on Seilerstätte. The Coburg facade lacks all sense of play compared to the Neupauer-Breuner and Rottal palaces. Its garden side, however, boasts a fine historical curiosity: a section of the ancient Viennese city walls, one of the few that managed to escape demolition during construction of the Ringstrasse.

Two blocks south of the Coburg Palace, turn west on Himmelpfortgasse. The modest house at **No. 15** possesses a curlicued gable that derives from the facade of the Dominikanerkirche (*see* Tour 1); the interior passageway remains much as it was 150 years ago—woodpile, communal water basin, Biedermeier carriage, and all. Next door, at No. 13, the **Erdödy-Fürstenberg Palace** (1724) has design motifs mostly lifted from the Neupauer-Breuner Palace.

㊲ The **Ministry of Finance** at No. 8, designed by Fischer von Erlach in 1697 and later expanded by Hildebrandt, was origi-

519 M.P.H.

190 M.P.H.

75 M.P.H.

0 M.P.H.

WE LET YOU SEE EUROPE AT YOUR OWN PACE.

Regardless of your personal speed limits, Rail Europe offers everything to get you over, around and through anywhere you want in Europe. For more information, call your travel agent or 1-800-4-EURAIL.

OFFICIAL DISTRIBUTOR

Rail Europe

OF THE EURAIL PASS

We can wire money to every major city in Europe almost as fast as you can say, "Zut alors! J'ai perdu mes valises".

How fast? We can send money in 10 minutes or less, to 13,500 locations in over 68 countries worldwide. That's faster than any other international money transfer service. And when you're *sans* luggage, every minute counts.

MoneyGram from American Express® is available throughout Europe. For more information please contact your local American Express Travel Service Office or call: 44-71-839-7541 in England; 33-1-47777000 in France; or 49-69-21050 in Germany. In the U.S. call 1-800-MONEYGRAM.

MoneyGram

INTERNATIONAL MONEY TRANSFERS.

nally the town palace of Prince Eugene of Savoy, who, as commander-in-chief of the Imperial Army in the War of the Spanish Succession, led Austrian forces (alongside the English under the Duke of Marlborough) to victory over the French at the Battle of Blenheim in 1704. The Baroque details here are among the most inventively conceived and beautifully executed in the city; all the decorative motifs are so softly carved that they appear to have been freshly squeezed from a pastry tube. The Viennese are lovers of the baroque in both their architecture and their pastry, and here the two passions seem visibly merged.

From Himmelpfortgasse, turn right onto Rauhensteingasse and then immediately right on Ballgasse, which winds to the left and then dwindles down to a short arched passageway leading into Franziskanerplatz. The **Moses Fountain** in the center of the square dates from 1798; the small **Franziskanerkirche** on the east side is an international hybrid, with a facade (1603) that imitates German churches of the early Renaissance and a later interior that imitates Italian churches of the Baroque. The small shopping arcade at the garishly painted No. 6 is worth exploring for its disturbingly surreal decoration.

From Franziskanerplatz, take Weihburggasse west to **Kärntner Strasse,** Vienna's leading shopping street. These days Kärntner Strasse is much maligned. Too commercial, too crowded, too many tasteless signs, too much gaudy neon—the complaints go on and on. Nevertheless, the Viennese continue to arrive regularly for their evening promenade, and it is easy to see why. Vulgar the street may be, but it is also alive and vital, possessing an energy that the more tasteful Graben and the impeccable Kohlmarkt lack. For the sightseer beginning to suffer from art-history overdose, a Kärntner Strasse window-shopping break will be welcome.

The short Donnergasse (across Kärntner Strasse from Himmelpfortgasse) leads into Neuer Markt. The square's centerpiece, Georg Raphael Donner's **Providence Fountain,** has not had a happy life. Put up in 1739, it was at the time the very latest word in civic improvements, with elegantly mannered nude statuary meant to personify the Danube and four of its tributaries. The Empress Maria Theresa, however, was offended; despite having had 16 children, she disapproved of nudity in art. The figures were removed and stored away and later nearly melted down for munitions. They were finally restored in 1801, but were once again moved away (to be replaced by the present copies) in 1873. The original figures can be studied in quiet at the Lower Belvedere Palace (*see* Tour 6).

The church at the southwest corner of the Neuer Markt is the Kapuzinerkirche; in its basement (entrance to the left of the church) is the **Kaisergruft,** or Imperial Burial Vault. The crypts contain the partial remains of some 140 Habsburgs (the hearts are in the Augustinerkirche and the entrails in St. Stephen's) plus one non-Habsburg governess ("She was always with us in life," said Maria Theresa, "why not in death?"). The sarcophagi are often elaborate and occasionally bizarre: Maria Theresa is shown in bed with her husband awaking to the Last Judgment as if it were just another weekday morning, while the remains of her son (the ascetic Joseph II) lie in a simple casket at the foot of the bed as if he were the family dog. The body of Empress Zita, widow of Austria's last Kaiser, lies in the most recent tomb dating from 1989. *Neuer Markt, tel. 0222/512–6853–12. Admission: AS30 adults, AS20 children. Open daily 9:30–4.*

From the southwest corner of Neuer Markt, walk south on Tegetthofstrasse to Albertinaplatz. On the square's west side ➌➒ the **Albertina Museum** houses a vast collection of drawings and prints dating to the 15th century. Because of their fragility, only a very small selection of the more than 200,000 pieces of art is on view at any one time, and most of the famous works (for example, Albrecht Dürer's *Praying Hands*) must usually be viewed in reproduction. *Augustinerstr. 1, tel. 0222/53483. Admission: AS45 adults, AS20 children. Open Mon., Tues., Thurs. 10–4; Wed. 10–6; Fri. 10–2; Sat. and Sun. 10–1; closed Sun. July and Aug.*

Time Out Take a coffee break at one of the nearby cafés. The **Café Sacher,** in the Hotel Sacher on Philharmonikerstrasse—the street leading east from the south end of Albertinaplatz—is the most formal (no shorts allowed inside during the summer); its famous Sachertorte can also be purchased at a small Kärntner Strasse shop on the hotel's east side. The **Café Tirolerhof,** on the north side of Albertinaplatz, is a less upscale (but more typically Viennese) alternative.

The collection of marble statuary in the triangle in front of the Albertina is the "Memorial to Victims of Fascism," a controversial work because of the location (the remains of hundreds of victims of a 1945 bombing lie in the ruined cellar of the building which stood here) and the sculptor, Alfred Hrdlicka (once an avowed communist).

From the north end of Albertinaplatz, Führichgasse leads east across Kärntner Strasse to Annagasse. The small neighborhood church at No. 2, the **Annakirche,** possesses a fine bulbous dome atop its tower and an unusually consistent Baroque decorative scheme inside, but the main attraction is the narrow street itself, with its fine collection of unpretentious facades. The high point, undoubtedly, is **No. 14,** with its carved frieze of impish, gossiping cherubs. The poses here are conventional, but the execution is not, for the frieze achieves with ease the spontaneity that Baroque sculpture always sought but too often failed to find.

Return to Kärntner Strasse, and follow it south to the Ringstrasse. The building on the right, facing Opernring, is the ➍➌ famous Vienna **Opera House.** The first of the Ringstrasse projects to be completed (in 1869), it suffered severe bomb damage during World War II (only the outer walls, the front facade, and the main staircase area behind it survived). Though it was rebuilt, it remains something of a shell, for the cost of fully restoring the 19th-century interior decor was prohibitive. Tours of the Opera are given regularly, but starting times vary according to opera rehearsals; the current schedule is usually posted at the west side entrance, where the tours begin.

The construction of the Opera is the stuff of legend. When the foundation was laid, the plans for Opernring were not yet complete, and in the end the avenue turned out to be several feet higher than originally planned. As a result, the Opera lacked the commanding prospect that its architects, Eduard van der Null and August Sicard von Sicardsburg, had intended, and even Emperor Franz Josef pronounced the building a bit low to the ground. For the sensitive van der Nüll (and here the story becomes a bit suspect), failing his beloved emperor was the last straw. In disgrace and despair, he committed suicide. Sicardsburg died of grief shortly thereafter. And the emperor, horrified at the deaths his innocuous remark had caused, limited all his future artistic pronouncements to a single immutable formula: *Es war sehr schön, es hat mich sehr gefreut* ("It was very nice, it pleased me very much").

Tour 6: South of the Ring to the Belvedere

Two blocks southwest of the Opera, facing the Schillerplatz, ❹ the **Academy of Fine Arts** was built in the late 19th century to house an institution founded in 1692. The academy's Renaissance Revival architecture was meant to instill in its students an appreciation of the past; traditional standards were staunchly maintained here in the face of the artistic rebellions of the early 20th century. In 1907 and again in 1908, an aspiring artist named Adolf Hitler was refused admission on the grounds of insufficient talent. Today the academy contains an old-master art collection that will be of interest mostly to specialists, the one exception being Hieronymus Bosch's famous *Last Judgment* triptych, which more than makes up in horrific imagination what it lacks in painterly sophistication. *Schillerplatz 3, tel. 0222/58816–225. Admission: AS30. Open Tues., Thurs., Fri. 10–2; Wed. 10–1, 3–6; weekends and holidays 9–1.*

If the Academy of Fine Arts represents the conservative attitude of the arts in the late 1800s, then its antithesis can be ❹ found immediately behind it to the southeast: the **Secession Building.** Restored in the mid-1980s after years of neglect, the Secession Building is one of Vienna's preeminent symbols of artistic rebellion; rather than look to the architecture of the past like the revivalist Ringstrasse, it looked to a new anti-Historicist future. It was, in its day, a riveting trumpet blast of a building, and is today considered by many to be Europe's first piece of full-blown 20th-century architecture.

The Secession movement began in 1897 when 20 dissatisfied Viennese artists headed by Gustav Klimt "seceded" from the Künstlerhausgenossenschaft, the conservative artists' society associated with the Academy of Fine Arts. The movement promoted the radically new kind of art known as Jugendstil, which found its inspiration in both the organic, fluid designs of Art Nouveau and the related but more geometric designs of the English Arts and Crafts movement. (The Secessionists founded an arts-and-crafts workshop of their own, the famous Wiener Werkstätte, in an effort to embrace the applied arts.) The Secession Building was the movement's exhibition hall, designed by the architect Joseph Olbrich and completed in 1898. The lower story, crowned by the entrance motto *Der Zeit Ihre Kunst, Der Kunst Ihre Freiheit* (To Every Age Its Art, To Art Its Freedom), is classic Jugendstil: The restrained but assured decoration (by Koloman Moser) beautifully complements the facade's pristine flat expanses of cream-colored wall. Above the entrance motto sits the building's most famous feature, the gilded openwork dome that the Viennese were quick to christen "the golden cabbage" (Olbrich wanted it to be seen as a dome of laurel, a subtle classical reference meant to celebrate the triumph of art). The plain white interior—"shining and chaste," in Olbrich's words—was also revolutionary; its most unusual feature was movable walls, allowing the galleries to be reshaped and redesigned for every show. One early show, in 1902, was an exhibition devoted to art celebrating the genius of Beethoven; Gustav Klimt's *Beethoven Frieze*, painted for the occasion, has now been restored and is permanently installed in the building's basement. *Friedrichstr. 12, tel. 0222/587–5307. Admission: AS60 adults, AS30 senior citizens, children free. Open Tues.–Fri. 10–6, weekends and holidays 10–4.*

To the south of the Secession Building run two parallel streets, the Linke (left) and Rechte (right) Wienzeile. Farther to the south, the River Wien, a tributary of the Danube, runs between them, but here the river was covered over at the turn of the century. The site is now home to the Naschmarkt, Vienna's main outdoor produce market.

Time Out   Explore the **Naschmarkt** and pick up a meal as you go. The stands marked *Imbisse* (Snack) will sell you a *Hühnerschnitzel-Semmel* (chicken schnitzel inside a Viennese roll), the **Meeres-Buffet** offers a vast array of seafood, **Heindl & Co. Palat-schinkenkuch'l** (pancake kitchen) sells a wide variety of meat and dessert crepes, and the **Naschmarkt Bäckerei** can supply the necessary pastry. If you want a more leisurely sit-down meal, try **Sopherl**, a favorite hangout of Naschmarkt vendors, on Linke Wienzeile on the market's west side.

The Ringstrasse-style apartment houses that line Linke Wienzeile are mostly an undistinguished lot, but four blocks south of the Secession Building, two unexpectedly stand out: **Nos. 38 and 40,** designed (1898–99) by the grand old man of Viennese fin-de-siècle architecture, Otto Wagner, during his Secessionist phase.

A good example of what Wagner was rebelling against can be seen next door, at **No. 42,** where Baroque decorative enthusiasm has degenerated into Baroque Revival decorative hysteria, and the overwrought facade seems to drown in a jumble of classical motifs. Wagner had come to believe that this sort of display was nothing but empty pretense and sham; modern apartment houses, he wrote in his pioneering text *Modern Architecture*, are entirely different from 18th-century town palaces, and architects should not pretend otherwise. Accordingly, Wagner banished classical decoration and introduced a new architectural simplicity, with flat exterior walls and plain, regular window treatments meant to reflect the orderly layout of the apartments behind them. For decoration, he turned to his younger Secessionist cohorts Joseph Olbrich and Koloman Moser, who designed the ornate Jugendstil patterns of red majolica-tile roses and gold stucco medallions that brighten the facades of Nos. 38 and 40.

More of Wagner's Secessionist work can be seen two blocks east of the Secession Building on the northern edge of Karlsplatz. In 1893 Wagner was appointed architectural supervisor of the new Vienna City Railway, and the matched **pair of small pavilions** he designed for the Karlsplatz station in 1898 are among the city's most ingratiating buildings. Their structural framework is frankly exposed (in keeping with Wagner's belief in architectural honesty), but they are also lovingly decorated (in keeping with the Viennese love of architectural finery). The result is Jugendstil at its very best, melding plain and fancy with grace and insouciance.

Like the space now occupied by the Naschmarkt, the Karlsplatz was formed when the River Wien was covered over at the turn of the century. At the time Wagner expressed his frustration with the result—too large a space for a formal square and too small a space for an informal park—and the awkwardness persists to this day. The buildings surrounding the Karlsplatz, on the other hand, are quite sure of themselves: on the south side the **Technical University** (1816–18) and on the north side the **Kunstlerhaus** (the exhibition hall in which the Secessionists refused to exhibit, built in 1881 and still in use) and the **Musikverein** (finished in 1869, now home to the Vienna Philharmonic). Much the most important building, however, is the oldest: the Church of Saint Charles Borromeo, familiarly known as ❹❸ the **Karlskirche,** built in the early 18th century on what was then the bank of the River Wien and is now the Karlsplatz's southeast corner.

The church had its beginnings in a disaster. In 1713, Vienna was hit by a brutal plague outbreak, and Emperor Charles VI made a vow: If the plague abated, he would build a church dedicated to his namesake Saint Charles Borromeo, the 16th-century Italian bishop who was famous for his ministrations to Milanese plague victims. In 1715 construction began, using an ambitious design by Johann Bernhard Fischer von Erlach that combined architectural elements from ancient Greece (the columned entrance porch), ancient Rome (the freestanding columns, modeled after Trajan's Column), contemporary Rome (the Baroque dome), and contemporary Vienna (the Baroque towers at either end). When it was finished, the church received (and continues to receive) a decidedly mixed press. History, incidentally, delivered a negative verdict: In its day the Karlskirche spawned no imitations, and it went on to become one of European architecture's most famous curiosities. Seen lit at night, the building is magical in its setting.

The main interior of the church utilizes only the area under the dome, and is surprisingly conventional given the unorthodox facade. The space and architectural detailing are typical High Baroque; the fine vault frescoes, by J. M. Rottmayr (1725-1730), depict Saint Charles Borromeo imploring the Holy Trinity to end the plague.

❹❹ Finally, one last Karlsplatz building remains: the **Historisches Museum der Stadt Wien** (Museum of Viennese History), hidden away at the east end of the square next to the Karlskirche. The museum possesses a dazzling array of Viennese historical artifacts and treasures: models, maps, documents, photographs, antiquities, stained glass, paintings, sculpture, crafts, reconstructed rooms. Paintings include Klimts and Schieles, and there's a life-size portrait of the composer Alban Berg painted by his contemporary Arnold Schönberg. Alas, display information and designations in the museum are only in German, and there's no guidebook in English. *Karlsplatz, tel. 0222/505–8747. Admission: AS30 adults, AS15 senior citizens, AS10 children. Open Tues.–Sun. 9–4:30.*

Beyond the Karlsplatz to the east is the **French Embassy,** built in 1909 in an Art Nouveau style that offers a clear contrast to the more geometric Austrian Jugendstil. Beyond the embassy lies **Schwarzenbergplatz.** The military monument occupying the south end of the square is the **Russian War Memorial,** set up at the end of World War II by the Soviets; the Viennese, remembering the Soviet occupation, call its unknown soldier "the unknown plunderer." South of the memorial is the formidable **Schwarzenberg Palace,** designed by Johann Lukas von Hildebrandt in 1697 and now (in part) a luxury hotel (*see* Dining and Lodging, *below*).

Hildebrandt's most important Viennese work is farther along, at Rennweg 6A: the **Belvedere Palace.** In fact the Belvedere is two palaces with extensive gardens between. Built just outside the city fortifications between 1714 and 1722, the complex originally served as the summer palace of Prince Eugene of Savoy; much later it became the home of Archduke Franz Ferdinand, whose assassination in 1914 precipitated World War I. Though the lower palace is impressive in its own right (it served as Prince Eugene's living quarters), it is the much larger upper palace, used for state receptions, banquets, and balls, that is Hildebrandt's acknowledged masterpiece.

Best approached through the gardens, the upper palace displays a remarkable wealth of architectural invention in its facade, avoiding the main design problem common to all palaces because of their excessive size: monotony on the one hand and pomposity on the other. Hildebrandt's decoration here approaches the Rococo, that final style of the Baroque era when traditional classical motifs all but disappeared in a whirlwind of seductive asymmetric fancy. The main interiors of the palace go even further: Columns are transformed into muscle-bound giants, pilasters grow torsos, capitals sprout great piles of symbolic Imperial paraphernalia, and the ceilings are set aswirl with ornately molded stucco. The result is the finest Rococo interior in the city.

Today both the upper and lower palaces are museums devoted to Austrian painting. **The Austrian Museum of Baroque Art,** in the lower palace, displays Austrian art of the 18th century (including the original figures from Georg Raphael Donner's *Providence Fountain* in the Neuer Markt). Next to the Baroque Museum (outside the west end) is the converted Orangerie, devoted to works of the medieval period. The main attraction, however, is the upper palace's collection of **19th- and 20th-century Austrian paintings,** centering on the work of Vienna's three preeminent early 20th-century artists: Gustav Klimt, Egon Schiele, and Oskar Kokoschka. Klimt was the oldest, and by the time he helped found the Secession movement, he had forged a highly idiosyncratic painting style that combined realistic and decorative elements in a way that was completely revolutionary. Schiele and Kokoschka went even further, rejecting the decorative appeal of Klimt's glittering abstract designs and producing works that completely ignored conventional ideas of beauty. Today they are considered the fathers of modern art in Vienna. *Upper Belvedere: Prinz-Eugen-Str. 27. Tel. 0222/784158. Admission: AS60 adults, AS30 children. Open Tues.–Sun. 10–5.*

Tour 7: Schönbrunn Palace

Schönbrunn Palace, the huge Habsburg summer palace laid out by Johann Bernhard Fischer von Erlach in 1696, lies well within the city limits, just a few subway stops west of Karlsplatz on line U4. The vast and elegantly planted gardens are open daily from dawn till dusk, and multilingual guided tours of the palace interior take place daily. The **Wagenburg** (Imperial Coach Collection) can be seen in the west wing, entered at the far end of the small courtyard off the main courtyard's southwest corner, and the **Tiergarten** (the Imperial Menagerie, now the Vienna Zoo), founded in 1752 during the reign of Maria Theresa, is on the west side of the gardens. On the grounds to the west is the **Palmenhaus,** a huge greenhouse filled with exotic trees and plants. Close by is the **Schmetterlinghaus,** given over to hordes of live butterflies, orchids, and other floral displays.

A visit inside the palace is not included in the general sightseeing tours, which merely offer a mercilessly tempting drive past. The four-hour sightseeing tours of Schönbrunn cost many times what you'd pay if you tackled the easy excursion yourself; their advantage is that they get you there and back with less effort. Go on your own if you want time to wander the magnificent grounds.

The best approach to the palace and its gardens is through the front gate, located on Schönbrunner Schloss-Strasse halfway between the Schönbrunn and Hietzing subway stations. The vast main courtyard is ruled by a formal design of impeccable order and rigorous symmetry: Wing nods at wing, facade mirrors facade, and every part stylistically complements every other. The courtyard, however, turns out to be a mere appetizer; the feast lies beyond. The breathtaking view that unfolds on the other side of the palace is one of the finest set pieces in all Europe and one of the supreme achievements of Baroque planning. Formal *allées* (garden promenades) shoot off diagonally, the one on the right toward the zoo, the one on the left toward a rock-mounted obelisk and a fine false Roman ruin. But these, and the woods beyond, are merely a frame for the astonishing composition in the center: the sculpted fountain, the carefully planted screen of trees behind, the sudden almost vertical rise of the grass-covered hill beyond. And at the crest of the hill, topping it all off, sits a Baroque masterstroke: Johann Ferdinand von Hohenberg's incomparable **Gloriette.** Perfectly scaled for its setting, the Gloriette holds the whole vast garden composition together, and at the same time crowns the ensemble with a brilliant architectural tiara.

After the superb gardens, the palace interior comes as something of an anticlimax. Of the 1,400 rooms, 45 are open to the public, and two are of special note: the Hall of Mirrors, where the six-year-old Mozart performed for the Empress Maria Theresa in 1762, and the Grand Gallery, where the Congress of Vienna (1815) danced at night after carving up Napoleon's collapsed empire during the day. The most unusual interior at Schönbrunn, however, is not within the palace at all. It is the newly restored Imperial subway station, known as the **Hofpavillon,** located just outside the palace grounds (at the northwest corner, a few yards east of the Hietzing subway station). Designed by Otto Wagner in conjunction with Joseph Olbrich and Leopold Bauer, the Hofpavillon was built in 1899 for the exclusive use of the Emperor Franz Josef and his entourage. Exclusive it was: the emperor used the station only once. The exterior, with its proud architectural crown, is Wagner at his best, and the lustrous interior is one of the finest examples of Jugendstil decoration in the city. *Schönbrunner Schloss-Str., subway stop Schönbrunn, tel. 0222/81113–238. Guided tours of palace interior AS80 adults, AS30 children. Open Apr.–Oct., daily 8:30–5; Nov.–Mar., daily 8:30–4:30. Gloriette roof admission: AS20 adults, AS10 children. Open May–Sept., daily 8–6; Oct., daily 8–5. Wagenburg, tel. 0222/ 877–3244. Admission: AS30 adults, children free. Open Nov.– Mar., daily 10–4; Apr.–Oct., daily 10–6. Tiergarten, subway stop Hietzing, tel. 0222/877–1237. Admission: AS60 adults, AS15 children. Open daily Nov.–Jan. 9–4:40, Oct. and Feb. 9–5, Mar. 9–5:30, Apr. 9–6, May–Sept. 9–6:30. Palmenhaus green house: nearest entrance Hietzing, tel. 0222/8775087–406. Admission: AS35 adults, AS20 senior citizens, AS15 children. Open daily May–Sept. 9:30–5:30, Oct.–Apr. 9:30–4:30. But-terfly house: nearest entrance Hietzing, tel. 0222/877–5087– 421. Admission AS35 adults, AS20 senior citizens, AS15 chil-dren. Open daily May–Sept. 10–4:30, Oct.–Apr. 10–3. Hof-pavillon, Schönbrunner Schloss-Str., next to Hietzing subway station, tel. 0222/877–1571. Admission: AS15. Open Tues.– Sun. 9–12:15, 1–4:30.*

The vast **Technical Museum,** located close by though not within the Schönbrunn grounds, is closed until 1996 for cellar-to-roof renovation and modernization. You may still be able to get a look at the outstanding display of steam locomotives to the west of the main building, but the other treasures of the house are under cover.

Vienna for Free

Vienna is not famous for its sightseeing generosity—there is even an admission charge when the Vienna Boys' Choir sings Mass at the Hofburgkapelle (in fairness, however, it should be noted that the musical masses at the nearby Augustinerkirche are free). A look through the **Dorothem** auction house costs nothing unless, of course, you decide to bid. Check with the tourist information office about free times at the museums; the Museum of the City of Vienna is free on Friday mornings, for example. Filmed operas, projected on a huge screen in front of City Hall several evenings a week, are a great summer attrac-tion; check the tourist office for program and times. The city's many public parks are the main no-cost attraction, notably the **Schönbrunn Gardens** (*see* Tour 7), the **Volksgarten** (*see* Tour 4), and the **Belvedere Gardens** (*see* Tour 6). In addition, the **Stadtpark** (on the Ringstrasse near its east end) offers early-evening band concerts in the summer; it also contains some fine turn-of-the-century architecture and a frothy monument to Jo-hann Strauss. The beautifully planted **Burggarten** (on the east side of the Neue Burg) is flanked at its north end by the imperi-al greenhouses, built in 1905. The famed **Wienerwald** (Vienna Woods) is not a park but a series of low wooded hills west of the city, actually the easternmost foothills of the Alps. Exploring the woods in fine weather is a time-honored Viennese pastime; the view of the city and the Danube from the Leopoldsberg Hill is especially cherished.

What to See and Do with Children

Vienna's main attraction for children is the famous **Wurstel-prater** (or Volksprater), Vienna's foremost amusement park (at the Prater's north end; take the U1 subway line to Prater-stern). It has all the traditional modern amusement-park rides plus a number of less innocent indoor, sex-oriented attractions and a museum devoted to the Wurstelprater's long history. The best-known attraction is the giant Ferris wheel that figured so prominently in the 1949 film *The Third Man.* One of three built in Europe at the end of the last century (the others were in England and France but have long since been dismantled), the wheel was badly damaged during World War II and restored shortly thereafter. Its progress is slow and stately (a revolution takes ten minutes), the views from its cars magnificent.

The **Vienna Zoo** will also appeal and possesses the added advantage of being located in the Schönbrunn Gardens (*see* Tour 7). In the basement of the **Theater Museum** is a children's museum that is reached by a slide (Lobkowitzpl., tel. 0222/512–3705). The **Doll and Toy Museum** (*see* Tour 2) has plenty of charm. Also see the specialty museums, below. Lesser attractions include the **Museum of Natural History** (*see* Tour 4) and a notably bizarre **aquarium,** grotesquely housed in a World War II flak-tower in the middle of the tiny Esterhazy Park between Mariahilfer Strasse and Gumpendorferstrasse (tel. 0222/587–1417; admission: AS50 adults, AS20 children; open daily 9–6). Finally, the climb to the top of the **south tower of St. Stephen's Cathedral** (*see* Tour 1) should work up an appetite for a visit, if the pocketbook allows, to **Demel's** (Kohlmarkt 14), Vienna's most famous pastry shop.

Off the Beaten Track

Vienna's most exalted piece of Jugendstil architecture is not in the inner city but in the suburbs to the west: the **Am Steinhof Church,** designed by Otto Wagner in 1904 during his Secessionist phase. Built on the grounds of the Lower Austrian State Asylum (now the Vienna City Psychiatric Hospital), Wagner's design united mundane functional details (rounded edges on the pews to prevent injury to the patients and a slightly sloped tile floor to facilitate cleaning) with a soaring, airy dome and glittering Jugendstil decoration (mosaics by Remigius Geyling and stained glass by Koloman Moser). The church is open once a week for guided tours (in German). *Baumgartner Höhe 1, tel. 0222/949060–2391. Admission free. Open Sat. 3–4. Subway stop: Unter-St.-Veit, then No. 47A bus to Psychiatrisches Krankenhaus.*

Music lovers will want to make a pilgrimage to the **Zentral-friedhof** (Central Cemetery, in the 11th District on Sim-meringer Hauptstrasse), which contains the graves of most of Vienna's great composers, some moved here from other cemeteries: Ludwig van Beethoven, Franz Schubert, Johannes Brahms, the Johann Strausses (father and son), and Arnold Schönberg, among others. The monument to Wolfgang Amadeus Mozart is a memorial only; the approximate location of his actual burial, in an unmarked grave, can be seen at the now deconsecrated St. Marx-Friedhof at Leberstrasse 6–8. *Street-car 71 to St. Marxer Friedhof, or on to Zentralfriedhof Haupttor/2. Tor for the composers' graves.*

Musical residences abound as well. Schubert—a native of the city, unlike most of Vienna's other famous composers—was born at Nussdorferstrasse 54 (tel. 0222/345–9924), in the Ninth

District, and died in the Fourth District at Kettenbrücken-gasse 6 (tel. 0222/573–9072). Joseph Haydn's house is at Hay-dngasse 19 (tel. 0222/596–1307) in the Sixth District; Beethoven's Heiligenstadt residence, where at age 32 he wrote the "Heiligenstadt Testament," an anguished cry of pain and protest against his ever-increasing deafness, is at Probusgasse 6 in the 19th District (tel. 0222/375–408). Finally, the home of the most popular composer of all, waltz king Johann Strauss the younger, can be visited at Praterstrasse 54 (tel. 0222/240–121), in the Second District; he lived here when he composed "The Blue Danube Waltz" in 1867. All the above houses contain commemorative museums (admission: AS15; open Tues.–Sun. 9–12:15 and 1–4:30); for subway stops, *see* Historic Buildings and Sights, *below*.

Two museums not covered on the walking tours are of special note. The **Museum of Applied Arts** (on the Ring at Stubenring 5, tel. 0222/71136; admission AS60 adults, AS30 senior citizens, children free; open Fri.–Wed. 10–6, Thurs. 10–9) contains a large collection of Austrian furniture and art objects; the Ju-gendstil display devoted to Josef Hoffman and his followers at the Wiener Werkstätte is particularly fine. And the **Museum of Military History** (south of the Belvedere on Ghegastr.; tel. 0222/782303; admission AS30; open Sat.–Thurs. 10–4) contains a vast array of Austro-Hungarian military relics and memen-tos, including the car in which Archduke Franz Ferdinand was riding when he was assassinated in 1914 at Sarajevo.

Sightseeing Checklists

This list includes both attractions that were covered in the pre-ceding tours and additional ones that are described here for the first time.

Historic Buildings and Sights

Beethoven Heiligenstadt residence (*see* Off the Beaten Track). *Subway stop: Heiligenstadt, then No. 38A bus to Armbrust-ergasse.*
Café Central (*see* Tour 2). *Subway stop: Herrengasse.*
Café Hawelka (*see* Tour 3). *Subway stop: Stephansplatz.*
City Hall (*see* Tour 4). *Subway stop: Rathaus.*
Dorotheum (Auction House; *see* Tour 3). *Subway stop: Steph-ansplatz.*
Figarohaus (Mozart Residence; *see* Tour 5). *Subway stop: Stephansplatz.*
Freud's apartment (*see* Tour 4). *Subway stop: Schottentor.*
Haydn residence (*see* Off the Beaten Track). *Subway stop: Pilgramgasse.*
Hofburg (Habsburg Imperial Palace; *see* Tour 4). *Subway stop: Herrengasse.*
Hofpavillon (*see* Tour 7). *Subway stop: Hietzing.*
Hundertwasserhaus. A 50-apartment public-housing complex designed by Friedrich Hundertwasser, Austria's best-known living painter. Looking as if it was painted by a crew of mischie-vous circus clowns wielding giant crayons, the building caused a sensation when it went up in 1985. It remains a tourist attrac-tion not to be missed. *Corner of Kegelgasse and Löwengasse. Subway stop: Schwedenplatz, then streetcar N to Hetzgasse.*

Imperial Burial Vault (*see* Tour 5). *Subway stop: Stephansplatz.*

Looshaus (House without Eyebrows; *see* Tour 3). *Subway stop: Herrengasse.*

National Library (in the Hofburg; *see* Tour 4). *Subway stop: Herrengasse.*

National Theater (*see* Tour 4). *Subway stop: Rathaus.*

Opera House (*see* Tour 5). *Subway stop: Karlsplatz.*

Palace of Justice (*see* Tour 4). *Subway stop: Volkstheater.*

Parliament (*see* Tour 4). *Subway stop: Lerchenfelder Strasse.*

Pasqualatihaus (Beethoven's residence; *see* Tour 2). *Subway stop: Schottentor.*

Schönbrunn Palace (*see* Tour 7). *Subway stop: Schönbrunn.*

Schubert's birthplace. (*see* Off the Beaten Track). *Subway stop: Schottentor, then No. 37 or No. 38 tram to Nussdorfer Strasse/ Canisiusgasse.* **The house where he died.** *Subway stop: Kettenbrückengasse.*

Strauss residence (*see* Off the Beaten Track). *Subway stop: Nestroyplatz.*

University of Vienna (*see* Tour 4). *Subway stop: Schottentor.*

Virgilkapelle. (*see* Tour 3). An old and mysterious chapel, uncovered during excavations for the subway system in the 1970s. It was probably constructed in the 13th century by hollowing out the ground underneath the charnel house next to St. Stephen's; no trace of an entrance door was found, its only possible means of access apparently being a trap door in the ceiling. Visible from the first underground level of the Stephansplatz subway station. *Subway stop: Stephansplatz.*

Winter Riding School (Hofburg; *see* Tour 4). *Subway stop: Herrengasse.*

Museums and Galleries

Academy of Fine Arts (*see* Tour 6). *Subway stop: Karlsplatz.*

Albertina Museum (*see* Tour 5). *Subway stop: Stephansplatz.*

Belvedere Palace (*see* Tour 6). *Subway stop: Karlsplatz; then for upper Belvedere, Streetcar D to Belvederegasse.*

Cathedral and Diocese Museum (*see* Tour 1). *Subway stop: Stephansplatz.*

Clock Museum (*see* Tour 2). *Subway stop: Stephansplatz.*

Collection of Musical Instruments (Hofburg; *see* Tour 4). *Subway stop: Babenbergerstrasse.*

Collection of Weapons (Hofburg; *see* Tour 4). *Subway stop: Babenbergerstrasse.*

Court Silver and Tableware Treasury (Hofburg; *see* Tour 4). *Subway stop: Herrengasse.*

Doll and Toy Museum. (*see* Tour 2). *Subway stop: Stephansplatz.*

Ephesus Museum (Hofburg; *see* Tour 4). *Subway stop: Babenbergerstrasse.*

Ethnological Museum (Hofburg; *see* Tour 4). *Subway stop: Babenbergerstrasse.*

Globe Museum. (*see* Tour 4). *Subway stop: Herrengasse.*

Imperial Apartments (Hofburg; *see* Tour 4). *Subway stop: Herrengasse.*

Imperial Coach Collection (Schönbrunn; *see* Tour 7). *Subway stop: Schönbrunn.*

Imperial Treasuries (Hofburg; *see* Tour 4). *Subway stop: Herrengasse.*

Museum of Applied Arts (*see* Off the Beaten Track) *Subway stop: Stubentor.*
Museum of Art History (*see* Tour 4). *Subway stop: Babenbergerstrasse.*
Museum of Military History (*see* Off the Beaten Track). *Subway stop: Südtiroler-Platz, then Streetcar 18 to Fasangasse.*
Museum of Modern Art (*see* Tour 4). *Subway stop: Schottentor, then Streetcar D to Fürstengasse.*
Museum of Natural History (*see* Tour 4). *Subway stop: Volkstheater.*
Museum of Viennese History (*see* Tour 6). *Subway stop: Karlsplatz.*
Secession Building (*see* Tour 6). *Subway stop: Karlsplatz.*

In addition to the above, which are mentioned in the walking tours, Vienna possesses an astonishing array of little specialty museums, some of which are free, most of which have small admission fees.

Bell Museum. Troststr. 38, tel. 0222/604–3460. Open Wed. 2–5. *Subway stop: Reumannplatz.*
Circus and Clown Museum. Karmelitergasse 9, tel. 0222/21106–127. Open Wed. 5:30–7 PM, Sat. 2:30–5 PM, Sun. 10–noon. *Subway stop: Schwedenplatz.*
Esperanto Museum. Hofburg (Michaelerplatz entrance), tel. 0222/535–5145. Open Mon., Fri. 10–4, Wed. 10–6. *Subway stop: Herrengasse.*
Film Museum. Augustinerstr. 1, tel. 0222/533–7054. Film showings Oct.–May, Mon.–Sat. 6 and 8 PM. *Subway stop: Karlsplatz.*
Firefighting Museum. Am Hof 7, tel. 0222/53199. Open Sat. 10–noon, Sun. 9–noon. *Subway stop: Herrengasse.*
Folk Art Museum. Laudongasse 15–19, tel. 0222/438905. Open Tues.–Fri. 9–4, Sat. 9–noon, Sun. 9–1. *Subway stop: Rathaus.*
Folk Art Museum (Religious art; original convent pharmacy). Johannesgasse 8, tel. 0222/512–1337. Open Wed. 9–4, Sun. 9–1. *Subway stop: Stephansplatz.*
Football (Soccer) Museum. Meiereistr. (in the Praterstadium), tel. 0222/21718. Open Mon., Fri. 10–1, Tues., Thurs. 2–6. *Subway stop: Praterstern, then streetcar 21.*
Glass Museum. Kärntner Str. 26 (Lobmeyr Store), tel. 0222/512–0508. Open weekdays 9–6, Sat. 9–noon. *Subway stop: Stephansplatz.*
Heating Technology Museum. Längenfeldgasse 13–15 (Berufschule), tel. 0222/4000–93231 or 0222/4000–93319. Open Tues. 1–6 PM. *Subway stop: Längenfeldgasse.*
Horsedrawn Cab Museum. Veronikagasse 12, tel. 0222/438852–0. Open first Wed. of every month 10–noon. *Subway stop: Josefstädter Strasse, then streetcar J to Gürtel.*
Horseshoeing, Harnessing and Saddling Museum. Linke Bahngasse 11, tel. 0222/71155–372. Open Mon.–Thurs. 1:30–3:30 PM by arrangement. *Subway stop: Rochusgasse.*
Jewish Museum. Seitenstättengasse 4, tel. 0222/535–5502. Open Sun.–Thurs. 10–5. *Subway stop: Schwedenplatz.* (The museum is scheduled to move to Dorotheergasse 11; check for location and opening hours.)
Medical History Museum. Währinger Str. 25/1 (in the Josephinum), tel. 0222/403–2154. Open weekdays 9–3. *Subway stop: Schottentor.*
Pathological Anatomy Museum. Spitalgasse 2 (in the Allgemeines Krankenhaus), tel. 0222/438672. Open Wed. 3–6,

Thurs. 8–11 AM, first Sat. each month 10–1; closed Aug. *Subway stop: Schottentor.*

Period Furniture Museum. Mariahilfer Str. 88, tel. 0222/523-424-99. Open Tues.–Fri. 9–4, Sat. 9–noon. *Subway stop: Zieglergasse.*

Postal and Telegraph Services Museum. Mariahilfer Str. 212, tel. 0222/89101. Closed until 1996 for renovation. *Subway stop: Schönbrunn.*

Railway Museum. Mariahilfer Str. 212, tel. 0222/89101. Closed until 1996 for renovation, although locomotive park may be viewable. *Subway stop: Schönbrunn.*

Streetcar Museum. Erdbergstr. 109, tel. 0222/712-1201. Open early May–early Oct., weekends and holidays 9–4. *Subway stop: Schlachthausgasse.*

Technology Museum. Mariahilfer Str. 212, tel. 0222/89101. Closed until 1996 for renovation. *Subway stop: Schönbrunn.*

Theater Museum. Lobkowitzplatz 2, tel. 0222/512-8800. Open Tues.–Sun. 10–5. *Subway stop: Stephansplatz.*

Tobacco Museum (smoking encouraged). Mariahilfer Str. 2 (Messepalast), tel. 0222/961716. Open Tues. 10–7; Wed.–Fri. 10–3; weekends 9–1. *Subway stop: Babenbergerstrasse.*

Treasury of the Order of Teutonic Knights. Singerstr. 7, tel. 0222/512-1065-6. Open Mon., Thurs., Sat., Sun. 10–noon, Wed., Fri., Sat. 3–5; closed Sun. Nov.–Apr. *Subway stop: Stephansplatz.*

Undertaker's Museum. Goldeggasse 19, tel. 0222/50195-227. Open weekdays noon–3 by prior arrangement only. *Subway stop: Südtiroler-Platz.*

Viticultural Museum. Döblinger Hauptstr. 96, tel. 0222/376939 or 0222/361-0042. Open Sat. 3:30–6 PM, Sun. 10–noon. Closed July and Aug. *Subway stop: Heiligenstadt; or (closer) Schottentor, then streetcar 37 to Pokornygasse.*

Churches and Temples

Am Steinhof Kirche (*see* Off the Beaten Track). *Subway stop: Unter St. Veit, then No. 47A bus to Psychiatrisches Krankenhaus.*

Annakirche (*see* Tour 5). *Subway stop: Stephansplatz.*

Augustinerkirche (Hofburg; *see* Tour 4). *Subway stop: Herrengasse.*

Dominikanerkirche (*see* Tour 1). *Subway stop: Stephansplatz.*

Franziskanerkirche (*see* Tour 5). *Subway stop: Stephansplatz.*

Jesuitenkirche (*see* Tour 1). *Subway stop: Stubentor/Dr. Karl-Lueger-Platz.*

Karlskirche (*see* Tour 6). *Subway stop: Karlsplatz.*

Kirche Am Hof (*see* Tour 2). *Subway stop: Stephansplatz.*

Maria am Gestade (*see* Tour 1). *Subway stop: Stephansplatz.*

Michaelerkirche (*see* Tour 3). *Subway stop: Herrengasse.*

Minoritenkirche (*see* Tour 2). *Subway stop: Herrengasse.*

Peterskirche (*see* Tour 3). *Subway stop: Stephansplatz.*

Ruprechtskirche (*see* Tour 1). *Subway stop: Schwedenplatz.*

Schottenhof (*see* Tour 2). *Subway stop: Schottentor.*

St. Stephen's Cathedral (*see* Tour 1). *Subway stop: Stephansplatz.*

Synagogue (*see* Tour 1). *Subway stop: Schwedenplatz.*

Votivkirche (*see* Tour 4). *Subway stop: Schottentor.*

Parks and Gardens

Burggarten (*see* Vienna for Free). *Subway stop: Babenber-gerstrasse.*
Prater. In 1766, to the dismay of the aristocracy, Emperor Joseph II decreed that the vast expanse of imperial parklands known as the Prater would henceforth be open to the public. East of the inner city between the Danube Canal and the Danube proper, the Prater is a public park to this day, notable for its long promenade (the Hauptallee, over 3 miles in length), its sports facilities (a golf course, a stadium, a race track, and a swimming pool, for starters), and the Wurstelprater with its giant Ferris wheel. *Subway stop: Praterstern.*
Schönbrunn Gardens (*see* Tour 7). *Subway stop: Schönbrunn.*
Stadtpark (*see* Vienna for Free). *Subway stop: Stadtpark.*
Volksgarten (*see* Tour 4). *Subway stop: Lerchenfelder Strasse.*
Wurstelprater (*see* What to See and Do with Children). *Subway stop: Praterstern.*

Other Places of Interest

Aquarium (*see* What to See and Do with Children). *Subway stop: Kettenbrückengasse.*
Central Cemetery (*see* Off the Beaten Track). *Subway stop: Karlsplatz, then streetcar 71 from Schwarzenbergplatz.*
Danube Tower. In the middle of the Danube Park (a reclaimed garbage dump), 827 feet high with two revolving restaurants and fine views. Tel. 0222/235368. *Subway stop: Kaisermühlen.*
Flea Market: (*see* Shopping). *Subway stop: Kettenbrücken-gasse.*
Naschmarkt (*see* Tour 6). *Subway stop: Karlsplatz.*
Roman ruins (Hoher Markt, Tour 1). *Subway stop: Steph-ansplatz.*
Vienna Zoo (Schönbrunn gardens; *see* Tour 7). *Subway stop: Hietzing.*

Shopping

Shopping Districts The **Kärntner Strasse, Graben,** and **Kohlmarkt** pedestrian areas claim to have the best shops in Vienna, and for some items, such as jewelry, some of the best anywhere, although you must expect high prices. The side streets within this area have developed their own character, with shops offering antiques, art, clocks, jewelry, and period furniture. Outside the center, concentrations of stores are on **Mariahilfer Strasse** straddling the Sixth and Seventh districts; **Landstrasser Hauptstrasse** in the Third District; and, still farther out, **Favoritenstrasse** in the 10th District.

A collection of attractive small boutiques has sprung up in the **Sonnhof** passage between Landstrasser Hauptstrasse 28 and Ungargasse 13 in the Third District and in the **Palais Ferstel** passage at Freyung 2 in the First District. The **Spittelberg** market, on the Spittelberggasse between Burggasse and Siebensterngasse in the Seventh District, has drawn small galleries and handicrafts shops (open on Saturdays from April to October) and is particularly popular in the weeks before Christmas. That is the time also for the tinselly **Christkindlmarkt** on Rathausplatz in front of city hall; in protest over its commercialization, smaller markets specializing in handicrafts have sprung up on such traditional spots as Am Hof and Freyung (First District).

Vienna's **Naschmarkt** (between Linke and Rechte Wienzeile, starting at Getreidemarkt) is one of Europe's great and most colorful food and produce markets. Stalls open at 5 or 6 AM, and the pace is lively until 1 or 2 PM. Saturday is the big day, when farmers come into the city to sell at the back end of the market. It's closed Sunday.

Department Stores The renovated, reopened **Steffl** department store (Kärntner Str. 19, tel. 0222/512–0685) is upscale without being overly expensive. The larger department stores are concentrated in Mariahilfer Strasse. By far the best is **Herzmansky** (Mariahilfer Str. 26–30, tel. 0222/931–6360), definitely upscale; outstanding gourmet shops and restaurants are in the basement. Farther up the street you will find slightly cheaper goods at **Gerngross** (Mariahilfer Str. and Kirchengasse, tel. 0222/932–5250) and **Stafa** (Mariahilfer Str. 120, tel. 0222/938621).

Flea Markets Every Saturday (except holidays) rain or shine, from about 7:30 AM to 4 or 5, the **Flohmarkt** in back of the Naschmarkt, stretching along the Linke Wienzeile from the Kettenbrücken subway station, offers a staggering collection of stuff ranging from serious antiques to plain junk. Haggle over prices.

Saturday and Sunday in summer from 2 to about 7:30 PM an outdoor **Art and Antiques** market takes place along the Danube Canal, stretching from the Schwedenbrücke to beyond the Salztorbrücke. Lots of books are sold, some in English, plus generally better goods than at the Saturday flea market. Bargain over prices all the same.

Auctions The **Dorotheum** (Dorotheergasse 17, tel. 0222/515600) is a state institution dating to 1707, when Emperor Josef I determined that he didn't want his people being taken advantage of by pawnbrokers. The place is intriguing, with goods ranging from furs to furniture auctioned almost daily. Information on how to bid is available in English.

Specialty Stores
Antiques You will find the best antiques shops located in the First District, many clustered close to the Dorotheum auction house, in the **Dorotheergasse, Stallburggasse, Plankengasse,** and **Spiegelgasse.** You'll also find interesting shops in the **Josefstadt** (Eighth) district, with prices considerably lower than those in the center of town. Wander up Florianigasse and back down Josefstädter Strasse, not overlooking the narrow side streets.

D & S (Plankengasse 6, tel. 0222/512–2972) specializes in old Viennese clocks. Look in at **Galerie Kovacek** (Stallburg 2, tel. 0222/512–9954) to see a remarkable collection of glass paperweights and other glass objects; you'll also find paintings and furniture here. **Peter Feldbacher** (Annagasse 6, tel. 0222/512–2408) has items ranging from glass to ceramics to furniture. For Art Deco, look to **Galerie Metropol** (Dortheergasse 12, tel. 0222/513–2208) or **Galerie bei der Albertina** (Lobkowitzplatz 1, tel. 0222/513–1416).

Books Several good stores with books in English as well are on the Graben and Kärntner Strasse in the First District. For bookstores specializing in English-language books, *see* Important Addresses and Numbers, above.

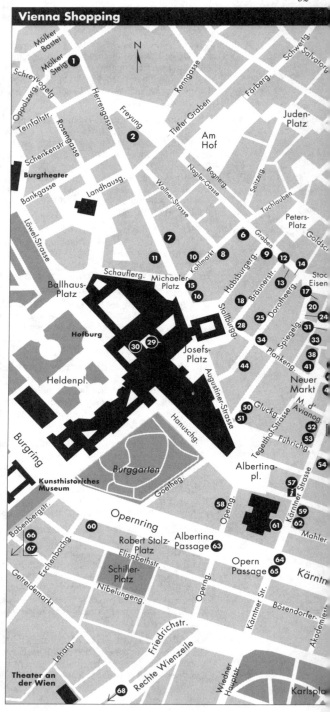

Vienna Shopping

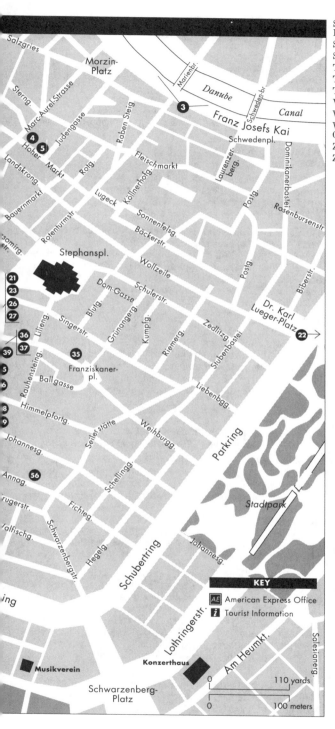

Men's Clothing Clothing in Vienna is far from cheap but is of good quality. The best shops are in the First District.

Sir Anthony (Kärntner Str. 21–23, tel. 0222/512–6835).
E. Braun (Graben 8, tel. 0222/512–5505).
House of Gentlemen (Kohlmarkt 12, tel. 0222/533–3258).
ITA (Graben 18, tel. 0222/533–6004).
Malowan (Opernring 23, tel. 0222/587–6296).
Silbernagel (Kärntner Str. 15, tel. 0222/512–5312).
Teller (Landstrasser Hauptstr. 88–90, tel. 0222/712–6397) for particularly good value.
Venturini (Spiegelgasse 9, tel. 0222/512–8845) for custom-made shirts.

For men's *Trachten,* or typical Austrian clothing, including lederhosen, try **Loden-Plankl** (Michaelerplatz 6, tel. 0222/533–8032), and go to **Collins Hüte** (Opernpassage, tel. 0222/587–1305) to get the appropriate hat.

Women's Clothing The couturier to Vienna is **Adlmüller** (Kärntner Str. 41, tel. 0222/512–6661). Check also **Flamm** (Neuer Markt 12, tel. 0222/512–2889), **E. Braun, ITA,** or **Malowan** (*see* Men's Clothing, *above*). You'll find modern young styling at **Maldone** (Kärntner Str. 4, tel. 0222/512–2761; Kärntner Str. 12, tel. 0222/512–2234; Graben 29, tel. 0222/533–6091; and Hoher Markt 8, tel. 0222/533–2555).

Check out the selection of dirndls and women's *Trachten,* the typical Austrian costume with white blouse, print skirt, and apron, at **Lanz** (Kärntner Str. 10, tel. 0222/512–2456), **Niederösterreichisches Heimatwerk** (Herrengasse 6–8, tel. 0222/533–3495), **Resi Hammerer** (Kärntner Str. 29–31, tel. 0222/512–6952), and **Tostmann** (Schottengasse 3a, tel. 0222/533–5331). (*See also* **Loden-Plankl** under Men's Clothing, *above*.)

The best shop for furs is **Liska** (Kärntner Str. 8, tel. 0222/512–4120; Hoher Markt 8, tel. 0222/533–2211). Be sure to arrange to get the value-added tax (VAT) returned on your purchase.

Ceramics and Porcelain Ceramics are anything but dull at **Berger** (Weihburggasse 17, tel. 0222/512–1434); the more standard patterns of Gmunden ceramics are at **Pawlata** (Kärntner Str. 14, tel. 0222/512–1764) and around the corner at **Plessgott** (Kärntnerdurchgang, tel. 0222/512–5824). Check out Viennese porcelain patterns at **Augarten** (Graben/Stock-im-Eisen-Platz 3, tel. 0222/512–1494) and **Albin Denk** (Graben 13, tel. 0222/512–4439), **Rosenthal** (Kärntner Str. 16, tel. 0222/512–3994), and **Wahliss** (Kärntner Str. 17, tel. 0222/512–3856).

Crystal and Glass Select famous Vienna glassware at **Bakalowits** (Spiegelgasse 3, tel. 0222/512–6351) and **Lobmeyr** (Kärntner Str. 26, tel. 0222/512–0508), which also has a small museum of its creations upstairs; the firm supplied the crystal chandeliers for the Metropolitan Opera in New York City, a gift from Austria. **Tabletop** (Passage, Freyung 2, tel. 0222/535–4256) has the exquisite Riedl glass (though readers have reported that goods were never received), as does **Rasper & Söhne** (Graben 15, tel. 0222/534330).

Gift Items **Österreichische Werkstätten** (Kärntner Str. 6, tel. 0222/512–2418) offers handmade handicrafts, gifts, and souvenirs ranging from jewelry to textiles.

Souvenir in der Hofburg (Hofburgpassage 1 and 7, tel. 0222/ 533–5053) is another source of gifts.

Niederösterreichisches Heimatwerk (*see* Women's Clothing, *above*) has handmade folk objects and textiles.

Wiener Geschenke (Reitschulgasse 4/Michaelerplatz, tel. 0222/ 533–7078, and Lobkowitzplatz 1, tel. 0222/513–3773) has a nice selection of quality gift and souvenir items.

Jewelry **Carius & Binder** (Kärntner Str. 17, tel. 0222/512–6750) is good for watches.

Haban (Kärntner Str. 2, tel. 0222/512–6730; Graben 12, tel. 0222/512–1220) has a fine selection of watches and jewelry.

A. Heldwein (Graben 13, tel. 0222/512–5781) sells elegant jewelry, silverware, and watches.

A. E. Köchert (Neuer Markt 15, tel. 0222/512–5828) has original creations.

Kunz (Neuer Markt 13, tel. 0222/512–7112) sells stunning modern pieces for men and women.

Schullin (Kohlmarkt 7, tel. 0222/533–9007) has some of the most original work found anywhere.

Jade Discover interesting pieces of Austrian jade at **Burgenland** (Opernpassage, tel. 0222/587–6266).

Needlework For Vienna's famous petit point, head for **Petit Point Kovacec** (Kärntner Str. 16, tel. 0222/512–4886) or **Stransky** (Hofburgpassage 2, tel. 0222/533–6098).

Records Look for records and tapes at **Arcadia** (Kärntner Str. 40, in the Staatsoper Passage, tel. 0222/513–9568), which also features books and music-related souvenirs.

Carola is best for pop LPs and CDs (Albertinapassage, by the Opera, tel. 0222/564114).

EMI (Kärntner Str. 30, tel. 0222/512–3675) and **da Caruso** (Operngasse 4, tel. 0222/513–1326) specialize in classics, with an emphasis on opera.

Havlicek (Herrengasse 5, tel. 0222/533–1964) features classics and is particularly knowledgeable and helpful.

Shoes and Leather Goods Try **Humanic** (Kärntner Str. 51, tel. 0222/512–5892 or Singerstr. 2, tel. 0222/512–9101). For exclusive styles, go to **Zak** (Kärntner Str. 36, tel. 0222/512–7257), **Popp & Kretschmer** (Kärntner Str. 51, tel. 0222/512–7801), and **Nigst** (Neuer Markt 4, tel. 0222/512–4303).

Wrought Iron *Weinhebers* (wine dispensers with pear-shape glass containers) and other iron items can be found at **Hemerle** (Annagasse 7, tel. 0222/512–4746) or **Zach** (Bräunerstr. 8, tel. 0222/533–9939).

Sports and the Outdoors

Participant Sports

Bicycling Vienna has more than 400 kilometers (about 250 miles) of cycling paths, including specially marked routes through the center of the city; look for the special pathways either in red brick or marked with a stylized cyclist in yellow. Note and observe the special traffic signals at some intersections. Excellent paved cycling trails run along the Danube, the Danube Canal, and through the *Donauinsel*, the artificial island on the north bank of the Danube. You can take a bike on the subway (except during rush hours) for half fare, but only in cars with a blue shield on the door, and only on stairs or elevators with the "bike" shield, not the escalators. The city tourist office has a brochure in German with useful cycling maps, plus a leaflet "See Vienna by Bike" with tips in English. At most bookstores you can purchase a cycling map of Vienna put out by a local cycling organization known as ARGUS (Frankenberggasse 11, tel. 0222/505–8435). You can rent a bike starting at about AS35 per hour, leaving your passport or other identification as a deposit. Rent a bike year-round at the Westbahnhof, Wien Nord (Praterstern), or Floridsdorf rail stations, or pick up a bike at **Radverleih Salztorbrücke** from April to mid-October (Franz-Josefs-Kai at Salztorbrücke, by the canal, tel. 0222/532–8234); at **Radverleih Hochschaubahn,** mid-March through October (in the Prater amusement park, by the Hochschaubahn, bear slightly right after you pass the Big Wheel, tel. 0222/260165); at **Radverleih Praterstern,** April–October (on the street level under Praterstern North rail station; or at **Fahrradstadl Semmering,** April–November (Ravelinstr. 2, under the railroad bridge, tel. 0222/749–8859). Other rental locations are available from tourist offices. Organized, two-hour bike tours with English-speaking guides leave the Danube Canal at the Salztorbrücke, May–September, Mondays at 4 PM.

Boating   Both the **Alte Donau** (Old Danube), a series of lakes to the north of the main stream, and the **Neue Donau,** on the north side of the Donauinsel (the artificial island in the river), offer good waters for paddleboats, rowboats, kayaks, sailboats, and windsurfing. The Danube itself is somewhat fast-moving for anything but kayaks. Rent boats from **Auzinger Boote** (Laberlweg 22, tel. 0222/235788), **Karl Hofbauer** (Neue Danube at Reichsbrücke, and Obere Alte Donau 186, tel. 0222/236733), **Eppel** (Wagramer Str. 48, tel. 0222/235168), **Irzl** (Florian Berndl-Gasse 33 and 34, tel. 0222/236743), and **Newrkla** (An der Obere Alte Donau, tel. 0222/386105). For details about sailing and sailing events, check with **Haus des Sports** (Prinz-Eugen-Str. 12, tel. 0222/505–3742).

Golf   The one in-town golf course is at **Freudenau** in the Prater (tel. 0222/218–9564). But this 18-hole par-70 course is so popular from April to November, even with the weekday AS700 fee, that you'll probably need to be invited or have an introduction from a member to play; on weekends, membership or an invitation is required. Alternatives are **Föhrenwald,** an 18-hole par-72 course about 43 kilometers (27 miles) away, at Wiener Neustadt (tel. 02622/21900 or 02622/29171), or **Ebrichsdorf,** 27 kilometers (17 miles) south of Vienna, an 18-hole par-72 course (tel. 02254/3888), but these, too, are generally overbooked. Weekdays, of course, will be best for either course.

Health and Fitness Clubs   Try **Gym and Art** (in Kursalon, Johannesgasse 33, tel. 0222/714–7775), **Fitness Center Harris** (Niebelungengasse 7, tel. 0222/587–3710; and in the SAS Palais Hotel, tel. 0222/51517–1944), or **Zimmermann Fitness** (Linke Bahngasse 9, tel. 0222/753212; Kaiserstr. 43, tel. 0222/526–2000; and Kreuzgasse 18, tel. 0222/434625, women only).

Hiking   The city has eight *Stadt-Wander-Wege,* marked routes whose starting points are reachable from a streetcar stop. Get route maps and information at the information office in City Hall (Friedrich Schmidt-Platz, tel. 0222/4000–2938). You can easily strike out on your own, city map in hand, taking a route

through the vineyards up and around Kahlenberg/Leopolds-
berg, starting either from the end station of the No. 38 streetcar (Grinzing) or from the Kahlenberg stop of the No. 38A bus
and heading back down to Nussdorf (streetcar D). Another possibility is to wander the Lainzer Tiergarten, an enormous nature preserve within the city, with deer, wild boar, and other
fauna; reach it via the No. 60 streetcar from Kennedybrücke/
Hietzing on the U4 subway, then the No. 60B bus.

Ice Skating The **Wiener Eislaufverein** (Lothringer Str. 22, behind the InterContinental Hotel, tel. 0222/713–6353) has outdoor skating
with skate rentals, October through March. Weekends are
crowded. For indoor skating, check the **Wiener Stadthalle**
(Vogelweidplatz 14, U6 to Urban Loritz-Platz, tel. 0222/981-
000).

Jogging Jogging paths run alongside the Danube Canal, and runners
also frequent the Stadtpark and the tree-lined route along the
Ring, particularly the Parkring stretch. Farther afield, in the
Second District, the Prater Hauptallee, from Praterstern to
the Lusthaus, is a favorite.

Riding Splendid bridle paths crisscross the Prater park. To hire a
mount, contact the **Reitclub Donauhof** (Hafenzufahrtstr. 63,
tel. 0222/218–3646 or 0222/218–9716).

Skiing Nearby slopes such as **Hohe Wand** (take No. 49B bus from the
Hütteldorf stop of the U4 subway), west of the city in the 14th
District, offer limited skiing, with a ski lift and man-made snow
when the heavens refuse, but serious Viennese skiers (that in-
cludes nearly everybody) will take a train or bus out to nearby
Niederösterreich (Lower Austria), with the area around the
Semmering (about an hour from the city) one of the favorite lo-
cations for a quick outing.

Swimming Vienna has at least one pool for each of its 23 districts; most are
indoor pools, but some locations have an outdoor pool as well.
For a less formal environment, head for the swimming areas of
the **Alte Donau** or the **Donauinsel**. The pools and the Alte
Donau (paid admission) will be filled on hot summer weekends,
so the Donauinsel can be a surer bet. Some beach areas are
shallow and suitable for children, but the Donauinsel has no
lifeguards, though there are rescue stations for emergencies.
Changing areas are few, lockers nonexistent, so don't take valuables. And don't be tempted to jump into the Danube Canal;
the water is definitely not for swimming, nor is the Danube itself, because of heavy undertows and a powerful current.

The city has information on all places to swim; contact City Hall
(Rathaus, Friedrich Schmidt-Platz, tel. 0222/40005). Ask for
directions on reaching the following:

Donauinsel Nord. A huge recreation area with a children's section and nude bathing.

Donauinsel Süd. Good swimming and boating and a nude bathing area. Harder to get to and less crowded than other areas,
and food facilities are limited.

Gänsehäufel. A bathing island in the Alte Donau (tel. 0222/
235392), with lockers, changing rooms, children's wading
pools, topless and nude areas, and restaurants; likely to be full
by 11 AM or earlier.

Krapfenwaldbad. An outdoor pool tucked among the trees on the edge of the Vienna Woods (tel. 0222/321501). Full of Vienna's beautiful people and singles. Get there early on sunny Sundays or you won't get in.

Stadionbad. A huge sports complex, popular with the younger crowd; go early. There is no direct transportation; take the No. 80B bus from Stadionbrücke in the Third District to the Hauptallee stop, or, for the fun of it, ride the miniature railway (*Liliputbahn*) from behind the Ferris wheel in the Prater amusement park to the Stadion station and walk the rest of the way (Prater, Marathonweg, tel. 0222/262102).

Tennis Though Vienna has plenty of courts, they'll be booked solid. Try anyway; your hotel may have good connections. **Sportservice Wien-Sport** (Bacherplatz 14, tel. 0222/543131) operates a central court-booking service (100 courts in summer, three halls in winter), and **Vereinigte Tennisanlagen** (Prater Hauptallee, tel. 0222/218–1811) has courts in other locations as well. Or you can try **Tennisplätze Arsenal** (57 sand courts; Arsenalstr. 1, by the Südbahnhof, tel. 0222/782132; Faradaygasse 4, tel. 0222/787265; Gudrunstr. 31, tel. 0222/621521), **Tennisplätze Stadionbad** (Prater Hauptallee, tel. 0222/248261), or **Wiener Eislaufverein** (Lothringer Str. 22, behind the Inter-Continental Hotel, tel. 0222/713–6353).

Spectator Sports

Football (Soccer) Matches are played mainly in the **Vienna Stadium** in the Prater (Meiereistr., tel. 0222/218–0854) and the **West Stadium** (Keisslergasse 6, tel. 0222/945519). Indoor soccer takes place in the **Stadthalle** (Vogelweidplatz 14, tel. 0222/98100). Tickets can usually be bought at the gate, but the better seats are available through ticket agencies. At the **Vienna Ticket Service** (Postfach 160, A-1060, tel. 0222/587–9843, fax 0222/587–9844), tickets must be ordered a month in advance. Otherwise try **American Express** (Kärntner Str. 21–23, tel. 0222/515–400, fax 0222/515–4070), **Cosmos** (Kärntner Ring 15, A-1010, tel. 0222/51533, fax 0222/513–4147), **Kartenbüro Flamm** (Kärntner Ring 3, A-1010, tel. 0222/512–4225, fax 0222/513–9962), or **Österreichische Verkehrsbüro** (Friedrichstr. 7, tel. 0222/588–000, fax 0222/587–7142).

Horse Racing The race track (both flat and sulky racing) is in the Prater (Trabbrennplatz, tel. 0222/218–9535), and the season runs April–November. The highlight is the Derby, which takes place the third Sunday in June.

Tennis Professional matches are played in the Prater or in the Stadthalle (*see* Football, *above*). Ticket agencies will have details.

Dining

In recent years Vienna, once a culinary backwater, has produced a new generation of chefs willing to slaughter sacred cows and create a New Vienna Cuisine. The movement is well past the "less is more" stage that nouvelle cuisine traditionally demands (and to which most Viennese vociferously objected), relying now on lighter versions of the old standbys and clever combinations of such traditional ingredients as liver pâtés and sour cream.

In a first-class restaurant you will pay as much as in most other Western European capitals. But you can still find good food at refreshingly low prices in the simpler restaurants, particularly at neighborhood *Gasthäuser* in the suburbs. If you eat your main meal at noon (as the Viennese do), you can take advantage of the luncheon specials.

Many restaurants are closed one or two days a week (often Saturday and Sunday), and most serve meals only 11:30–2:30 and 6–10. An increasing number now serve after-theater dinners, but reserve in advance. *Wien wie es isst* (in German; from almost any bookstore) gives up-to-date information on the restaurant, café, and bar scene.

Vienna's restaurant fare ranges from Arabic to Yugoslav, but assuming you've come for what makes Vienna unique, our listings focus not on the exotic but on places where you'll meet the Viennese and experience Vienna. Highly recommended restaurants are indicated by a star ★ .

Category	Cost*
Very Expensive	over AS500
Expensive	AS300–AS500
Moderate	AS150–AS300
Inexpensive	under AS150

per person, excluding drinks but including service (usually 10%) and sales tax (10%)

Very Expensive

★ **Korso.** For some, Vienna's top restaurant, in the Bristol Hotel; you're surrounded with subdued dark-paneled and gold elegance; tables are set with fine linen, glassware, and silver. The food matches the setting; chef Reinhard Gerer is one of Austria's great creative cooks. Try such specialties as scallops in white tomato butter or *Rehnüsschen*, tiny venison fillets. Ask sommelier Christian Zach to recommend an appropriate wine. *Mahlerstr. 2, tel. 0222/515–16–546, fax 0222/515–16–550. Reservations required. Jacket and tie required. AE, DC, MC, V. Closed Sat. lunch, Aug.*
Palais Schwarzenberg. This restaurant, in a former private palace, has one of the most impressive settings in Vienna, but be sure to book a table on the glassed-in terrace; you'll be surrounded inside by greenery, with a view out over the formal gardens. The food is a notch or two below Korso's (above), but still extremely good. The service may lag if the restaurant is full, so be prepared to relax and enjoy the setting. You can't go wrong with the fillet of beef in red wine sauce or the delicate pike. The wine list is excellent but the prices exaggerated; the house wines are a fully acceptable substitute. *Schwarzenbergplatz 9, tel. 0222/784515, fax 0222/784714. Reservations required. Jacket and tie required. AE, MC, V.*
★ **Steirer Eck.** Critics are in agreement that this is Austria's top restaurant. You dine handsomely in classical elegance, among businesspeople at noon, amid politicians and personalities at night. Tables are set with flower arrangements and elegant crystal, with a flair that matches the food. Chef Helmut

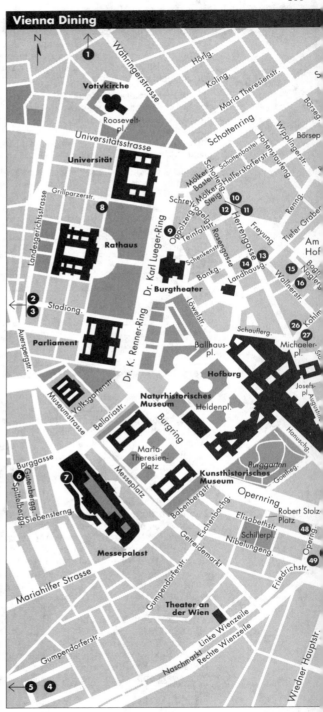

Vienna Dining

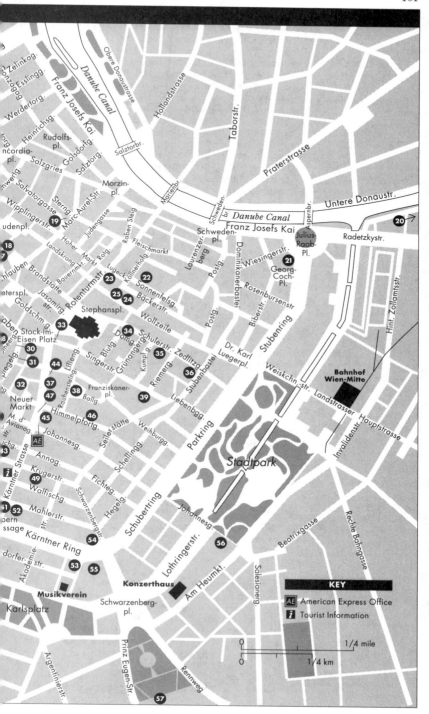

Obere Donaustrasse

Danube Canal

Franz Josefs Kai

Zelinkog.
Esslingg.
Werdertorg.
Heinrichsg.
Rudolfs-
pl.
ncordia-
pl.
Salzgries
Goldorg.
Salztorg.
Salvatorgasse
Sterng.
Morzin-
pl.
Wipplingerstr.
Marc-Aurel-Str.
Judengasse
udenpl.
19
18
7
Hoher Markt
Rotg.
Landskrong.
Raben Steig
Fleischmarkt
Lugeck
Köllnerhofg.
hlauben
Brandstätte
Bauernmkt.
Sonnenfelsg.
22
Rotenturmstr.
23
25
24
Bäckerstr.
eterspl.
Jasomirg.
str.
Goldschm.g.
Stephanspl.
Wollzeile
33

Hollandstrasse

Taborstr.

Praterstrasse

Salztorbr.

Marienbr.

Untere Donaustr.

Danube Canal
Franz Josefs Kai
Radetzkystr.
20

Schweden-
pl.
Julius-
Raab-
Pl.
Schwedenbr.
aspernbr.

Schwedenbr.
Laurenzerberg
Postg.
Wiesingerstr.
21
Georg-
Coch-
Pl.
Dominikanerbastei
Rosenbursenstr
Biberstr.

34
Schulerstr.
Zedlitzg.
Dr. Karl
Luegerpl.
35
36
Stubenbastei
Stubenring

Stock-im-
Eisen Platz
30
31
44
Lilieng.
Domg.
Blutg.
Singerstr.
Grünangerg.
Kumpfg.
Riemerg.
Liebenbgg.
Weiskchn.str. Landstrasser Hauptstrasse

8
piegelg.
32
37
38
47
Rauhensteing.
Franziskaner-
pl.
39
Ballg.
Neuer
Markt
M. d.
Avianog.
str.
45
Himmelpfortg.
46
Johannesg.
Annag.
Krugerstr.
Walfischg.
Schwarzenbergstr.
Seilerstätte
Weihburgg.
Schellingg.
Fichteg.
Hegelg.
Parkring
Johannesg.
Stadtpark
**Bahnhof
Wien-Mitte**
Hint. Zollamtsstr.
Invalidenstr.
Beatrixgasse
Rechte Bahngasse

Kärntner Strasse
3
i
1
52
bern
ssage
Mahlerstr.
str.
Kärntner Ring
54
56
Lothringerstr.
Am Heumkt.
Salesianerg.
dorfer-
str.
Akademie-
str.
53
55
Musikverein
Schwarzenberg-
pl.
Konzerthaus
Karlsplatz

Argentinierstr.
Prinz Eugen-Str.
Rennweg
57

KEY
AE American Express Office
i Tourist Information

0 _____ 1/4 mile
0 _____ 1/4 km

Österreicher is a genius at combining ideas and tastes; artichoke with lobster is a successful example, rack of wild boar with tiny sausages another, but creations are constantly changing. The house wine list is overwhelming; you can ask sommelier Adolf Schmid for advice with the assurance that it will be good. *Rasumofskygasse 2, tel. 0222/713–3168, fax 0222/ 713–5168. Reservations required. Jacket and tie required. AE, V. Closed weekends.*

★ **Vier Jahreszeiten.** The InterContinental's restaurant is an excellent if conservative choice for both the ample noontime buffet and evening dining. The atmosphere is elegant without being overdone. Service, too, is attentive but discreet, the wine list impressive but not overwhelming. The delicate roast lamb is consistently delicious; so is the fillet of beef with raw mushrooms. For dessert, ask for a *Mohr im Hemd,* literally, a moor in a shirt, a chocolate sponge-cake confection with chocolate sauce and whipped cream. *Johannesgasse 28, tel. 0222/ 71122–143, fax 0222/713–4489. Reservations advised. Jacket and tie required. AE, DC, MC, V.*

Zu den Drei Husaren. The Three Hussars has rejoined the ranks of Vienna's gourmet temples; the house remains embalmed in its draped red velvet and gold. If you don't mind the heavy hand (which occasionally carries over to the food and service), you may enjoy this touch of "old" Vienna, evening piano music included. Evenings are enjoyed by celebrities, lunchtime is for business, and both are for tourists. Beware the enticing but unpriced hors d'oeuvre trolley; a single dip here can double your bill. The Husaren does best with standards: *Leberknödelsuppe* (liver-dumpling soup), Wiener schnitzel, roast beef, and the like. *Weihburggasse 4, tel. 0222/512–1092, fax 0222/512–1092–18. Reservations advised at lunch, required in the evening. Jacket and tie required. AE, DC, MC, V. Closed mid-July–mid-Aug.*

Expensive

Hedrich. This tiny, unassuming restaurant offers astonishingly fine food. Richard Hedrich, the owner and chef, decided to go into business for himself and cook to his and his guests' pleasure. The daily noontime special is a bargain for its quality. Or try the lobster risotto or sole with scampi. *Stubenring 2, tel. 0222/512–9588. Reservations essential for lunch, useful for dinner. Jacket and tie advised. No credit cards. Closed Fri., weekends, Aug.*

★ **Imperial Café.** In the Imperial Hotel, the café is much more than just a (very good) meeting spot for coffee or *Torte;* both lunch and after-concert supper are popular and reasonably priced. The rooms are understated by local standards; crystal and velvet are evident but not overdone. The city's politicians, attorneys, and business types gather here for solid Viennese fare, selecting either from the choice daily specialties, which generally include a superb cream soup, or relying on such standards as Leberknödelsuppe and *Tafelspitz,* Viennese boiled beef. In summer, the terrace outside is enticing but noisy. The wine list includes French and German selections, but many prefer an open wine by the glass. *Kärntner Ring 16, tel. 0222/ 501–10389, fax 0222/501–10–410. Reservations recommended. Jacket and tie advised. AE, DC, MC, V.*

Kaiserwalzer. The "old Vienna" atmosphere is a bit heavy, but puts the menu—focusing on Austrian and Hungarian specialties—in just the right setting. Come for red beet soup, Wiener schnitzel or *Fogosch*, the tasty Danube fish. Service is attentive and open wines are fine. *Esterházygasse 9, tel. 0222/587–0494, fax 0222/587–0494. Reservations useful. Jacket and tie recommended. AE, DC, MC, V. Closed lunch and Sun.*

König von Ungarn. In the hotel of the same name, the wood-paneled restaurant, with its comfortable atmosphere, is jammed at noon with businesspeople who come to deal and to sample the roast meats from the carvery trolley. When the relatively small space is packed, service can get lax. *Schulerstr. 10, tel. 0222/512–5319, fax 0222/512–4593. Reservations required at lunch, advised in the evening. Jacket and tie advised. MC. Closed Sat.*

★ **Sirk.** This comfortable restaurant in traditional style is ideal for a light lunch or an evening snack. The sidewalk terrace is perfect for afternoon coffee and dessert, but for more privacy, take a table upstairs; those overlooking the Opera are best, but you'll have to fight Vienna's power brokers for one of them at noon. The daily menu is excellent value, or you might choose the rare roast beef with black-mushroom sauce. The post-opera menu is consistently good. *Kärntner Str. 53, tel. 0222/51516–552, fax 0222/51516–550. Reservations required at lunch, recommended at dinner. Jacket and tie advised. AE, DC, MC, V.*

Zum Kuckuck. This intimate, wood-paneled restaurant, in a building many hundreds of years old, draws its clientele from the ministries in the neighborhood at noon. The kitchen does such variations on regional themes as fillet of pork Hungarian style (with a cabbage-tomato sauce) and fillet of venison in puff pastry. Try the warm fig cake with rum sauce for dessert. *Himmelpfortgasse 15, tel. 0222/512–8470, fax 0222/523–3818. Reservations required. Jacket and tie advised. AE, MC. Closed weekends.*

Moderate

Am Lugeck. At lunchtime you'll mingle with lawyers and businesspeople who appreciate the central location and the choice of Viennese food in an architecturally mixed but pleasant atmosphere. The modern grill-bar with a spiral stair is good for a quick snack; the great arched *Keller* rooms downstairs are more suited to a relaxed lunch or dinner. At the outdoor tables the generally good service tends to suffer. If you have the chance, choose any of the game dishes; the *Rehragout* (venison stew) is outstanding. The spareribs are more than ample. *Lugeck 7, tel. 0222/512–7979. Reservations advised. Jacket and tie advised indoors; outdoor dress, casual but neat. AE, DC, MC, V.*

Bastei Beisl. You'll find good basic Viennese cuisine in this unpretentious, friendly, pine-paneled restaurant. Try the *Zwiebelrostbraten*, a rump steak smothered in fried onions. The tables outside in summer add to the pleasure at noon or in the evening. *Stubenbastei 10, tel. 0222/512–4319. Reservations advised. Dress: casual but neat. AE, DC, MC. Closed Sun. and holidays; also Sat. during July and Aug.*

Bei Max. The decor is somewhat bland, but the tasty Carinthian specialties—the cheese-and-meat-filled ravioli known as *Kasnudeln* and *Fleischnudeln* in particular—pack this friendly restaurant. You'll also find such classic standards as *Tafelspitz* (boiled beef), as well as outstanding desserts.

Landhausgasse 2/Herrengasse, tel. 0222/533–7359. Reservations advised. No credit cards. Closed Sat., Sun., and Aug.

★ **Glacis-Beisl.** This restaurant, tucked beneath a section of the old city wall, is no longer the secret it once was, but the charm of the indoor rooms is still appealing, and its garden under grape arbors is unique. Alas, a proposed rebuilding of the Messepalast into a museum threatens the existence of this fascinating corner of Vienna. The menu is long; ask the waiter for help. You'll find most of the Viennese standards, but the place seems right for grilled chicken (*Brathendl*) and a mug of wine. *Messepalast (follow signs to the rear right corner), Messeplatz 1, tel. 0222/930–7374. Reservations required for the garden in summer. Dress: informal but neat. No credit cards. Closed Sat. lunch, Sun., and Jan.–Mar.*

Gösser Bierklinik. The rooms go on and on in this upstairs (more formal) and downstairs (preferred) complex that dates back four centuries. The fare is as solid as the house; the Wiener schnitzel here is first class. The salad bar is new. And there's a menu in English. The beer, of course, is Austrian, from the Gösser brewery in Styria. *Steindlgasse 4, tel. 0222/ 535–6897. Reservations advised, particularly at lunch. Jacket and tie advised upstairs; downstairs dress, casual but neat. AE, DC, MC, V. Closed Sun.*

★ **Gösser Brau.** This vast *Keller* with a (dummy) copper brewing vat is a noontime hangout of businesspeople who appreciate the good food and generally prompt service. Go for the game when it's available. *Rehrücken* (rack of venison) is a specialty. The appropriate accompaniment is Gösser beer, of course. *Elisabethstr. 3, tel. 0222/587–4750. Reservations suggested at noon. Jacket and tie advised. AE, DC, MC, V.*

Königsbacher bei der Oper. The small, paneled and arched rooms or the tables outside seem just right for Viennese standards such as schnitzel and boiled beef. The daily special—this might be ravioli or meat loaf—is an excellent value. Service is friendly, beer is German. *Walfischgasse 5, tel. 0222/513–1210. Reservations advised. Dress: casual but neat. No credit cards. Closed Sat. dinner, Sun.*

★ **Martinkovits.** If you have time, head out to this typical "old Vienna" wine restaurant in the shadow of the Sievering vineyards, for grilled chicken of a quality and flavor you'll not soon forget. And the wines are excellent. The rooms inside are pleasant, but the garden is sheer delight. *Bellevuestr. 4, No. 39A bus from U6/U4 Heiligenstadt, Windhabergasse stop, tel. 0222/321546. Reservations advised on weekends. Dress: casual but neat. No credit cards. Closed all day Mon. and Tues.– Thurs. lunch. Check for winter closing months.*

★ **Ofenloch.** Unique for its turn-of-the-century ambience, this restaurant features waitresses in costume and a menu in miniature newspaper form. The fare is based on original recipes. Garlic fans will find the *Vanillerostbraten*, a rump steak prepared not with vanilla but with garlic, delicious. The misleading name came about because in early days, no one would admit to ordering anything with garlic. *Kurrentgasse 8, tel. 0222/ 533–8844. Reservations required. Jacket and tie advised. AE, DC, MC, V.*

Stadtbeisl. The smallish dark-paneled rooms are packed at noon, as is the summer garden amid the ivy outside. Take the game in season; otherwise try one of the good Viennese standards. *Naglergasse 21, tel. 0222/533–3507. Reservations advised. Jacket advised inside, casual but neat outside. V.*

Zu den Drei Hacken. This is one of the last of the old *Gasthäuser* in the center of town; Schubert, among other luminaries of the past, is alleged to have dined here. You will find excellent Viennese fare, from schnitzel to Tafelspitz. The outdoor garden is attractive, but jammed in summer. *Singerstr. 28, tel. 0222/512–5895. Reservations advised. Dress: casual but neat. AE, DC, Closed Sat. evening, Sun.*

★ **Zu ebener Erde und im ersten Stock.** This gem of a historic house has an upstairs/downstairs combination: In the tiny room upstairs, done in old Vienna decor, the cuisine is adventurous, with such dishes as breast of duck with julienned zucchini and stuffed leg of hare, but you'll find old Viennese favorites as well. There's simpler (and cheaper) fare on the ground floor. *Burggasse 13, tel. 0222/936254. Reservations required. Jacket and tie required. AE. Closed Sat. noon, Sun. and Mon.*

Inexpensive

★ **Figlmüller.** If you'll accept the style of the house (you sit at a series of benches elbow-to-elbow with the other guests), this is *the* spot for Wiener schnitzel—one that overhangs the plate. (Waiters understand the doggie-bag principle.) Other choices are somewhat limited, and you'll have to take wine or mineral water with your meal because no beer or coffee is served. But Figlmüller is an experience you'll want to repeat. *Wollzeile 5, tel. 0222/512–6177. Reservations advised. Dress: casual but neat. No credit cards. Closed weekends.*

★ **Gigerl.** This charming and original wine restaurant offers a hot and cold buffet, specializing in vegetable and pasta dishes; try the macaroni salad or the *Schinkenfleckerl*, a baked noodle and ham dish. They go remarkably well with the light wines that the costumed waitresses keep pouring into your glass. In winter the rooms can get smoky and stuffy; in summer, the outside tables are delightful. *Rauhensteingasse 3/Blumenstockgasse 2, tel. 0222/513–4431. Reservations advised. Dress: casual but neat. AE, DC, MC, V.*

Göttweiger Stiftskeller. In this traditional, basic restaurant, look for grilled and fried chicken, schnitzel variants, tasty liver dishes such as Leberknödelsuppe, plus occasional surprises like oxtail soup. The food helps compensate for the rather unexciting rooms. The wines, on the other hand, are outstanding. *Spiegelgasse 9, tel. 0222/512–7817. Reservations not required. Dress: casual but neat. No credit cards. Closed weekends.*

★ **Gulaschmuseum.** The original idea behind this modern restaurant is literally dozens of tasty variants on the theme of goulash. They're just right for a between-meal snack, although most of the goulashes served are filling enough for a complete meal. *Schulerstr. 20, tel. 0222/512–1017. Reservations not required. Dress: casual but neat. No credit cards.*

Lustig Essen. The name means "amusing dining." The concept in these modern rooms involves smaller portions (although generous enough for most) at remarkably reasonable prices, so that you can sample more of the outstanding dishes on the menu. Try the cream of garlic soup, the lamb ragout or grilled shrimp. *Salvatorgasse 6, tel. 0222/533–3037. Reservations useful. Dress: casual but neat. No credit cards.*

Naschmarkt. In this attractive cafeteria the food is good, of excellent value, and of far more variety than at the next-door McDonald's. Look for the daily specials on the blackboard. You'll also find good soups (chilled gazpacho on hot summer days), sandwiches, a salad bar, and a nonsmoking area. *Schwarzenbergplatz 16, tel. 0222/505–3115. Reservations not required. Dress: casual. No credit cards. Also at Schottengasse 1, tel. 0222/533–5186. Schottengasse is closed Sun. evening.*

Reinthaler. The atmosphere is thick enough to cut in this convenient neighborhood establishment, full of regulars. The fare is genuine Viennese: schnitzel, chicken, roast pork with *Knödel* (bread dumpling), and such. The ivy-fenced tables outside in summer are particularly popular. *Glückgasse 5, tel. 0222/512–3366. Reservations not required. Dress: casual. No credit cards. Closed Fri. evening and weekends.*

Rosenberger Marktrestaurant. Downstairs under a huge (artificial) tree you'll find a cluster of cafeteria islands offering soups, excellent grilled specialties, vegetables, pastas, salads, desserts, and fresh juices and other beverages, all prepared to order and attractively (if somewhat confusingly) presented. You can leave your valuables in one of the free lockers while you make and enjoy your selection. Look for seasonal specialties such as asparagus and fresh chilled melon. Take your choice to any of the side rooms, some decorated with musical instruments, some with antique kitchenware and dishes. *Maysedergasse 2/Fürichgasse 3, tel. 0222/512–3458. No reservations. No credit cards. Street floor Bistroette café open from 8 AM.*

Trzesniewski. "Unpronounceably good" is the (correct) motto of this tiny sandwich shop, a Viennese tradition for decades. If a quick snack will suffice, three or four of the open sandwiches and a *Pfiff* (⅛ liter) of beer, or a vodka, may be just the needed pickup. Share one of the few tables, or stand up at one of the counters. You'll be surprised at the elegance of many of the customers. *Dorotheergasse 1, tel. 0222/512–3291. Reservations not required. Dress: casual. No credit cards. Closed Sat. evening and Sun.*

Wine Taverns

In-town wine restaurants cannot properly be called *Heurige*, since they are not run by the vintner, so the term is "wine restaurant," or "cellar" (*Keller*). Many of them extend a number of levels underground, particularly in the older part of the city. Mainly open in the evening, they are intended primarily for drinking, though you can always get something to eat from a buffet, and increasingly, full dinners are available. Some of the better wine restaurants follow; no credit cards except where noted.

Piaristen Keller. The atmosphere, with live music, is sufficiently genuine that you can overlook the occasionally lax service. This is a dining Keller; the food is good and the house wines are excellent. *Piaristengasse 45, tel. 0222/429152, fax 0222/434173. Reservations advised. Jacket and tie suggested. AE, DC, MC, V. Evenings only. Expensive.*

Antiquitäten-Keller. The fare is authentic Viennese cuisine, served among authentic antiques to the strains of classical music. *Magdalenenstr. 32, tel. 0222/566–9533. Reservations advised. Jacket and tie required. AE, DC, MC, V. Closed Sun. Moderate.*

★ **Esterhazykeller.** This maze of rooms offers some of the best Keller wines in town plus a hot-and-cold buffet. *Haarhof 1, tel. 0222/533–3482. Reservations advised on weekends. Jacket rec-*

ommended. Stüberl closed Sat., Sun. lunch; Keller closed weekends. Moderate.

★ **Melker Stiftskeller.** Down and down you go, into one of the friendliest Kellers in town, where *Stelze* (roast knuckle of pork) is a popular feature, along with outstanding wines by the glass. *Schottengasse 3, tel. 0222/533–5530. Reservations advised. Jacket recommended. Evenings only, closed Sun. Moderate.*

Augustinerkeller. This upstairs Keller is open at noontime as well. The grilled chicken is excellent. *Augustinerstr. 1/ Albertinerplatz, tel. 0222/533–1026. Reservations not required. Dress: casual but neat. Inexpensive.*

Zwölf Apostel-Keller. You pass a huge wood statue of St. Peter on the way down to the two underground floors in this cellar in the oldest part of Vienna. The young crowd comes for the good wines and the atmosphere, and there's buffet food as well. *Sonnenfelsgasse 3, tel. 512–6777. Reservations advised on weekends. Dress: casual but neat. Inexpensive.*

Heurige

These taverns in the wine-growing districts on the outskirts of the city vary from the simple front room of a vintner's house to ornate establishments. (The name means "new wine," and that's what is chiefly served.) The true Heuriger is open for only a few weeks a year to allow the vintner to sell a certain quantity of his production tax-free for consumption on his own premises. The commercial establishments keep to a somewhat more regular season, but still sell only wine from their own vines.

The choice is usually between a "new" and an "old" white wine and a red, but you can also ask for a milder or sharper wine according to your taste. Most Heurige are happy to let you sample the wines before ordering. You can also order a *Gespritzter*, half wine and half soda water. The waitress will bring you the wine, usually in quarter-liter mugs, but you get your own food from the buffet. The wine tastes as mild as lemonade, but it packs a punch. If it isn't of good quality, you will know by a raging headache the next day.

Summer and fall are the seasons for visiting the Heurige, though often the more elegant and expensive establishments, called *Noble-Heuriger*, stay open year-round. No credit cards except where noted.

Heurige are concentrated in several outskirts of Vienna: Stammersdorf, Grinzing, Sievering, Nussdorf, Neustift, and a corner of Ottakring. Perchtoldsdorf, just outside Vienna, is also well known for its wine taverns.

Our favorite district is Stammersdorf, across the Danube. Try **Robert Helm.** *Stammersdorfer Str. 121, tel. 0222/391244. Reservations advised on weekends and in winter. Dress: casual but neat.* Wine and food are both excellent at **Wieninger,** with its spacious garden and series of typical vintner's rooms. *Stammersdorfer Str. 78, tel. 0222/394106. Reservations advised in winter. Dress: casual but neat. Closed Mon. and mid-Dec.–Jan. 2.*

The Grinzing district today suffers from mass tourism, with very few exceptions; one is **Zum Martin Sepp,** where the wine, food, service, and ambience are excellent. *Cobenzlgasse 32, tel.*

0222/324–4875. Reservations suggested on weekends. Jacket advised. DC, V. East of the village center, **Zimmermann** has good wines and buffet foods, a charming tree-shaded garden, and an endless collection of paneled rooms and vaulted cellars. *Armbrustergasse 5/Grinzinger Str., tel. 0222/372211 or 0222/371–7074. Reservations advised. Jacket and tie advised. AE, DC, MC, V. Closed Sun.*

In Sievering try **Haslinger.** *Agnesgasse 3, tel. 0222/441347. Reservations useful on weekends. Dress: casual but neat.*

In Neustift, **Wolff** has a gorgeous garden and outstanding food, as well as good wine. *Rathstr. 46, tel. 0222/442335. Reservations advised. Jacket suggested.*

In Nussdorf seek out **Schübl-Auer.** *Kahlenberger Str. 22, tel. 0222/372222. Reservations not required. Dress: casual but neat. Closed Sun., Jan., July.*

Cafés

The typical Viennese café, with polished brass or marble-topped tables, bentwood chairs, supplies of newspapers, and tables outside in good weather, is a fixed institution of which there are literally hundreds. All cafés serve pastries and light snacks in addition to beverages. Many offer a menu or fixed lunch at noon, but be aware that some can get rather expensive. No credit cards except where noted.

When you want a quick (but excellent) coffee and dessert, look for an **Aida** café; they are scattered throughout the city. Here's a sampling of the best of the traditional cafés: **Alte Backstübe** (Lange Gasse 34, tel. 0222/431101; AE, MC, V; closed Mon. and Aug.), in a gorgeous Baroque house, was once a bakery and is now a museum with a café in back; **Bräunerhof** (Stallburggasse 2, tel. 0222/512–3893) has music on some afternoons; **Café Central** (Herrengasse 14, tel. 0222/535–4176; AE, DC, MC, V; closed Sun.) is where Stalin and Trotsky played chess; **Frauenhuber** (Himmelpfortgasse 6, tel. 0222/512–4323; closed Sat. evening and Sun.) has its original turn-of-the-century interior and a good choice of desserts; **Haag** (Schottengasse 2, tel. 0222/533–1810; closed Sun., June–Aug.), with crystal chandeliers and a shaded courtyard garden in summer, serves snacks and desserts; **Landtmann** (Dr. Karl Lueger-Ring 4, tel. 0222/532–0621; AE, DC, MC, V) is where government officials gather; **Museum** (Friedrichstr. 6, tel. 0222/565202), original interior by the architect Adolf Loos, draws a mixed crowd and has lots of newspapers; **Schwarzenberg** (Kärntner Ring 17, tel. 0222/512–7393; AE, DC, MC, V), with piano music in late afternoons, is highly popular, particularly its sidewalk tables in summer; **Tirolerhof** (Tegetthofstr. 8/Albertinaplatz, tel. 0222/512–7833), with its excellent desserts, is popular with students.

Café Hawelka (Dorotheergasse 12, tel. 0222/512–8230; closed Tues., Sun. noon) deserves special mention; whole books have been written at and about this gathering place. Its international clientele ranges from artists to politicians; Hawelka is jammed any time of day, so you share a table (and the smoky atmosphere). In a city noted for fine coffee, Hawelka's is superb, even more so when accompanied by a freshly baked *Buchterln* (sweet roll, evenings only).

So, you're getting away from it all.

Just make sure you can get back.

AT&T Access Numbers
Dial the number of the country you're in to reach AT&T.

*ANDORRA	19◇-0011	GERMANY**	0130-0010	*NETHERLANDS	06◇-022-9111
*AUSTRIA	022-903-011	*GREECE	00-800-1311	*NORWAY	050-12011
*BELGIUM	078-11-0010	*HUNGARY	00◇-800-01111	POLAND¹◆²	0◇010-480-0111
BULGARIA	00-1800-0010	*ICELAND	999-001	PORTUGAL¹	05017-1-288
CROATIA¹◆	99-38-0011	IRELAND	1-800-550-000	ROMANIA	01-800-4288
*CYPRUS	080-90010	ISRAEL	177-100-2727	*RUSSIA¹ (MOSCOW)	155-5042
CZECH REPUBLIC	00-420-00101	*ITALY	172-1011	SLOVAKIA	00-420-00101
*DENMARK	8001-0010	KENYA¹	0800-10	SPAIN	900-99-00-11
*EGYPT¹ (CAIRO)	510-0200	*LIECHTENSTEIN	155-00-11	*SWEDEN	020-795-611
*FINLAND	9800-100-10	LITHUANIA◆	8◇196	*SWITZERLAND	155-00-11
FRANCE	19◇-0011	LUXEMBOURG	0-800-0111	*TURKEY	9◇9-8001-2277
*GAMBIA	00111	*MALTA	0800-890-110	UK	0800-89-0011

Countries in bold face permit country-to-country calling in addition to calls to the U.S. *Public phones require deposit of coin or phone card. **Western portion. Includes Berlin and Leipzig. ◇Await second dial tone. ¹May not be available from every phone. ◆ Not available from public phones. ¹Dial "02" first, outside Cairo. ²Dial 010-480-0111 from major Warsaw hotels. ©1993 AT&T.

Here's a travel tip that will make it easy to call back to the States. Dial the access number for the country you're visiting and connect right to AT&T **USADirect®** Service. It's the quick way to get English-speaking operators and can minimize hotel surcharges.

If all the countries you're visiting aren't listed above, call **1 800 241-5555** before you leave for a free wallet card with all AT&T access numbers. International calling made easy—it's all part of **The i Plan.**℠

THE *i* PLAN℠

AT&T

All The Best Trips Start with Fodor

Fodor's Affordables

Titles in the series: Caribbean, Europe, Florida, France, Germany, Great Britain, Italy, London, Paris.

"Travelers with champagne tastes and beer budgets will welcome this series from Fodor's." — *Hartford Courant*

"These books succeed admirably; easy to follow and use, full of cost-related information, practical advice, and recommendations...maps are clear and easy to use." — *Travel Books Worldwide*

The Berkeley Guides

Titles in the series: California, Central America, Eastern Europe, France, Germany, Great Britain & Ireland, Mexico, The Pacific Northwest, San Francisco.

The best choice for budget travelers, from the Associated Students at the University of California at Berkeley.

"Berkeley's scribes put the funk back in travel." — *Time*

"Hip, blunt and lively."
— *Atlanta Journal Constitution*

"Fresh, funny and funky as well as useful." — *The Boston Globe*

Fodor's Bed & Breakfast and Country Inn Guides

Titles in the series: California, Canada, England & Wales, Mid-Atlantic, New Englan, The Pacific Northwest, The South, The Upper Great Lakes Region, The West Coast.

"In addition to information on each establishment, the books add notes on things to see and do in the vicinity. Tha alone propels these books to the top of the heap."— *San Diego Union-Tribune*

Exploring Guides

Titles in the series: Australia, California, Caribbean, Florida, France, Germany, Great Britain, Ireland, Italy, London, New York City, Paris, Rome, Singapore & Malaysia, Spain, Thailand.

"Authoritatively written and superbly presented, and makes worthy reading before, during or after a trip. "
— *The Philadelphia Inquirer*

"A handsome new series of guides, complete with lots of color photos, geared to the independent traveler."
— *The Boston Globe*

Visit your local bookstore
or call 1-800-533-6478 24 hours a day.

Fodor's The name that means smart travel

Pastry Shops

Viennese pastries are said to be the best in the world. In all shops you can buy them to eat on the premises as well as to take out. **Kurkonditorei Oberlaa** (Neuer Markt 16, tel. 0222/513–2936) has irresistible confections, cakes, and bonbons, as well as light lunches and salad plates, served outdoors in summer. Traditionalists and tourists with fat pocketbooks still go to **Demel** (Kohlmarkt 14, tel. 0222/533–5516), where the value is arguable but turn-of-the-century atmosphere prevails among velvet and polished brass. The newer **Demel Vis-à-vis** opposite (Kohlmarkt 11, tel. 0222/533–6020) has an elegant buffet and stand-up tables, plus a mail-order service for Demel specialties. **Gerstner** (Kärntner Str. 15, tel. 0222/512–4963) is also recommended, and **Heiner** (Kärntner Str. 21–23, tel. 0222/512–6863, and Wollzeile 9, tel. 0222/512–4838) is dazzling for its crystal chandeliers as well as for its pastries. **Sluka** (Rathausplatz 8, tel. 0222/427172) has special dietetic desserts, snacks, and an appetizer buffet and serves outdoors in summer.

Lodging

In Vienna's best hotels the staff seems to anticipate your wishes almost before you have expressed them. Such service of course has its price, and if you wish, you can stay in Vienna in profound luxury. For those with more modest requirements, ample rooms are available in less expensive but entirely adequate hotels. Pensions, mainly bed-and-breakfast establishments often managed by the owner, generally represent good value. A number of student hostels are run as hotels in summer, offering about the most reasonable quarters of all. And several apartment hotels accommodate those who want to stay longer.

When you have only a short time to spend in Vienna, you will probably want to stay in the inner city (the First District, or 1010 postal code) or fairly close to it, within walking distance of the most important sights, restaurants, and shops. Although most of the hotels there are in the upper categories, excellent and reasonable accommodations can be found in the Eighth District, which borders the First and puts you close to the major museums. You'll also find a group of moderate and inexpensive hotels in the Mariahilfer Strasse–Westbahnhof area, within easy reach of the city center by streetcar.

For the high season, Easter through October, and around the Christmas–New Year holidays, make reservations a month or more in advance. Vienna is continually the site of some international convention or other, and the city fills up quickly.

Our hotel categories correspond more or less to the official Austrian rating system, with five stars the equivalent of our Very Expensive category. All rooms have bath or shower unless otherwise stated; color television is usual in the top two categories; breakfast is included with all *except* the highest category. Highly recommended lodgings are indicated by a star ★.

Category	Cost*
Very Expensive	over AS2,200
Expensive	AS1,200–AS2,200
Moderate	AS850–AS1,200
Inexpensive	under AS850

All prices are for a standard double room, including local taxes (usually 10%) and service (15%).

Very Expensive

Ambassador. This superbly located dowager (from 1866) wears well. An air of decadent elegance radiates from the red velvet and crystal chandeliers in the high-ceilinged guest rooms. The trade-off is room air conditioners and rather stuffy period furniture. But what was once good enough for Mark Twain—yes, he stayed here, but long before the renovations of 1990–91—is still very good, and you will know instantly that you are in Vienna. Unless you want the excitement of a direct view into the lively pedestrian Kärntner Strasse, ask for one of the quieter rooms on the Neuer Markt side. *Neuer Markt 5/Kärntner Str. 22, A–1010, tel. 0222/514660, fax 0222/513–2999. 107 rooms. Facilities: restaurant, bar. AE, DC, MC, V.*

★ **Bristol.** This hotel has one of the finest locations in Europe, on the Ring next to the opera house. The accent here is on tradition, from the brocaded walls to the Biedermeier period furnishings in the public rooms and many of the bedrooms. The house dates to 1896; renovations have left no trace of the fact that the Bristol was the U.S. military headquarters during the 1945–55 occupation. Like an old shoe, the hotel is seductively comfortable from the moment you arrive. The rooms on the Mahlerstrasse (back) side of the house are quieter, but the view isn't as spectacular as from rooms on the Kärntner Strasse. *Kärntner Ring 1, A–1010, tel. 0222/515160, fax 0222/515–16–550. 152 rooms. Facilities: Korso, one of the 2 restaurants, is rated among Vienna's best; American bar, sauna, exercise room. AE, DC, MC, V.*

Hilton. The public areas have been restyled for a more contemporary look and the bedrooms are a cut above the usual Hilton standard in size and individuality of decor. The suites are particularly spacious; who could resist breakfast on a suite balcony with a 180-degree view of the city? The upper rooms are quietest; the no-smoking floor is so popular that you need to book at least a week in advance. The airport bus terminal is next door to the Hilton; the U3 and U4 subway lines, trains, and buses stop at the terminal across the street; yet you're within an easy walk of the city center. *Am Stadtpark, A–1030, tel. 0222/717000, fax 0222/713–0691. 620 rooms. Facilities: 2 restaurants, café, Klimt lobby bar, sauna, fitness center. AE, DC, MC, V.*

Imperial. The hotel is as much a palace today as when it was completed in 1869. The emphasis is on old Vienna elegance and privacy; heads of state stay here when they're in town. Service is deferential; the rooms have high ceilings and are furnished in classic antiques and Oriental carpets. The bath areas, in contrast, are modern and inviting; many are as large as guest rooms in lesser hotels. The staff will adjust the hardness (or softness) of the beds to your specific wants. Don't overlook the

ornate reception rooms to the rear or the formal marble staircase to the right of the lobby. Rooms on the back overlooking
the Musikverein are the quietest. *Kärntner Ring 16, A–1010,
tel. 0222/501100, fax 0222/501–10–410. 158 rooms (nonsmoking rooms available). Facilities: 2 restaurants (the Café is excellent), piano bar. AE, DC, MC, V.*

InterContinental. This "first" among Vienna's modern hostel-
ries (1964) has taken on the Viennese patina, and its public
rooms, with glittering crystal and red carpets, suggest luxurious comfort. The guest rooms lean more toward the chain's
norm, adequate though unexciting, but you will get either a
view over the city park across the street (preferred) or over the
city itself. The higher you go, the more dramatic the perspec-
tive. *Johannesgasse 28, A–1030, tel. 0222/711220, fax 0222/
713–4489. 498 rooms (nonsmoking rooms available). Facilities: 2 restaurants (Vier Jahreszeiten is recommended), 2 bars,
sauna. AE, DC, MC, V.*

★ **Palais Schwarzenberg.** You will know from your first glimpse of
the elegant facade that this is no ordinary hotel. Set in a vast
formal park, the palace, built in the early 1700s, seems like a
country estate, and you can even jog in the formal garden. Your
room will be furnished in genuine (but surprisingly comfortable) antiques, with some of the Schwarzenberg family's art on
the walls. The baths are modern, although you might miss a
shower curtain. Each room is individual; duplex suites 24 and
25 have upstairs bedrooms and views over the park; Room 26
has exquisite furniture, gorgeous draperies, and a winding
stair leading up to the bedroom. If you have any reason to celebrate, do it here; this is the genuine old Vienna at its most elegant. *Schwarzenbergplatz 9, A–1030, tel. 0222/784515, fax
0222/784714. 38 rooms. Facilities: restaurant, bar. AE, DC,
MC, V.*

Sacher. Few hotels in the world have been featured so often in
films or in history; you'll sense the musty atmosphere of tradition when you arrive. This is the house where the legendary ci-
gar-smoking Frau Sacher reigned; Emperor Franz Josef was a
regular patron. The Sacher dates to 1876; the patina remains
(Room 329 exudes a sense of well-being) despite the elegant
new baths installed in 1990. The corridors are a veritable art
gallery, and the location directly behind the Opera House could
hardly be more central. The staff is particularly accommodating; it has long been an open secret that the concierge at the
Sacher can miraculously produce concert and opera tickets
when all other possibilities are exhausted. The restaurant isn't
quite up to the rest of the house. *Philharmonikerstr. 4, A–
1010, tel. 0222/514560, fax 0222/514–57–810. 125 rooms, 117
with bath (nonsmoking rooms available). Facilities: restaurant, café, 2 bars (the Blue is recommended). AE, DC, MC, V.*

Vienna Marriott. The metal-and-glass exterior gives the impression of a giant greenhouse, borne out by the inviting mini-
jungle of green trees and plants in the vast atrium lobby. Some
guests object to the perpetual waterfall in the bar/café area,
but for Vienna the effect is certainly original. Despite the size,
a friendly atmosphere pervades. For a hotel built in 1984, the
rooms and suites are unusually spacious and furnished with extra attention to detail; the corner suites (No. 24 on each floor)
give a superb view out over the city park opposite. The upper
rooms in back offer a panorama of the inner city; these and the
rooms on the inner court are the quietest. You're an easy stroll
from the city center. *Parkring 12A, A–1010, tel. 0222/51518,*

Altstadt, **7**
Ambassador, **20**
Austria, **16**
Biedermeier im
Sünnhof, **15**
Bristol, **23**
Europa, **19**
Fürstenhof, **5**
Hilton, **28**
Hotel-Pension
Zipser, **2**
Ibis Wien, **6**
Imperial, **29**
InterContinental, **30**
Kärntnerhof, **17**
König von Ungarn, **18**
Mailberger Hof, **26**
Opernring, **21**
Palais
Schwarzenberg, **31**
Pension Aclon, **10**
Pension Baroness, **1**
Pension Christina, **14**
Pension City, **12**
Pension Nossek, **8**
Pension Pertschy, **9**
Pension Suzanne, **24**
Pension Wild, **4**
Rathaus, **3**
Sacher, **22**
Schweizerhof, **13**
Vienna Marriott, **27**
Wandl, **11**
Zur Wiener
Staatsoper, **25**

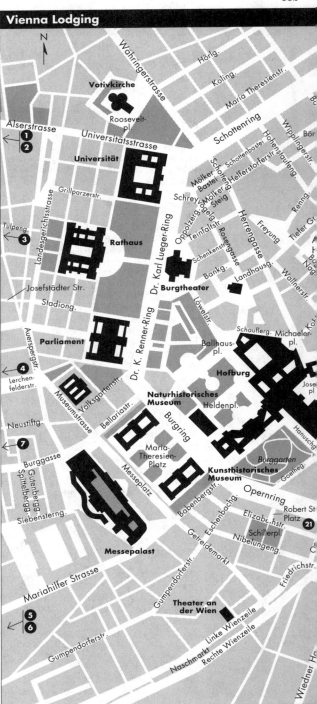

Vienna Lodging

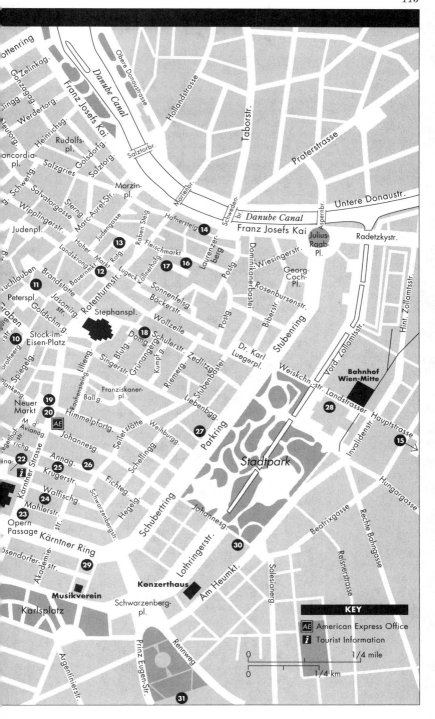

KEY

AE American Express Office

i Tourist Information

0   1/4 mile

0   1/4 km

fax 515–18–6722. 304 rooms (nonsmoking rooms available). Facilities: 2 restaurants, café, 2 bars, sauna, pool, fitness room. AE, DC, MC, V.

Expensive

Altstadt. You're one streetcar stop or a short walk from the main museums in this newly renovated, old-Vienna residential building. Each of the spacious rooms has individual decor focusing mainly on period furniture, with fine wood set against light and blue-gray walls. The upper rooms have views out over the city roofline. *Kirchengasse 41, tel. 0222/526–3399, fax 0222/ 523–4901. 25 rooms with bath or shower. Facilities: bar. AE, DC, MC, V.*

Biedermeier im Sünnhof. This jewel of a hotel is tucked into a renovated 1820s house that even with all modern facilities still conveys a feeling of old Vienna. The rooms are compact but efficient, the public areas tastefully done in the Biedermeier style, and the service is friendly. The courtyard passageway around which the hotel is built has attracted a number of interesting boutiques and handicrafts shops, but at times there is an excess of coming and going as tour groups are accommodated. It's about a 20-minute walk or a six-minute subway ride to the center of the city. *Landstrasser Hauptstr. 28, A–1030, tel. 0222/ 716–710, fax 0222/716–71–503. 204 rooms. Facilities: restaurant, bar. AE, DC, MC, V.*

Europa. The Europa had a face-lift in 1989, which almost worked, but the hotel cannot quite hide its 1957 birth year, and the garish blue-and-pink entry canopies don't help. But the rooms are comfortable without being luxurious, and the baths are modern. You couldn't find a more central location. Rooms on the Neuer Markt side are quieter than those on Kärntner Strasse, and the best rooms are those on the corners. *Neuer Markt 3/Kärntner Str. 18, A–1010, tel. 0222/515940, fax 0222/ 513–8138. 102 rooms. Facilities: restaurant, café, bar. AE, DC, MC, V.*

König von Ungarn. In a 16th-century house in the shadow of St. Stephen's Cathedral, this hotel began catering to court nobility in 1815. (Mozart lived in the house next door when he wrote *The Marriage of Figaro*). A superb redesign has turned it into a modern hotel, and you could hardly hope for a happier result. The hotel radiates charm, from the greenery in the wood-paneled atrium lobby to the antiques of various periods and the pine country furnishings in the bedrooms. The rooms are not overly large, but each is individually and appealingly decorated. Those in back are somewhat quieter. Insist on written confirmation of bookings. *Schulerstr. 10, A–1010, tel. 0222/ 515840, fax 0222/515–848. 32 rooms. Facilities: restaurant, lobby bar. DC, MC, V.*

★ **Mailberger Hof.** This 14th-century house on a pedestrian street just off the Kärntner Strasse was once a Baroque town palace. In 1976 it was turned into an intimate family-run hotel with great success and is a favorite of stars from the nearby state opera. The rooms are so attractively decorated it's hard to imagine you're in a hotel; colors and furniture have been coordinated without fussiness to create a setting you won't want to leave. You'll have to book about a month ahead to get a room. *Annagasse 7, A–1010, tel. 0222/512–0641, fax 0222/512–0641– 10. 40 rooms. Apartments with kitchenettes available by the month. Facilities: restaurant. AE, MC, V.*

★ **Opernring.** This establishment's spacious, comfortable rooms, with homelike furnishings and bright, attractive tiled baths, are only one reason guests come back. The unusually friendly, personal attention of the owner, Susie Riedl, makes you feel as though you're the only guest. The hotel has Best Western affiliation. The rooms on the inner courtyard are sunny and quieter but have a dreary outlook; disregard the traffic noise (there's no air-conditioning, so you may want the windows open) and enjoy the extraordinary view of the Opera, diagonally across the Ring. *Opernring 11, A–1010, tel. 0222/587–5518, fax 0222/ 587–5518–29. 35 rooms. AE, DC, MC, V.*

Moderate

★ **Austria.** This older house, tucked away on a tiny cul-de-sac, offers the ultimate in quiet and is only five minutes' walk from the heart of the city. The high-ceilinged rooms are pleasing in their combination of dark wood and lighter walls; the decor is mixed, with Oriental carpets on many floors. You'll feel at home here, and the staff will help you find your way around town or get opera or concert tickets. *Wolfengasse 3 (Fleischmarkt), A–1010, tel. 0222/515230, fax 0222/512–4343. 51 rooms, 40 with bath or shower. AE, DC, MC, V.*

Fürstenhof. This turn-of-the-century building, directly across from the Westbahnhof, describes its large rooms as "old-fashioned comfortable," and you reach them via a marvelous hydraulic elevator. Furnishings are a mixed bag. The side rooms are quieter than those in front. *Neubaugürtel 4, A–1070, tel. 0222/933267, fax 0222/933267–26. 60 rooms. AE, DC, MC, V.*

★ **Hotel-Pension Zipser.** This 1904 house, with an ornate facade and gilt-trimmed coat of arms, is one of the city's very best hotel values. It's in a fascinating district of small cafés, shops, jazz clubs, and excellent restaurants, yet within steps of the J streetcar line direct to the city center. The rooms are newly redone in browns and beiges, with modern furniture to match; the baths are elegant and well lit. The balconies of some of the back rooms overlook tree-filled neighborhood courtyards. The friendly staff will help get theater and concert tickets. Book ahead a month or two to be sure of a room. *Lange Gasse 49, A– 1080, tel. 0222/408–5266, fax 0222/408–5266–13. 47 rooms. Facilities: coffee bar. AE, DC, MC, V.*

Ibis Wien. About an eight-minute walk from the Westbahnhof and easily identifiable by its bronze metal exterior, the Ibis offers its standard chain accommodations in contemporary rooms that are compact, complete, and very good value. The blue and blue-gray accents are refreshing against the white room walls. The rooms on the shady Wallgasse side are more comfortable; those on the upper floors have a superb panoramic view. You may have to contend with some tour groups. *Mariahilfer Gürtel 22–24/Wallgasse 33, A–1060, tel. 0222/565626, fax 0222/ 564368. 341 rooms. Facilities: restaurant, Weinstube, garage. AE, DC, MC, V.*

★ **Kärntnerhof.** Behind the "Schönbrunn yellow" facade of this elegant 100-year-old house on a quiet cul-de-sac lies one of the friendliest small hotels in the center of the city. Don't let the dated and uninteresting lobby put you off; take the gorgeously restored Art Deco elevator to the rooms upstairs. They have just been done over in either brown or white reproduction furniture, and the baths are modern. Room 205, in its combination of blue and white, is stunning. The staff is adept at getting theater and concert tickets for "sold out" performances and happily puts together special outing programs for guests. For a small fee, parking can be arranged in the abbey courtyard next door. *Grashofgasse 4, A–1010, tel. 0222/512–1923, fax 0222/513–2228–33. 43 rooms. AE, DC, MC, V.*

Pension Christina. This quiet pension, just steps from Schwedenplatz and the Danube Canal, offers mainly smallish modern rooms, warmly decorated with attractive dark-wood furniture set off against beige walls. Room 524 is particularly spacious and inviting. *Hafnersteig 7, A–1010, tel. 0222/533–2961, fax 0222/533–2961–11. 33 rooms. MC.*

★ **Pension Pertschy.** Housed in a former town palace just off the Graben, this pension is as central as you can get. A massive arched portal leads to a yellow courtyard, around which the house is built. Anybody who has stayed in Room 220 with its stylish old blue ceramic stove (just for show) would be happy again with nothing less. Most rooms are spacious with antique furniture of mixed periods, but even the small single rooms are charming. Baths are satisfactory. Use the elevator, but don't overlook the palatial grand staircase. *Habsburgergasse 5, A–1010, tel. 0222/534–490, fax 0222/534–4949. 43 rooms. MC.*

Schweizerhof. Occupying floors 4, 5, and 6 of an Art Deco building in the heart of the city, this hotel will make you feel comfortably at home with its pleasantly mixed decor, parquet floors, and Oriental carpets. Ask for Room 527, with unusual and valuable hand-carved pine country furniture. Corner Room 523 gives you a look at the Anker Clock; from corner Room 508, you can glimpse the spires of St. Stephen's Cathedral. *Bauernmarkt 22, A–1010, tel. 0222/533–1931, fax 0222/533–0214. 55 rooms. AE, MC, V.*

Wandl. The restored facade identifies a 300-year-old house that has been in family hands as a hotel since 1854. You couldn't find a better location, tucked behind St. Peter's Church, just off the Graben. The hallways are punctuated by cheerful, bright openings along the glassed-in inner court. The rooms are modern, but some are a bit plain and charmless, despite parquet flooring and red accents. Ask for one of the rooms done in period furniture, with decorated ceilings and gilt mirrors; they're palatial, if a bit overdone. *Petersplatz 9, A–1010, tel. 0222/534550, fax 0222/534–55–77. 138 rooms. Facilities: bar. No credit cards.*

Zur Wiener Staatsoper. The hotel's florid facade, with oversize torsos supporting its upper bays, is pure 19th-century Ringstrasse style. The rooms are less well defined in style, small yet comfortable. The baths are adequate. And you'll find yourself within steps of the Opera and Kärntner Strasse. *Krugerstr. 11, A–1010, tel. 0222/513–1274, fax 0222/513–1274–15. 22 rooms. AE, MC, V.*

Inexpensive

Pension Aclon. On the third floor of a gray but gracious older building just off the Graben (with the famous Café Hawelka downstairs), this family-run hostelry (complete with sheepdog) is attractively done up in old-Vienna style, with lots of plants, 19th-century furniture, dark woods, and elegant marble baths. Rooms on the inner court are quieter, though the street in front carries no through traffic. *Dorotheergasse 6–8, A–1010, tel. 0222/512–7949, fax 0222/513–8751. 22 rooms. AE, DC, V.*

Pension Baroness. One flight up, behind the drab facade of this turn-of-the-century apartment house, are comfortable rooms with contemporary furnishings, many quite spacious and many completely renovated in 1990. The front rooms are noisy, but the nearby streetcar is a convenience. *Lange Gasse 61, A–1080, tel. 0222/405–1061, fax 0222/405–1061–61. 39 rooms. MC.*

★ **Pension City.** You'll be on historic ground here: In 1791 the playwright Franz Grillparzer was born in the house that then stood here; a bust and plaques in the entryway commemorate him. On the second floor (the Viennese call it the mezzanine) of the present 100-year-old house, located about three minutes away from St. Stephen's Cathedral, the rooms are newly outfitted in a successful mix of modern and 19th-century antique furniture against white walls. The baths are small but complete, and the amenities (minibars, TV, telephones) are remarkable at the price. *Bauernmarkt 10, A–1010, tel. 0222/533–9521, fax 0222/535–5216. 19 rooms. AE, DC, MC, V.*

Pension Nossek. This family-run establishment on the upper floors of a 19th-century office and apartment building lies at the heart of the pedestrian and shopping area. The rooms have high ceilings and are eclectically but comfortably furnished; those on the front have a magnificent view of the Graben. Do as the many regular guests do and book early. *Graben 17, A–1010, tel. 0222/533–7041, fax 0222/535–3646. 26 rooms, 16 with bath or shower. No credit cards.*

★ **Pension Suzanne.** This 1950s building on a side street is just steps away from the Opera. The rooms are smallish but comfortably furnished in 19th-century Viennese style; baths are modern, although short on shelf space. Suzanne has regular guests who book months in advance, so you'd be well advised to do the same. *Walfischgasse 4, A–1010, tel. 0222/513–2507, fax 0222/513–2500. 24 rooms, 7 apartments with kitchenette. No credit cards.*

Pension Wild. This friendly, family-run pension on several floors of an older apartment house draws a younger crowd to one of the best values in town. Rooms are simple but modern, with light-wood furniture and pine-paneled ceilings. Each wing has a kitchenette. The breakfast room/TV lounge is bright and attractive, and you're close to the major museums. *Lange Gasse 1, A–1080, tel. 0222/435174, fax 0222/402–2168. 14 rooms without bath. Facilities: sauna, solarium, fitness room. AE, DC, MC, V.*

★ **Rathaus.** This friendly hotel, under the same management as the nearby Zipser, is in a 1908 building that has been attractively renovated: The spacious rooms have contemporary furnishings. You'll be within an easy walk of the main museums and close to public transportation. *Lange Gasse 13, A–1080, tel. 0222/434302, fax 0222/408–4272. 40 rooms. No credit cards.*

Seasonal Hotels (Inexpensive–Moderate)

Student residences, which operate as hotels July–September, are an excellent bargain. They have single or double rooms, all, unless noted, with bath or shower. You can book any of the Rosenhotels by phoning 0222/597–0680, fax 0222/597–0689–89. Central booking for several of the student residence hotels is 0222/431661, fax 0222/426397. Credit cards in general are not accepted; exceptions are noted.

Academia (fairly luxurious). *Pfeilgasse 3a, A–1080, tel. 0222/
431661–55, fax 0222/426397. 368 rooms. Facilities: restaurant,
bar. AE, MC, V.*

Alsergrund. *Alser Str. 33, A–1080, tel. 0222/4332–317 or 0222/
512–7493, fax 0222/512–1968. 58 rooms without bath.*

Auersperg (inexpensive). *Auerspergstr. 9, A–1080, tel. 0222/
4325490 or 0222/512–7493, fax 0222/512–1968. 76 rooms. MC.*

Auge Gottes. *Nussdorfer Str. 75, A–1090, tel. 0222/342585. 79
rooms without bath.*

Avis. *Pfeilgasse 4, A–1080, tel. 0222/426374, fax 0222/426397.
72 rooms. Facilities: restaurant, bar. AE, MC, V.*

Haus Döbling (inexpensive). *Gymnaṣiumstr. 85, A–1190, tel.
0222/347631, fax 0222/347631–25. 308 rooms without bath.*

Haus Technik. *Schäffergasse 2, A–1040, tel. 0222/587–6569,
fax 0222/512–1968. 104 rooms with shower. Facilities: restaurant, garage.*

Josefstadt. *Buchfeldgasse 16, A–1080, tel. 0222/435211 or 0222/
512–7493, fax 0222/512–1968. 40 rooms without bath. MC, V.*

Panorama (slightly farther than most from the city center).
*Brigittenauer Lände 224, A–1200, tel. 0222/331090, fax 0222/
331–09–274. 270 rooms, 136 with shower. Facilities: restaurant, bar, sauna, parking.*

Rosenhotel Burgenland 3. *Bürgerspitalgasse 19, A–1060, tel.
0222/597–9475, fax 0222/597–9475–9. 140 rooms. Facilities:
restaurant, bar, garage. AE, MC, V.*

Rosenhotel Europahaus (well outside the center but clean, very
reasonable, and with a lovely garden; bus and direct streetcar
to city center). *Linzer Str. 429, A–1140, tel. 0222/972538, fax
0222/972538–101. 31 rooms. Facilities: parking.*

Studentenheim der Musikhochschule (offers the most central
location of any of the seasonal hotels, in the heart of the city).
*Johannesgasse 8, A-1010, tel. 0222/51484, fax 0222/51484–49.
85 rooms, some with bath or shower. Facilities: bicycle storage.*

The Arts and Nightlife

The Arts

Vienna is one of the main music centers of the world. Contemporary music gets its hearing, but it's the hometown standards—the works of Beethoven, Brahms, Haydn, Mozart,
Schubert—that draw the Viennese public. A monthly program, put out by the city tourist board and available at any
travel agency or hotel, gives a general overview of what's going
on in opera, concerts, jazz, theater, and galleries, and similar
information is posted on billboards and fat advertising columns
around the city.

Most theaters now reserve tickets by telephone against a credit
card; you pick up your ticket at the box office with no surcharge. The same applies to concert tickets. Ticket agencies
charge a minimum 22% markup and generally deal in the more
expensive seats. Expect to pay (or tip) a hotel porter or concierge at least as much as a ticket agency. You might try **Vienna
Ticket Service** (Postfach 160, A–1060, tel. 0222/587–9843, fax
0222/587–9844), **American Express** (Kärntner Str. 21–23, A-
1015, tel. 0222/515–400, fax 0222/515–40–70), **Kartenbüro
Flamm** (Kärntner Ring 3, A–1010, tel. 0222/512–4225), or **Cos-**

mos (Kärntner Ring 15, A–1010, tel. 0222/515330, fax 0222/513–4147).

Tickets to the state theaters (Opera, Volksoper, Burgtheater, or Akademietheater) can be charged against your credit card. You can order them by phone up to six days before the performance (tel. 0222/513–1513) or buy them in person up to seven days in advance at the central box office. *Theaterkassen, back of the Opera, Hanuschgasse 3, in the courtyard, tel. 0222/51444–2959 or –2960. AE, DC, MC, V. Open weekdays 8–6, Sat. 9–2, Sun. 9–noon.*

You can also write ahead for tickets. The nearest Austrian National Tourist Office can give you a schedule of performances and a ticket order form. Send the form (no payment is required) to the ticket office (Kartenvorverkauf Bundestheaterverband, Goethegasse 1, A–1010 Vienna), which will mail you a reservation card; when you get to Vienna, take the card to the main box office to pick up and pay for your tickets.

Opera The **Staatsoper,** one of the world's great houses, has been the scene of countless musical triumphs and a center of unending controversies over how it should be run and by whom. (When Lorin Maazel was unceremoniously dumped as head of the opera not many years ago, he pointed out that the house had done the same thing to Gustav Mahler a few decades earlier.) A performance takes place virtually every night from September through June, drawing on the vast repertoire of the house, with emphasis on Mozart and Verdi. (Opera here is nearly always performed in the original language, even Russian.) And guided tours of the opera house are held year-round. The 1994–95 season will get off to a late start, as the house is closed for alterations until December 15. Check for possible November performances in the Theater an der Wien (*see below*). The opera in Vienna is a dressy event. Evening dress and black tie, though not compulsory, are recommended for first-night performances and in the better seats.

Light opera and operetta are performed at the **Volksoper,** outside the city center at Währingerstrasse and Währinger Gürtel (third streetcar stop on No. 41, 42, or 43 from "downstairs" at Schottentor on the Ring). Prices here are significantly lower than in the main opera, and performances can be every bit as rewarding. Mozart is sung here, too, but in German, the language of the house.

You'll find musicals and operetta also at the **Theater an der Wien** (Linke Wienzeile 6, tel. 0222/588300), the **Raimundtheater** (Wallgasse 18, tel. 0222/599770), and **Ronacher** (Seilerstätte/Himmelpfortgasse, tel. 0222/513–8565). Opera and operetta are performed on an irregular schedule at the **Kammeroper** (Fleischmarkt 24, tel. 0222/512–0100–31).

In summer, chamber opera performances by the Kammeroper ensemble are given in the exquisite **Schlosstheater** at Schönbrunn Castle. Ticket agencies will have details.

Music Vienna is the home of four full symphony orchestras: the great Vienna Philharmonic, the Vienna Symphony, the broadcasting service's ORF Symphony Orchestra, and the Niederösterreichische Tonkünstler. There are also hundreds of smaller groups, from world-famous trios to chamber orchestras.

The most important concert halls are in the buildings of the Gesellschaft der Musikfreunde, called the **Musikverein** (*Dumbastr. 3; ticket office at Karlsplatz 6, tel. 0222/505–8190, fax 0222/505–9409; AE, DC, MC, V; open weekdays 9–6, Sat. 9–noon*) and the **Konzerthaus** (*Lothringerstr. 20, tel. 0222/712–1211, fax 0222/712–1211–4; AE, DC, MC, V; open weekdays 9–6, Sat. 9–1*). Both houses contain several halls; tickets bear their names: **Grosser Musikvereinssaal, Brahmssaal,** or **Kammersaal** in the Musikverein; **Grosser Konzerthaussaal, Mozartsaal,** or **Schubertsaal** in the Konzerthaus.

Concerts are also given in the small **Figarosaal** of Palais Palffy (Josefsplatz 6, tel. 0222/512–5681), the concert studio of the broadcasting station (Argentinierstr. 30A, tel. 0222/50101–881), and the **Bösendorfersaal** (Graf Starhemberg-Gasse 14, tel. 0222/504–6651).

Although the **Vienna Festival** (late May to mid-June) wraps up the primary season, the summer musical scene is bright, with something scheduled every day. Outdoor symphony concerts are performed twice weekly in the vast arcaded courtyard of the Rathaus (entrance on Friedrich Schmidt-Platz). You can catch musical events in the Volksgarten and in the Schwarzenberg, Rasumofsky, and Trautson palaces; at Schönbrunn they're part of an evening guided tour.

Mozart concerts are performed in 18th-century costumes and powdered wigs in the Mozartsaal of the Konzerthaus; operetta concerts are held in the Musikverein and the Hofburg; tickets are available through hotels and travel and ticket agencies. Note, however, that some of these concerts are rather expensive affairs put on for tourists, lasting possibly an hour, with intermission.

Church music, the Mass sung in Latin, can be heard on Sunday morning during the main season at **St. Stephen's;** in the Franciscan church, **St. Michael's;** and, above all, in the **Augustinerkirche.** The Friday and Saturday newspapers carry details. St. Stephen's also has organ concerts most Wednesday evenings from early May to late November.

The **Vienna Choirboys** sing Mass at 9:15 AM in the **Hofburgkapelle** from mid-September to late June. Written requests for seats (standing room is free but limited) should be made at least eight weeks in advance to Hofmusikkapelle Hofburg, A–1010 Vienna. You will be sent a reservation card, which you exchange at the box office (in the Hofburg courtyard) for your tickets. Tickets are also sold at ticket agencies and at the box office every Friday at 5 PM, but you should be in line by 4:30. Each person is allowed a maximum of two tickets.

Theater Vienna's **Burgtheater** (Dr. Karl Lueger-Ring 2, A–1010 Vienna; *see above* for ticket details) is one of the leading German-language theaters of the world. Its current directors have replaced the German classics with more modern and controversial pieces. The Burg's smaller house, the **Akademietheater** (Lisztstr. 1), draws on much the same group of actors, for classical and modern plays. Both houses are closed during July and August.

The **Theater in der Josefstadt** (Josefstädterstr. 26, tel. 0222/402–5127) stages classical and modern works year-round in the house once run by the great producer and teacher Max Reinhardt. The **Volkstheater** (Neustiftgasse 1, tel. 0222/932776) presents dramas, comedies, and folk plays; the **Kammerspiele** (Rotenturmstr. 20, tel. 0222/533-2833) does modern plays.

For theater in English (mainly standard plays), head for **Vienna's English Theater** (Josefsgasse 12, tel. 0222/402-1260) or the equally good **International Theater** (Porzellangasse 8, tel. 0222/319-6272), which also has a small cellar theater, **The Fundus,** next door in Müllnerstrasse.

Dance Other than ballet companies in the opera and Volksoper, Vienna offers nothing in the way of dance. Under new directors, the ballet evenings that are on the opera-house schedules are now much improved, if not yet up to international standards.

Film Film has enjoyed a recent renaissance, with viewers seeking original rather than German-dubbed versions. Look for films in English at **Burgkino** (Opernring 19, tel. 0222/587-8406)—in summer, Carol Reed's classic *The Third Man* with Orson Welles is a regular feature; **City** (Tuchlauben 13, tel. 0222/533-5232); **de France** (Schottenring 5/Hessgasse 7, tel. 0222/345236); **Top-Kino** (Rahlgasse 1, tel. 0222/587-5557); and **Votiv-Kino** (Währinger Str. 12, tel. 0222/343571). The film schedule in the daily newspaper *Der Standard* lists foreign-language films (*Fremdsprachige Filme*) separately. In film listings, *OmU* means original language with German subtitles.

The **Filmmuseum** in the Albertina (Augustinerstr. 1, tel. 0222/533-7054; screenings Mon.–Sat. 6 and 8 PM; AS 45) shows original-version classics like *Birth of a Nation, A Night at the Opera,* and *Harvey* and organizes retrospectives of the works of artists, directors, and producers. The monthly program is posted outside, and guest memberships (AS40 per day) are available. It is closed July, August, and September.

Nightlife

Bars and Lounges Vienna has blossomed in recent years with delightful and sophisticated bars. Head for the Bermuda Triangle, an area in the First District roughly defined by Judengasse, Seitenstättengasse, Rabensteig, and Franz-Josefs-Kai. Here you will find dozens of bars, both intimate and large, like **Salzamt, Krah-Krah,** and **Ma Pitom.** Around Concordiaplatz and in Heinrichsgasse, **Puerto** and **Domicil** are highly popular. Back toward Stephansplatz, on Bäckerstrasse, check out **Weinorgel, Oswald & Kalb;** on Blutgasse, **Chamäleon;** on Singerstrasse, the **Galerie Bar. The American Bar** on Kärntner Durchgang has an original Adolf Loos turn-of-the-century interior.

Cabaret Cabaret has a long tradition in Vienna. **Simpl** (Wollzeile 36, tel. 0222/512-4742) continues earning its reputation for barbed political wit but has had to give way to some newcomers at **K&K** (Linke Wienzeile 4, tel. 0222/587-2275) and **Kabarett Niedermair** (Lenaugasse 1A, tel. 0222/408-4492). To get much from any of these, you'll need good German plus knowledge of local affairs and dialects.

Casinos Try your luck at the casino **Cercle Wien** (Kärntner Str. 41, tel. 0222/512-4836) in a former town palace. You'll need your passport for entry identification.

Discos The disco scene is big in Vienna, and the crowd seems to follow the leader from one "in" spot to the next. A few continually draw full houses. Try **Atrium** (Schwarzenbergplatz 10, tel. 0222/505–3594); **Queen Anne,** still very much "in" (Johannesgasse 12, tel. 0222/512–0203); and U–4, popular with a mixed group, early thirties and younger (Schönbrunner Str. 222, tel. 0222/858307).

Jazz Clubs Vienna is increasingly good for jazz, though places where it can be heard tend to come and go. Nothing gets going before 9 PM. Try **Jazzclub Sixth** (Gumpendorferstr. 9, tel. 0222/568710); **Jazzland** (Franz-Josefs-Kai 29, tel. 0222/533–2575); **Opus One** (Mahlerstr. 11, tel. 0222/513–2075); **Papa's Tapas** (Schwarzenbergplatz 10, tel. 0222/505–0311); and **Roter Engel** (Rabensteig 5, tel. 0222/535–4105).

Nightclubs Vienna has no real nightclub tradition, although there are a number of clubs in town. Most of the ones with floor shows are horribly expensive and not very good. The two where you run the least risk are **Casanova,** where singles can sit reasonably peacefully at the upstairs bar (Dorotheergasse 6, tel. 0222/512–9845; open daily till 4 AM), and **Moulin Rouge** (Walfischgasse 11, tel. 0222/512–2130; open Mon.–Sat. 10 PM–6AM).

The leading spots for dancing are the **Eden Bar,** which always has a live band and is for the well-heeled mature crowd (Liliengasse 2, tel. 0222/512–7450; open 10 PM–4 AM); **Chattanooga,** which often has a live band and draws a younger crowd (Graben 29, tel. 0222/533–5000); and **Volksgarten** (in the Volksgarten, Burgring 1, tel. 0222/533–0518), where a mixed younger set comes, particularly in summer for outdoor dancing.

Excursions from Vienna

Baden

This short tour takes you to Baden through the band of rolling wooded hills called the Vienna Woods (Wienerwald) that border Vienna on the west. The hills are skirted by vineyards forming a "wine belt," which also follows the valleys south of Vienna. You can visit this area easily in a day's outing, either by car or by public transportation, or you can spend the night in Baden, Mödling, or Alland for a more leisurely tour, visiting Mayerling, Heiligenkreuz, and a few other sights in the area.

Tourist Get information in Vienna before you start out, at the tourist
Information office of Lower Austria (Heidenschuss 2, tel. 0222/533–4773, fax 0222/535–0319). Other tourist offices are for Perchtoldsdorf (tel. 0222/867634–34); Mödling (tel. 02236/26727); Gumpoldskirchen (tel. 02252/62101); and Baden (tel. 02252/86800–310).

Escorted Tours This is one of the standard routes offered by the sightseeing-bus tour operators in Vienna, and it usually includes a boat ride through the "underground sea" grotto near Mödling. For details, check with your hotel or **Cityrama** (tel. 0222/534130) or **Vienna Sightseeing Tours** (tel. 0222/712–4683).

Getting Around You can get to Baden directly from Vienna by bus or, far more
By Bus or Train fun, interurban streetcar in about 40 minutes; the bus departs from the Ring directly opposite the Opera; the streetcar, from the Ring across from the Bristol Hotel. It is possible, with advance planning, to go on to Mayerling and Heiligenstadt on

post office buses (tel. 0222/71101), but schedules are infrequent, and driving is preferable.

By Car Head for Liesing (23rd District), then take Wiener Strasse to Perchtoldsdorf; from there, follow the signs south to Mödling and Baden. From Baden, take Route 210 (marked "Helenental") to Mayerling and on to Alland; return to Vienna via Route 11, stopping in Heiligenkreuz en route.

Exploring *Numbers in the margin correspond to points of interest on the Baden, Carnuntum, and Rohrau map.*

❶ Just over the Vienna city line is **Perchtoldsdorf,** a picturesque market town with many wine taverns; a 13th-century Gothic parish church; and the symbol of the town, an imposing stone defense tower completed in 1511. Locally known as Pedersdorf, this is a favorite excursion spot for the Viennese, who come mainly for the good local wines. Continue south 8 kilometers (5 **❷** miles) to **Mödling,** founded in the 10th century, where you'll find another Gothic parish church; a Romanesque 12th-century charnel house (where the bones of the dead were kept); and the town hall, which has a Renaissance loggia.

❸ A few kilometers east of Mödling—about 16 kilometers (10 miles) south of Vienna—is **Schloss Laxenburg,** a complex consisting of a large Baroque Neues Schloss (New Castle), a small 14th-century Altes Schloss (Old Castle), and an early 19th-century neo-Gothic castle set into the sizable lake. The large park is full of birds and small game, such as roe deer and hare, and is decorated with statues, cascades, imitation temples, and other follies. The Altes Schloss was built in 1381 by Duke Albrecht III as his summer residence, and several Habsburg emperors spent summers in the Neues Schloss, which now houses the International Institute of Applied Systems Analysis. Opposite is the large Baroque Convent of the Charitable Sisters.

❹ West of Mödling on Route 11 is the **Seegrotte Hinterbrühl,** a fascinating but now somewhat commercialized underground cave, created years ago when a mine filled up with water (Grutschg. 2, tel. 02236/26364). You can take a motorboat trip and look at the reflections through the arched caverns of the mine. Not far is the Höldrichsmühle, a mill that's now a restaurant, made famous by Franz Schubert's song about the linden tree.

❺ Back in Mödling, follow the "wine road" through the lush vineyard country to the famous wine-producing village of **Gumpoldskirchen,** the home of one of Europe's pleasantest white wines. Vintners' houses line the main street, many of them with the typical large wooden gates that lead to the vine-covered courtyards where the Heuriger (wine of the latest vintage) is served by the owner and his family at simple wooden tables with benches. Gumpoldskirchen also has an arcaded Renaissance town hall, a market fountain made from a Roman sarcophagus, and the castle of the Teutonic knights, whose descendants still own some of the best vineyard sites in the area.

❻ Continuing on the wine road brings you to the famous spa of **Baden.** Since antiquity, Baden's sulphuric thermal baths have attracted the ailing and the fashionable from all over the world. When the Romans came across the springs, they dubbed the town Aquae; the Babenbergs revived it in the 10th century, and when the Russian Czar Peter the Great visited in 1698, Baden's golden age began. Austrian Emperor Franz II spent the sum-

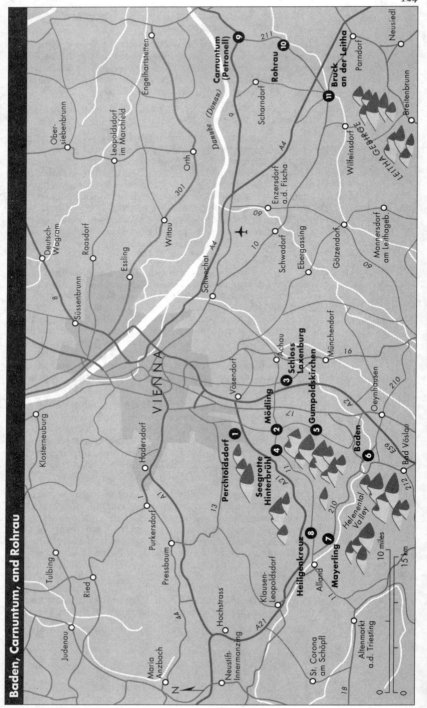

Baden, Carnuntum, and Rohrau

mers here; every year for 12 years before his death in 1835, the royal entourage moved from Vienna for the season. In Baden, Mozart composed his "Ave Verum"; Beethoven spent 15 summers here and wrote large sections of his Ninth Symphony and *Missa Solemnis;* here Franz Grillparzer wrote his historical dramas; and Josef Lanner, both Johann Strausses (father and son), Carl Michael Ziehrer, and Karl Millöcker composed and directed many of their waltzes, marches, and operettas.

The loveliest spot in Baden, and the main reason for a visit, is the huge and beautiful **Kurpark,** where many outdoor public concerts still take place. Operetta is given under the skies in the Summer Arena (the roof closes if it rains); in winter, it is performed in the Stadttheater. People sit quietly under the old trees or walk through the upper sections of the Kurpark for a view of the town from above. The old Kurhaus, now enlarged and renovated, incorporates a convention hall. The ornate casino, with its 19th-century decor, is a marvelous sight.

Other attractions include a **Beethoven House** (Rathausgasse 10, no phone; admission: AS15 adults, AS5 children; open Tues.–Fri. 4–6, weekends and holidays 9–11 and 4–6) and an enchanting **Doll and Toy Museum** (Erzherzog Rainer-Ring 23, tel. 02252/41020; admission: AS15 adults, AS5 children; open Tues.–Fri. 4–6, weekends and holidays 9–11 and 4–6).

7 Route 210 takes you through the quiet Helenental Valley west of Baden to **Mayerling,** scene of a suicide pact in 1889 between the 30-year-old Habsburg heir, Crown Prince Rudolf, Emperor Franz Josef's only son, and his 17-year-old mistress, Baroness Marie Vetsera. The mystery surrounding the tragedy is still a juicy subject for speculation. In an attempt to suppress the scandal—the full details are not known to this day—the baroness's body, propped up between two uncles, was smuggled back into the city by carriage. The Mayerling story surfaces regularly in books, films, and tabloid-newspaper gossip. The hunting lodge where the suicide took place is no longer there; it was replaced by a Carmelite convent, built by the bereaved emperor.

8 About 4 kilometers (2.5 miles) northeast of Mayerling, in the heart of the southern section of the Vienna Woods, is **Heiligenkreuz,** a magnificent Cistercian abbey with a famous Romanesque and Gothic church, founded in 1135 by Leopold III. The church itself is lofty and serene, with beautifully carved choir stalls (the Cistercians are a singing order) surmounted by busts of Cistercian saints. The cloisters are interesting for the Chapel of the Dead, where the brothers lie in state guarded by four gesticulating skeletons holding candelabra. The chapter house contains the tombs of Babenberg rulers.

Dining and Lodging

Alland **Marienhof.** Close to both Mayerling and Heiligenkreuz, this stylish building set in a beautiful park has immaculate rooms, each with a whirlpool bath. The **Kronprinz** restaurant serves outstanding, adventuresome fare, and there's a simpler and cheaper restaurant as well. *A–2534, tel. 02258/2378, fax 02258/ 237841. 25 rooms. Facilities: restaurant (reservations useful, jacket and tie advised; closed Sun. evening, Mon., and two weeks in Feb.), sauna, tennis. AE. Expensive.*

Baden **Sauerhof.** "Schönbrunn yellow" marks this appealing country house that's been elegantly renovated, with rooms in old-Vienna style. The hotel caters to seminars and group activities. Nevertheless, the restaurant is excellent (try the veal steak with mushrooms, or for dessert, the famous house crepes). *Weilburgstr. 11–13, A–2500, tel. 02252/41251, fax 02252/48047. 88 rooms. Facilities: restaurant (reservations not required, jacket and tie advised; open evenings only except Sun. and holidays), bar, indoor pool, sauna, fitness room, tennis. AE, DC, MC, V. Very Expensive.*

Krainerhütte. This friendly house, in typical Alpine style, with balconies and lots of natural wood, is family-run. *Helenental, A–2500, tel. 02252/44511, fax 02252/445–1499. 60 rooms. Facilities: restaurant, indoor pool, sauna, solarium, tennis. DC, MC, V. Expensive.*

Mödling **Babenbergerhof.** Rooms in this renovated, older hotel are comfortably up-to-date. You're in the quiet pedestrian zone (parking available) and upper rooms on the street side have views of the ancient parish church. The garden is particularly pleasant for summer dining; try the fried chicken or boiled beef. *Babenbergergasse 6, A–2340, tel. 02236/22246, fax 02236/22246–6. 50 rooms. Facilities: restaurant (reservations not required; dress: casual but neat; closed Mon. and Jan.), bar. MC, V. Restaurant moderate–expensive, hotel moderate.*

Perchtoldsdorf **Jahreszeiten.** This elegant, formal restaurant is now in the capable hands of Günter Winter, who achieved an excellent reputation with Hauswirth in Vienna, although both food and service are variable. The menu offers international cuisine with an Austrian flair. Beyond the kitchen, the atmosphere, like the tables, is set to perfection, and the menu is supplemented by wines from an outstanding cellar, international as well as local. *Hochstr. 17, tel. 0222/865–3129. Reservations required. Jacket and tie advised. AE, DC, MC, V. Closed Sat. lunch, Sun. dinner, Mon., one week in Feb., mid-July–mid-Aug. Expensive.*

Carnuntum and Rohrau

As the Romans moved up the Danube, they set up installations and fortresses along the way, mainly on the south side of the river. The Roman ruins in Vienna have long since been covered by later generations of buildings and can now be seen only in the handful of underground museums in the First District. But about 20 km (12 mi) east of the airport, one of the more impressive Roman camps, Carnuntum, has been extensively excavated, and in an easy day trip by car or public transportation you can see this ancient community and the nearby towns of Rohrau and Bruck an der Leitha.

Escorted Tours With the opening of the Czech and Slovak republics, more tours may be offered to the eastern part of Lower Austria, but for now this is one area you'll probably have to explore on your own.

Getting Around The suburban rail line from Wien-Mitte (Landstrasser
By Train or Bus Hauptstr.) stops at Petronell, with service about once an hour. Carnuntum is about a 10-minute walk from the Petronell station. You can also take a post office bus, from the Wien-Mitte bus station, which drops you at the ruins. From Petronell, a bus runs to Rohrau (check schedules), and from Rohrau you can either return to Petronell or take a bus on to Bruck an der Leitha and from there a bus or train back to Vienna.

By Car In leaving the city, follow signs to "Airport/Bratislava" (A4). Leave the divided highway for the more scenic Route 9, which will be marked to Hainburg. At Petronell, you will have to take a sharp left off the bypass road, but signs are clear for the Roman ruins (Carnuntum). From Petronell, take Route 211 to Rohrau and on to Bruck an der Leitha; from there, Route 10 or the A4 autobahn takes you back to Vienna.

Exploring The Roman town and military camp of **Carnuntum** was the larg-
❾ est garrison on the Roman "Amber Road" leading south from the Baltic Sea. At its peak it had a population of 30,000 and boasted two amphitheaters. The settlement collapsed following a defeat by the Germans in the third century. You can take a guided tour or wander through the excavations, arranged as an open-air museum, with the remains of Roman houses, the amphitheater that once held 25,000 people, and the Heidentor (Heathen Gate), in a nearby field (tel. 02165/2480; admission: AS30 adults, AS25 children; guided tour AS20 extra; open Apr.–Oct., daily 10–5). New buildings are being completed to house the artifacts found in the course of the diggings, many of which are now on display in the Museum Carnuntinium in Bad Deutsch-Altenburg, 4½ kilometers (2.8 miles) east. The Danube Museum in the great castle at Petronell contains some relics from the excavations (it is the only part of the castle open to visitors).

❿ About 8 kilometers (5 miles) south of Petronell is **Rohrau,** the birthplace of the composers Franz Josef (1732–1809) and Michael (1737–1806) Haydn. The compact straw-roofed house in which the family with 12 children lived is now a museum that gives a good idea of country life of the time (tel. 02165/2268; admission: AS20 adults, AS10 children; open Tues.–Sun. 10–5). Down the road is the 16th-century **Harrach Castle,** with an entry bridge (over the former moat) and a lake at the back. The art gallery contains the largest private collection in Austria (dating to 1668), with works by Rubens, Van Dyck, Breughel, and many Spanish and Italian artists. Haydn's mother was a cook at the castle, and Count Harrach became one of Haydn's first patrons. *Tel. 02164/22530. Admission: AS50 adults, AS20 children. Open Easter–end-Oct., Tues–Sun. 10–5.*

Time Out **Schlosstaverne.** The restaurant tucked into the front corner of the castle serves substantial portions of good country food and wines from the region. Service slows somewhat when tour groups appear. The terrace is particularly inviting on a warm, sunny day. *Tel. 02164/2487. Reservations advised on weekends. Dress: casual but neat. AE, DC. Closed Mon. Inexpensive.*

⓫ If you return to Vienna via **Bruck an der Leitha,** take time to look around this walled community, which until 1921 marked the border with Hungary. Note the town square, with the 15th-century Holy Trinity church and the town hall with its arcaded court and Rococo balcony. The 17th-century Prugg castle (once moated) is not open to the public, but you can wander under tall trees in the surrounding park.

The Waldviertel

The "Forest District" north of the Danube and to the northwest of Vienna was long dormant, out of the mainstream and cut off from neighboring Czechoslovakia by a sealed border. Today, with the collapse of communism in Czechoslovakia and the re-opening of many crossing points, the Waldviertel has reawakened. Here gentle hills bearing stands of tall pine and oak are interspersed with small farms and friendly country villages. The region can be seen in a couple of days, longer when you pause to explore the museums, castles, and other attractions. **Zwettl** and **Raabs an der Thaya,** where facilities are more modest and much less expensive than those of the major tourism routes, make good bases for discovering this area.

Tourist Information The tourist office for Lower Austria in Vienna (Heidenschuss 2, tel. 0222/533–4773, fax 0222/535–0319) has ample material on the Waldviertel. Other tourist offices within the region are those at Gars am Kamp (tel. 02985/2680), Horn (tel. 02982/2372), Zwettl (tel. 02822/52233), Gmünd (tel. 02852/53212, fax 02852/54713), Waidhofen an der Thaya (tel. 02842/503–17), and Raabs an der Thaya (tel. 02846/365).

Escorted Tours The Waldviertel remains undiscovered for organized tourism; for the time being, visitors are on their own.

Getting Around *By Bus or Train* The main rail line from Vienna to Prague passes through the Waldviertel, making the region accessible by train. In addition, post office buses cover the area fairly well and with reasonable frequency. Bus hubs are Horn, Waidhofen, and Zwettl. An express bus service runs between Vienna and Heidenreichstein via Waidhofen an der Thaya.

By Car Signs for Prague will head you in the right direction out of Vienna. At Stockerau take Route 4 to Horn, Route 38 west to Zwettl, an unnumbered road to Weitra, Route 41 to Gmünd and Schrems, Route 30 north to Heidenreichstein, Route 5 to Waidhofen an der Thaya, an unnumbered road via Gross Siegharts to Raabs an der Thaya, Route 30 to Riegersburg, an unnumbered road to Hardegg. Return on Route 30 to Geras, Route 4 to Horn, Route 34 down the Kamp valley past Langenlois, and Route 3 back to Vienna.

Exploring The successful Austrian field marshall Radetzky (1766–1858) is buried at **Heldenberg** in the tiny village of **Kleinwetzdorf,** in elegant but lugubrious surroundings. His tomb, arranged for by a wealthy uniform supplier, is set in a park studded with dozens of larger-than-life busts of Austrian royalty and nobility. The small castle has a Radetzky museum. *Tel. 02956/2751. Park free. Museum admission (guided tours only): AS30 adults, AS60 family. Open May–Oct., weekends, tours at 10, 1, 2, 3, and 4.*

Time Out **Restaurant Naderer** at the top of the hill above Maissau is an ideal stop for coffee: The house cakes are particularly good. A full meal can be enjoyed in summer on the terrace overlooking the valley.

At **Horn** are remnants of the impressive fortification walls built in 1532 to defend against invading Turks. Note the painted Renaissance facade on the house (1583) at Kirchenplatz 3.

About 5 kilometers (3 miles) outside Horn, at **Altenburg** on Route 38, **Altenburg abbey** was built in 1144 and rebuilt in 1645–1740 after its destruction by the Swedes. The library and the frescoed ceilings are glorious. *Tel. 02982/3451. Admission: AS45 adults, AS20 children. Open (with guided tours) Easter–end-Oct., daily 9–noon and 1–5.*

Almost 25 kilometers (15 miles) west of Altenburg, the castle at **Ottenstein,** now a hotel-restaurant, has a number of impressive reception rooms and parts dating to 1178. Ottenstein defied the Swedes only to be devastated by the Russians in 1945. Sports enthusiasts will find boating and swimming in the reservoir-lake and golf at Niedergrünbach. The ruined **Lichtenfels castle** nearby can be explored.

Zwettl is known for the vast **Cistercian abbey,** dating to 1138, about 2¼ kilometers (1½ miles) west of the town. Later renovations added the glorious Baroque touches. *Tel. 02822/550–17. Admission: AS35 adults, AS20 children. Open (with guided tours) May–Oct., Mon.–Sat. 10–noon and 2–4, Sun. 11–noon (tour at 11) and 2–4.*

About 2 kilometers (1 mile) north of Zwettl on Route 36, at Dürnhof, a fascinating **museum of medicine and meteorology** is housed in a cloister chapel built in 1294. Exhibits follow the development of medicine from earliest times to the present, and the courtyard garden of medicinal herbs adds another dimension to the history. *Tel. 02822/53180. Admission: AS40 adults, AS15 children. Open May–early Nov., daily 10–6.*

Time Out   In the Zwettl abbey the **Stiftsrestaurant,** a spacious tavern complex, serves good Austrian country fare such as grilled chicken and roast pork with bread dumplings. The beer is fresh from the nearby brewery.

About 7½ kilometers (almost 5 miles) west of Zwettl (follow the road signs), the **castle** at **Rosenau** is an impressive Renaissance structure built in 1590 with later Baroque additions. The castle was ravaged by the Soviets in 1945, then rebuilt as a hotel and museum complex housing the unique **Freemasonry museum,** with a secret room once used for lodge ceremonies that was discovered during the renovations. Displays show the ties of Haydn and Mozart to freemasonry, and many exhibit labels are in English, reflecting the origins of the brotherhood. *Tel. 02822/8221. Admission: AS45 adults, AS35 senior citizens, AS25 children. Open mid-Apr.–mid-Nov., daily 9–5.*

On the main road, turn west 20 kilometers (12½ miles) to the small town of **Weitra,** whose ornate painted houses (sgraffiti) dating from the 17th and 18th centuries are stunning. A charming small brewery here has been in business since 1321! And the tradition is well founded: In 1645, 33 citizens held the right to operate a brewery. At the new Brauhotel, you can even take a course in brewing. The domineering 15th-century **castle** with its Renaissance features is privately owned and normally closed, but it will be open to the public from mid-April to October, 1994, for the Lower Austrian regional exhibition.

Gmünd, a town that lies 16 kilometers (10 miles) north of Weitra on Route 41, was divided when the border with Czechoslovakia was established. The actual line passes through a few houses and backyards, but with the barbed-wire defenses removed, the border is now a harmless affair. Railroad fans have a field day here; the Czechs still use some steam locomotives for switching, and on the Austrian side Gmünd is one of the main points on the narrow-gauge Waldviertler Bahn, which runs occasional steam excursions (tel. 02852/52588–365 or 02852/54386). The nature park to the northeast of the center, open to the public all year, includes a geological open-air museum and a stone marking the 15th meridian east of Greenwich.

North of Schrems a detour west from Route 30, on Route 303, leads to **Neunagelberg,** a center of glass making since 1740. Among the glassworks you can visit is Glasstudio Zalto (tel. 02859/237). Another, Stölzle Kristall (tel. 02859/531), has a showroom and factory outlet.

At **Heidenreichstein** on Route 30, the massive moated **castle** with its corner towers has never been captured since it was built in the 15th century; some of the walls, 3 meters (10 ft) thick, went up in the 13th century. *Tel. 02862/52268. Admission (with guided tour): AS40 adults, AS20 children. Open mid-Apr.–mid-Oct., Tues.–Sun. 9–noon and 2–5; guided tours only at 9, 10, 11, 2, 3, and 4.*

Route 5 leads east to **Waidhofen an der Thaya,** a three-sided walled defense city typical of the 13th century. Fires destroyed much of the early character of the town, but the town square, rebuilt at the end of the 19th century, has a pleasing unity. The town is dominated by its Baroque parish church; the Rococo chapel to Mary includes a madonna of 1440 and distinguished portraits marking the stations of the cross. Outside the city walls, the **Bürgerspitalkapelle** has a side altar with a Gothic carved-wood relief of Mary and child and 13 assistants, from about 1500.

An unnumbered road continues east 21 kilometers (13 miles) via Gross-Siegharts to **Raabs an der Thaya,** an attractive village watched over by an 11th-century castle perched dramatically on a rock outcropping and reflected in the river below (tel. 02846/659; admission AS45 adults, AS35 senior citizens, AS25 children; guided tour AS30 extra; open May–Sept., daily 10–5). The intriguing ruins of the Kollmitz castle to the southeast of Raabs can be explored, and a bit farther along are the ruins of Eibenstein castle, another link in the 16th- and 17th-century defense chain along the border with Bohemia.

Route 30 leads to **Drosendorf,** with a castle built in 1100 and a town center typical of a small walled community. Farther along—27 kilometers (17 miles) from Raabs—lies **Riegersburg.** The **castle** here was originally moated, then the substantial edifice was given a Baroque rebuilding in 1731 and again virtually rebuilt after heavy damage inflicted by the Russians in 1945. Note the window variations and the figures that ornament the roofline. The whole castle was renovated in 1992–93, highlighting the elegance of the public rooms. *Tel. 02916/332. Admission (on guided tour only): AS70 adults, AS35 children. Combination ticket with Hardegg: AS120. Open Apr.–June, Sept.–Oct. daily 9–5; July–Aug. daily 9–7.*

About 6 kilometers (4 miles) east of Riegersburg on an unnumbered road, **Hardegg** has a **castle** that stands mightily on a rock promontory high above the Thaya river, watching over the Czech republic. (The river midstream marks the boundary; as recently as 1990, the pedestrian bridge was unpassable, the border sealed, and Czech border defenses concealed in the woods opposite.) The earliest parts of the castle date to 1140. The armory and armament collection, chapel, and the museum's exhibits on the emperor Maximilian in Mexico are alone worth the visit. In addition, the kitchen and other working rooms of the castle give a real feeling of the daily life of an earlier era. *Tel. 02949/8225. Admission: AS55 adults, AS50 senior citizens, AS27 children. Guided tour (an English-speaking guide may be available) AS20 extra. Open Apr.–June, Sept.–mid-Nov. daily 9–5; July–Aug. daily 9–6.*

From Hardegg, retrace your steps on Route 30 to **Geras,** where the impressive abbey has a marvelous Baroque interior. Continue south on Route 4 to Horn and take Route 34 south to Rosenburg and on through the Kamp river valley.

The castle at **Rosenburg** dates to 1200 and dominates the north entrance to the valley. Its features include the jousting field, the reception rooms, and the Renaissance balconies and small courtyards incorporated into the design. *Tel. 02982/2911. Admission (with guided tour): AS60 adults, AS30 children. Falconry demonstration daily at 11 and 3, AS60 adults, AS30 children; combination ticket (castle and falconry) AS90 adults, AS50 children. Open Apr.–end-Oct. daily 9–5.*

The scenic Kamp valley technically belongs to the Waldviertel, though for the amount of wine produced here, it might as well be a part of the Weinviertel, the wine district to the east. The villages along the route—Gars am Kamp, Schönberg am Kamp, Zöbing, Strass, and Langenlois—are all known for excellent wines, mainly varietal whites. **Strass** in particular has become an active center of viticulture, and many vintners offer wine tastings. Castle ruins dot the hilltops above the vineyards; the area has been populated since well before 900 BC.

Route 34 takes you through more vineyards to Kollersdorf, where Route 3 east will return you to Vienna.

Dining and Lodging

Grafenegg
★

Schlosstaverne Grafenegg. Behind the golden facade of the elegant tavern waits a friendly and welcoming atmosphere. Rooms are comfortably furnished in beiges and reds. The restaurant offers game in season and local cuisine with international touches. The strawberries in early summer taste even better outdoors on the sunny dining terrace. *A–3485 Haitzendorf, tel. 02735/2616. 6 rooms. Facilities: restaurant (reservations advised on weekends). No credit cards. Closed Jan.–Feb. Moderate.*

Kirchberg am Wagram
★

Gut Oberstockstall. A former cloister houses this country inn where the rustic setting indoors is charming and the courtyard garden idyllic in summer. The menu promises lamb, duck, game in season, and tempting desserts such as grilled apricots—all to the accompaniment of the house's own wines. *Tel. 02279/2335. Reservations advised. Dress: casual chic. No credit cards. Closed Sun.–Tues.; mid-Dec.–Feb.; last 2 weeks in Aug. Expensive.*

Langenlois

Brundlmayer. This country Heuriger offers outstanding wines from one of Austria's top vintners, as well as a tasty hot-and-cold buffet, all in a rustic setting or in the Renaissance courtyard. The simple but delicious fare includes *Schinkenfleckerl,* a baked dish of noodles and ham. *Walterst. 14, tel. 02734/2883. Reservations advised in winter. Dress: casual chic. No credit cards. Closed Mon.–Wed.; Jan.–Feb. Moderate.*

Raabs an der Thaya
★

Hotel Thaya. A family-run hotel directly on the river, the Thaya offers modern rooms in the new annex. Rooms overlooking the river are the favorites. The restaurant prepares such solid local specialties as roast pork and veal. *Hauptstr. 14, A–3820 Raabs an der Thaya, tel. 02846/2020. 25 rooms. Facilities:*

restaurant, bar, beer garden, disco, sauna, solarium, fitness room, parking. No credit cards. Moderate.

★ **Pension Schlossblick.** This small modern pension has a homey atmosphere in its spacious lounge and cheery breakfast room. The rooms on the town side looking through the trees to the castle are the nicest. *Eduard Braith-Str. 7, A-3820 Raabs an der Thaya, tel. 02846/437. 13 rooms. Facilities: restaurant for hotel guests, parking. No credit cards. Inexpensive.*

Rosenau **Schloss Rosenau.** Set in an elegant palace, this small hotel of-
★ fers country quiet and modern rooms furnished in period style. The wood-paneled restaurant is one of the best in the area, fea-turing garlic soup, bread soup, and lamb or game in season. In summer food seems to taste even better on the sunny outdoor terrace. *A-3924 Rosenau, tel. 02822/8221. 18 rooms. Facili-ties: restaurant (reservations advised on weekends), indoor pool, sauna, solarium, fishing. AE, DC, MC, V. Closed mid-Jan.-Feb. Moderate.*

The Weinviertel

The "Wine District," the rolling countryside north of Vienna, earns its name from the ideal terrain and climate here for wine. Both reds and whites come from this region bounded by the Danube on the south, the Thaya river and the reopened Czech border on the north, the March river and Slovakia to the east. No well-defined line separates the Weinviertel from the Waldviertel to the west; the Kamp river valley, officially part of the Waldviertel, is an important wine region. Whether wine, crops, or dairying, this is farming country, its broad expanses of vineyards and farmlands broken by patches of forest and neat villages. A tour by car, just for the scenery, can be made in a day; you may want two or three days to savor the region and its wines—generally on the medium-dry side. Don't expect to find here the elegant facilities you found elsewhere in Austria; prices are low by any standard, and village restaurants and ac-commodations are mainly *Gasthäuser* that meet local needs. This means that you'll rub shoulders over a glass of wine or a beer with country folk.

Tourist The tourist office for Lower Austria in Vienna (Heidenschuss
Information 2, tel. 0222/533-4773, fax 0222/535-0319) has basic information on the Weinviertel. Other tourist offices within the region are those at Poysdorf (Liechtensteinstr. 1, tel. 02552/3515), Retz (Herrenplatz 30, tel. 02942/2700), Laa an der Thaya (Rathaus, tel. 02522/5010), Mistelbach (Hauptplatz 6, tel. 02572/2515-248), Poysdorf (Singergasse 2, tel. 02552/220017), and Gänsern-dorf (Rathausplatz 1, tel. 02282/26510).

Escorted Tours The Weinviertel has yet to be exploited by tour operators, and visitors are on their own.

Getting Around Bus service to and through the area is good, with direct ser-
By Bus or Train vices available between Vienna and Retz, Laa an der Thaya, and Poysdorf as well as buses between the region's larger towns. Trains run from Vienna to Mistelbach, and to Gän-serndorf and beyond to Bernhardsthal on the Czech border.

By Car Roads are good and well marked. Head out of Vienna to Stockerau on Route 3 or the autobahn A22/E49/E59, following the signs to Prague. After Stockerau, turn north on Route 303 to beyond Hollabrun, then Routes 2 and 30 to Retz. From Retz, backtrack on Route 30 to Route 45 and head east to Laa an der Thaya. Then follow Route 46 to Staatz, Route 219 to Poysdorf, Route 7/E461 south beyond Gaweinstal, Route 220 to Gänserndorf, and Route 8 back to Vienna.

Exploring Like Linz, **Korneuburg** is winding down as a center of Austrian shipbuilding; many Danube passenger ships, including those under Russian and other flags, were built here. The massive Gothic-style town hall dominates the main square. The Augustine church has a *Last Supper* (1770) by the Austrian painter Maulpertsch as part of the altar.

Schloss Schönborn at **Göllersdorf** was laid out in 1712 by that master of Baroque architecture, Lukas von Hildebrandt. Today the castle is in private hands, but the harmony of design can be appreciated from the outside.

Retz, at the northwest corner of the Weinviertel, is known for its red wines. Here you can tour Austria's largest wine cellar, tunneled 20 m (65 ft) under the town, and at the same time taste wines of the area. Some of the tunnels go back to the 13th century, and at the end of the 15th century each citizen was permitted to deal in wines and was entitled to storage space in the town cellars. Efforts to use the cellars for armaments production during World War II failed because of the 88% humidity. The temperature remains constant at 8–10°C (47–50°F). Entrance to the cellars is at the Rathauskeller. *Tel. 02942/2700 or 02942/2379. Guided tour (includes a commemorative glass and a wine sample): AS50 adults, AS15 children. Tours Mon.–Sat. 2 PM, Sun. 10:30, 2, 4. Check first to be sure tours are on.*

The Retz town square is an attractive mixture of Sgraffito (painted) facades, Biedermeier, and other styles. Most buildings date to 1660 or later; during the Thirty Years' War the Swedes occupied Retz and left only 28 buildings standing. The Dominican church (1295) at the southwest corner of the square survived, and it is interesting for its long, narrow design.

To the northwest of the center, outside the walls on a hillcrest at Kalvarienberg 1, the **windmill**—the town's emblem—dates to 1830. It was in commercial use until 1927 as a gristmill and is still operational.

Retrace your way south on Route 30 to Route 45 and turn east to **Laa an der Thaya,** once an isolated town but increasingly a commercial center for Czech shoppers now that the border is open. (As long as you have your passport with you, you can cross the border and return without complication.) Laa boasts a **Beer Museum,** located in the town fortress, that traces the history of beer (the nearby Hubertus brewery has been in business since 1454) and maintains an imposing collection of beer bottles. *Tel. 02522/501–29. Admission: AS20 adults, AS15 children. Open May–Oct., weekends 2–4.*

Time Out If a coffee break is in order, **Café Weiler,** upstairs on the main square at Stadtplatz 2, has outstanding cakes and pastries.

Driving Route 46 from Laa, you'll find that the impressive hilltop castle ruin at **Staatz** loses significance the closer you get. It's possible to wander through the ruin, but little is left of the onetime fortress other than a pile of stone and a strategic view of the countryside.

Route 219 leads to **Poysdorf** and the heart of the Weinviertel. Poysdorf vintages, mainly whites, rank with the best Austria has to offer. The town museum includes a section on viticulture and wine making. *Brunner Str. 9, tel. 02552/220025. Admission: AS20 adults. Open Easter–Oct., Sun. and holidays 10– noon and 2–4.*

South of **Gänserndorf**, the **auto safari park** allows visitors to drive through re-created natural habitats of live wild animals, many of which (lions and tigers) are hardly indigenous to Austria. The adventure takes five to six hours. For those without a car, a safari bus leaves for the circuit every hour. *Siebenbrunner Str., tel. 02282/7261. Admission: AS145 adults, AS90 children. Open Palm Sunday–Oct., daily 9:30–4:30.*

North of **Strasshof**, the **Heizhaus** is a fascinating private collection of dozens of steam locomotives and railroad cars stored in a vast engine house. Enthusiasts have painstakingly rebuilt and restored many of the engines, which are operated on weekends. The complex includes transfer table, water towers, and coaling station, and visitors can climb around among many of the locomotives awaiting restoration. *Sillerstr. 123, tel. 02287/3027. Admission (with parking and guided tour): AS60 adults, AS30 children. Open Apr.–Sept., Sun. and holidays 10–4.*

Route 8 returns you to Vienna, passing through one of Austria's few oil fields, where operating pumps patiently pull up crude to be piped to the refinery about 20 km (12½ mi) south.

Dining and Lodging

Deutsch Wagram **Marchfelderhof.** This sprawling complex, with its eclectic series of rooms decorated with everything from antiques to hunting trophies, has a reputation for excess in the food department as well. The menu's standards—Wiener schnitzel, roast pork, lamb—are more successful than the more expensive efforts at innovation. *Tel. 02247/2243. Reservations advised. Jacket and tie advised. AE, DC, MC, V. Closed Mon. and late Dec.–early Feb. Expensive.*

Laa an der Thaya **Restaurant Weiler.** Light woods and country accessories set the
★ tone in this family-run restaurant, and in summer dinner is served in the outdoor garden. Try the delicate cream of garlic soup and a house specialty is game in season. For dessert, the delicious cakes of the house are temptingly displayed in a showcase. *Staatsbahnstr. 60, tel. 02522/379. Reservations advised on weekends. Dress: casual but neat. No credit cards. Closed Sun. dinner, Mon., and late June–mid-July. Moderate.*

Mistelbach **Zur Linde.** This friendly restaurant with rustic decor is setting higher standards for such traditional fare as roast pork, flank steak, and fresh game in season. But the major attraction here is the remarkable range of wines from the neighborhood at altogether reasonable prices. *Bahnhofstr. 49, tel. 02572/2409. Dress: casual but neat. AE, MC, V. Closed Sun. dinner, Mon.; mid-Jan.–mid-Feb., end-July–mid-Aug. Moderate.*
Gasthof Goldene Krone. This friendly, traditional house offers simple but adequate accommodation. Rooms are quaintly old-fashioned yet comfortable, and guests are in the heart of the Weinviertel for excursions. *Oberhofer Str. 15, A–2130, tel. 02572/27295. 22 rooms. Facilities: restaurant, bar, garage. No credit cards. Inexpensive.*

Poysdorf **Schreiber.** Choose the shaded garden under huge trees or the country rustic decor indoors. The typical Austrian fare—roast pork, stuffed breast of veal, boiled beef, filet steak with garlic—is commendable, as is the house-made ice cream. The wine card lists more than 60 area labels. *Bahnstr. 2, tel. 02552/2348. Dress: casual but neat. No credit cards. Closed Mon. dinner, Tues., and mid-Jan.–mid-Feb. Moderate.*

4 The Danube Valley

Vienna to Linz

By George W. Hamilton

In this chapter we follow the course of the Danube upstream from Vienna as it winds through Lower Austria (Niederösterreich) and a bit of Upper Austria (Oberösterreich) to Linz, past castles and industrial towns, the vineyards of the Weinviertel, and apricot and apple orchards. This is a wonderful trip in early spring, when the fruit trees are in bloom, or in fall after the grape harvest, when the hillside vineyards turn reddish blue and a crisp autumn chill settles over the Danube at dusk. This is where Lorelei lured sailors to the shoals, where Richard the Lionheart was locked in a dungeon for years, where marvelous castles suddenly appear at a turn in the road.

Linz, Austria's third-largest city (and perhaps its most underrated), is a key industrial center. It's a fine town for shopping; the stores are good, and prices are more reasonable than in Vienna or the big resorts. Concerts and opera at Linz's modern *Brucknerhaus* can be every bit as good as those in Vienna or Salzburg. From Linz, we explore several nearby towns and return along the Danube's south bank, visiting the great abbey at Melk, the Göttweig abbey above the river opposite Krems, and the abbey at Klosterneuburg.

The Danube, rising in Germany's Black Forest and emptying into the Black Sea, is our focal point: The route that brought the Romans to the area and contributed to its development remains one of Europe's important waterways, with three national capitals on its banks—Vienna, Budapest, and Belgrade. Many of the hilltop castles along the route were built to give an overview of this vital channel; the cities developed as ports for the salt, wood, ores, and other cargo it carried; and the railroads and highways of today largely parallel its course. With the opening of the Rhine-Main-Danube canal, river traffic is now possible to Rotterdam.

Essential Information

Important Addresses and Numbers

Tourist Information For general information on the area, check with the district tourist offices for **Lower Austria** (Heidenschuss 2, A–1010 Vienna, tel. 0222/533–4773, fax 0222/535–0319), **Upper Austria** (Schillerstr. 50, A–4010 Linz, tel. 0732/600–2210, fax 0732/600220), and **Linz** (Hauptplatz 34, tel. 0732/2393–1777, fax 0732/772873). Tourist offices for the towns are:

Bad Hall (Kurhaus, A–4540, tel. 07258/20310, fax 07258/2031–25).

Dürnstein (Parkplatz Ost, A–3601, tel. 02711/219, 02711/442).

Eferding (A–4070 Eferding, tel. 07272/555520, fax 07272/5555–33).

Freistadt (Hauptplatz 12, A–4240, tel. 07942/2974, fax 07942/3207).

Grein (Hauptstr. 3, A–4360, tel. 07268/680, fax 07268/4784).

Klosterneuburg (Niedermarkt, A–3400, tel. 02243/2038, fax 02243/86773).

Krems/Stein (Undstr. 6, A–3500, tel. 02732/82676, fax 02732/70011).

Melk (Linzer Str. 3–5, A–3390, tel. 02752/2307–32, fax 02752/2307–37).

Pöchlarn (Regensburger Str. 11, A–3380, tel. 02757/231040, fax 02757/2310–66).

St. Polten (Rathausplatz 1, A–3100, tel. 02742/53354, fax 02742/52531–492).

Steyr (Stadtplatz 27, A–4400, tel. 07252/53229 or 48154, fax 07252/48154–15).

Tulln (Albrechtsg. 32, A–3430, tel. 02272/5836).

Wachau (Undstr. 6, A–3500 Krems, tel. 02732/85620, fax 02732/87471).

Waidhofen an der Ybbs (Obere Stadtplatz 28, A–3340, tel. 07442/2511–165, fax 07442/2511–77).

Weissenkirchen (Gemeinde Weissenkirchen, A–3610, tel. 02715/2232–11 or 02715/2221, fax 02715/2221).

Arriving and Departing

Linz is served mainly by Austrian Airlines, plus Lufthansa, KLM, Swissair, and Air France. Regular flights connect it with Vienna, Amsterdam, Berlin, Düsseldorf, Frankfurt, Paris, Stuttgart, and Zürich. The Linz airport (tel. 07221/72700–0) is in Hörsching, about 12 km (7.5 mi) southwest of the city. *See also* Chapter 3, Vienna: Arriving and Departing by Car, Train, Boat and Bus.

Getting Around

By Car   A car is certainly the pleasantest way to make this trip. Roads are good and well marked, and you can switch over to the A1 autobahn, which parallels the general east-west course of the route. (*See* Renting and Leasing Cars in Chapter 1.)

By Train   Every larger town and city on this tour can be reached by train, but the train misses the Wachau valley along the Danube's south bank. The rail line on the north side of the river literally clings to the bank in places, but service is infrequent. You can combine rail and boat transportation along this route, taking the train upstream and crisscrossing your way back on the river. From Linz, the delightful LILO interurban line (tel. 0732/654376) makes the run up to Eferding, and you can also get to Bad Hall by train.

By Bus   If you link them together, bus routes will get you to the main points of this trip and even to the hilltop castles and monasteries, assuming you have the time. If you coordinate your schedule to arrive at a point by train or boat, you can usually make reasonable bus connections to outlying destinations. In Vienna you can book bus tours (*see* Guided Tours, *below*); in Linz, ask at the municipal bus station (Bahnhofplatz 12, tel. 0732/2160).

By Boat   Large riverboats with sleeping accommodations ply the route between Vienna and Linz and on to Passau on the German border. Smaller day boats go between Vienna and the Wachau valley, and there you can change to local boats that crisscross the river between the colorful towns. Bridges across the river are few along this stretch, so boats are essential transportation; service is frequent enough that you can cross the river, visit a town, catch a bus or the next boat to the next town, and cross the river farther up- or downstream. You can take a day trip from Vienna and explore one of the stops, such as Krems, Dürnstein, or Melk. Boats run from May to late September. For information on boat schedules, contact DDSG/Danube

Steamship Company (Handelskai 265, A–1020 Vienna, tel. 0222/217500, fax 0222/218–9238, or Regensburger Str. 9, A–4010 Linz, tel. 0732/783607, fax 0732/783607–9).

By Bicycle A bicycle trail parallels the Danube from considerably southeast of Vienna to Passau. Tourist offices (*see* Tourist Information, above) have information, maps, and recommendations for sightseeing and overnight and mealtime stops.

Guided Tours

Tours out of Vienna take you to Melk and back by bus and boat in eight hours, with a stop at Dürnstein. Bus tours operate year-round, but the boat runs only April–October. **Cityrama/Gray Line,** *Börsegasse 1, tel. 0222/534130, fax 0222/534–1322; adults AS720, children AS350, lunch not included;* **Vienna Sightseeing Tours,** *Stelzhammergasse 4/11, tel. 0222/712–4683, fax 0222/712–4683–77; adults AS880, children AS100;* **Vienna Line,** *Johannesgasse 14, tel. 0222/512–8091, fax 0222/513–9397; adults AS880, children AS100, lunch and hotel transfer included.*

Day boat trips with loudspeaker announcements in English run daily from mid-April to late October. Contact the DDSG/Danube Steamship Company (Handelskai 265, tel. 0222/217500, fax 0222/218–9238).

Exploring the Danube Valley and Linz

This trip can be done in as little as three days, allowing one day along the north Danube side (Tour 1), a day in Linz and surroundings (Tours 2 and 3), and a day to return along the south shore (Tour 4). You could also happily spend a week—adding time in Eferding and Freistadt, a day in Kremsmünster and Steyr, a day for Waidhofen an der Ybbs, and returning by ship.

Highlights for First-time Visitors

Burg Kreuzenstein (*see* Tour 1).
Dürnstein castle ruins (*see* Tour 1).
Freistadt (*see* Tour 3).
Carved wood altar at Kefermarkt (*see* Tour 3).
The library at the great abbey at Melk (*see* Tour 4).
100-year-old open streetcars in Linz (*see* Tour 2).
Stift Göttweig (*see* Tour 4).
Town square in Steyr (*see* Tour 3).
Weinkolleg Kloster Und (*see* Tour 1).

Tour 1: The North Bank of the Danube, the Wachau

Numbers in the margin correspond to points of interest on the Danube Valley maps.

If you're taking the tour by train, take streetcar D to the Franz Jozefs Bahnhof. If you're driving, the trickiest part may be getting out of Vienna. Follow signs to Prague to get across the Danube. Avoid the right-hand exit marked Prague, which leads to the autobahn, and continue ahead, following signs for

Prager Strasse and turning left at the traffic light. Prager Strasse (Route 3) heads you toward Langenzersdorf and Korneuburg.

Until recently, **Korneuburg** was the center of Austrian shipbuilding, where river passenger ships, barges, and transfer cranes were built for Russia, among other customers. Stop for a look at the imposing neo-Gothic city hall (1864), which dominates the central square and towers over the town.

Continue on Route 3 about 3 km (2 mi) beyond Korneuburg, and atop a hillside to your right you'll spot **Burg Kreuzenstein,** a fairyland castle with turrets and towers. Using old elements and Gothic and Romanesque bits and pieces brought here for the purpose, Count Wilczek built Kreuzenstein, from 1879 to 1908, on the site of a destroyed castle, to house his Late Gothic collection. You wouldn't suspect the building wasn't absolutely authentic if the tour guides weren't so honest. You'll see rooms full of armaments, the festival and banquet halls, library, chapel, even the kitchens. You can also reach Kreuzenstein via the suburban train *(S-Bahn)* to Leobendorf and a ¾ hour hike up to the castle. *Leobendorf bei Korneuburg, tel. 02262/66102. Admission: AS60 adults, AS40 children. Open for guided tours mid-Mar.–mid-Nov., Tues.–Sun. 9–5 (last tour at 4).*

Route 3 continues past Stockerau, through a lush meadow and woodland area, and after about 33 km (21 mi), at Grafenwörth, you'll see signs pointing to your right to **Schloss Grafenegg.** The moated Renaissance castle dating to 1533 was stormed by the Swedes in 1645 and rebuilt from 1840 to 1873 in the English Gothic Revival style. Greatly damaged during the 1945–1955 occupation, it was extensively restored in the 1980s. Look for such fascinating detail as the gargoyle waterspouts, and don't miss the chapel. *Haitzendorf, tel. 02735/220527. Admission: AS70 adults, AS30 children. Open mid-May–Oct., daily 10–6.*

Time Out The **Schlosstaverne** in Haitzendorf (tel. 02735/2616) offers excellent food in a delightful setting, either in the Biedermeier dining room or under an umbrella in the garden. In season, you'll find game; otherwise, turn to the excellent Austrian standards such as *Tafelspitz.*

Return to Route 3 or follow signs over the back roads to **Krems.** This Renaissance town is closely tied to Austrian history; here the ruling Babenbergs set up a dukedom in 1120, and the earliest Austrian coin was struck in 1130. In the Middle Ages, Krems looked after the iron trade, while neighboring Stein traded in salt and wine. Today the area is the center of a thriving wine production. Krems over the years became a center of culture and art, and today it is an attractive city to wander through, with narrow streets and a pedestrian zone.

Among the sights of Krems–Stein is the **Steiner Tor,** the massive square gate protected by two stubby round towers, once set into the wall of the moated city. The oldest part of town is to the east. Follow along the Obere and Untere Landstrasse, and you'll spot dozens of eye-catching buildings in styles ranging from Gothic to Renaissance to Baroque. It's easy to pick out the heavy Gothic **Piaristenkirche,** begun in 1470, with its distinctive square tower, central peak, and minitowers at each corner. The main altar and most of the side altars incorporate paintings by the local artist Martin Johann Schmidt (1718–1801), popu-

American Express offers Travelers Cheques built for two.

American Express® Cheques *for Two*. The first Travelers Cheques that allow either of you to use them because both of you have signed them. And only one of you needs to be present to purchase them.

Cheques *for Two* are accepted anywhere regular American Express Travelers Cheques are, which is just about everywhere. So stop by your bank, AAA* or any American Express Travel Service Office and ask for Cheques *for Two*.

AMERICAN EXPRESS **Travelers Cheques** ®

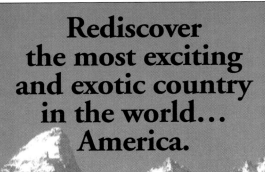

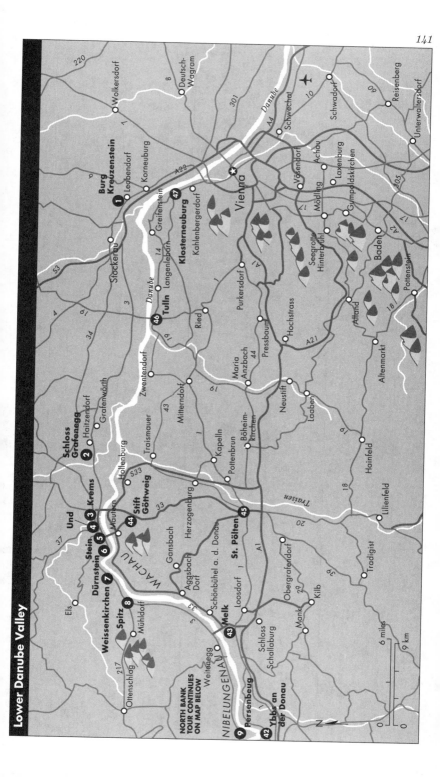

Lower Danube Valley

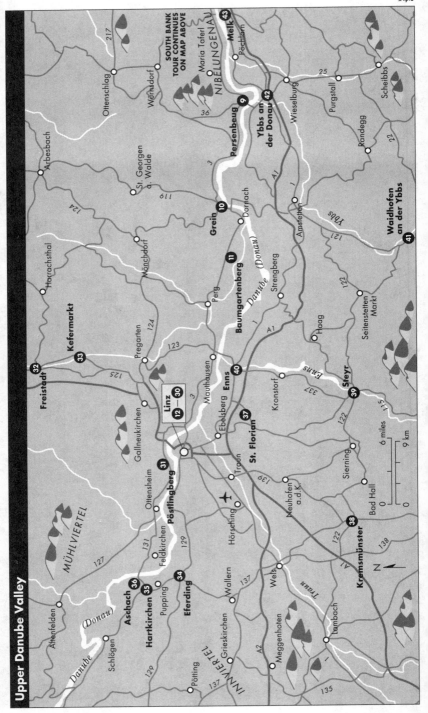

Upper Danube Valley

larly known as Kremser Schmidt, whose translucent works you will repeatedly come across in the course of this trip. Close by is the parish church of **St. Veit,** completed in 1630. The interior is surprisingly spacious; Schmidt did the ceiling frescoes.

The 14th-century former Dominican cloister, farther along the street, now serves as the **city historical museum,** with a wine museum that holds tastings. *Tel. 02732/84927. Admission: AS20 adults, AS10 children. Open Easter–late Oct., Tues.– Sat. 9–noon and 2–5; Sun., holidays 9–noon.*

On the entry portal of the **Bürgerspitalkirche** at Obere Landstrasse 15, you'll see Friedrich III's legend *AEIOU,* standing for *Austria Erit In Orbe Ultima,* Latin for "Austria will reach to the ends of the earth."

❹ Between Krems and Stein, in a beautifully restored Capucin cloister in the tiny town of **Und,** is the **Weinkolleg Kloster Und.** The building also houses the tourist office and a small wine museum, where you can taste (and buy) more than 100 Austrian wines. *Undstr. 6, Krems–Stein, tel. 02732/73073, fax 02732/ 73074–85. Admission (with tasting): AS130. Open daily 11–7.*

❺ In **Stein,** the former 14th-century **Minoritenkirche,** just off the main street in the pedestrian zone, now serves as a museum with changing displays. A few steps beyond, an imposing square Gothic tower identifies the 15th-century St. Nicholas parish church, whose altar painting and ceiling frescoes were done by Kremser Schmidt. The upper part of the Gothic charnel house (1462), squeezed between the church and the hillside, has been converted to housing. Notice, too, the many architecturally interesting houses in Stein, among them the former tollhouse, with rich Renaissance frescoes. Stein was the birthplace of Ludwig Köchel, the cataloguer of Mozart's works, which are referred to by their Köchel numbers.

❻ Moving along Route 3, you'll see **Dürnstein** ahead, distinguished by its prominent Baroque church and castle ruin on the hill overlooking the town. In the tower of this castle, Richard I of England was imprisoned (1192–1193), until he was rescued by Blondel, the faithful minnesinger. It's said that Blondel, located his imprisoned king when he heard the sound of his master's voice completing the verse of a song he was singing. The town is small; leave the car at one end and walk the narrow streets. A rather steep 30-minute climb to the ruins will earn you a breathtaking view up and down the Danube valley and over the hills to the south. The gloriously Baroque former **Stiftskirche,** from the early 1700s, sits on a cliff overlooking the river. More than 100 tiny angels decorate the heavens of its ceiling, and couples come from near and far to be married in the romantic setting.

❼ Tucked among vineyards, just around the bend in the Danube, is **Weissenkirchen,** a picturesque town that was fortified against the Turks in 1531. A fire in 1793 laid waste to much of the town, but the 15th-century parish church of **Maria Himmelfahrt,** built on earlier foundations, largely survived the conflagration. The south nave dates to 1300, the middle nave to 1439, the chapel to 1460. The madonna on the triumphal arch goes back to the Danube school of about 1520; the Baroque touches date to 1736; and to complete the picture, the Rococo organ was installed in 1777. On the Marktplatz, check out the 15th-century *Teisenhoferhof,* which has a charming Renaissance arcaded courtyard. The building now houses the Wachau museum and contains many paintings by Kremser Schmidt. *Tel. 02715/2268. Admission: AS20 adults, AS10 children. Open Apr.–Oct., Tues.–Sun. 10–5.*

About 4 kilometers (2½ miles) farther along Route 3 is **St. Michael** at Wösendorf, noted for the Late Gothic parish church dating to 1500, with its choir roof ridge ornamented by curious ceramic deer, horses, and hares. They are copies; the originals are in the museum in Krems. The church's Baroque interior has traces of late 16th-century frescoes. The charnel house contains mummified remains from 1150 to 1300 and a rather grotesque altar made of skulls.

8 Less than 1 kilometer farther, a road swings off to the right into **Spitz,** set like a jewel in the surrounding vineyards and hills. One vineyard, the "thousand bucket" hill, is said to produce a thousand buckets of wine in a good year. A number of interesting houses in Spitz go back to the 16th and 17th centuries. The Late Gothic 15th-century parish church contains Kremser Schmidt's altar painting of the martyrdom of St. Mauritius. Note the carved wood statues of Christ and the 12 apostles, dating to 1380, on the organ loft.

Just beyond Spitz and above the road is the ruin of the castle Hinterhaus, to which you can climb. A side road here marked to Ottenschlag (Route 217) leads up the hill, and about 7 kilometers (4½ miles) beyond Mühldorf, to **Burg Ranna,** a well-preserved castle surrounded by a double wall and dry moat. The original structure dates to 1114–1125, the St. George chapel possibly even earlier. *Ober-Ranna 1, Mühldorf, tel. 02713/8221. Admission: AS19. Open May–Oct., weekends and holidays 3–5.*

You can return on a back road via Jauerling and Maria Laach to Route 3 at Aggsbach. The views are now mainly of the other side of the Danube, as you look across at Schönbühel and Melk. Shortly after Weitenegg the Wachau ends, and you come into the part of the Danube valley known as the Nibelungenau, where the mystical race of dwarfs, the Nibelungen of legend, are supposed to have settled for a while.

Crowning a hill on the north bank is the two-towered **Maria Taferl,** a pilgrimage church with a spectacular outlook. It's a bit touristy, but the church and the view are worth the side trip. About 5 kilometers (3 miles) up a back road is **Schloss Artstetten,** a massive square castle with four round defense towers at the corners. This is the burial place of Archduke Franz Ferdinand and his wife Sophie, whose double assassination in 1914 in Sarajevo was one of the triggers that set off World War I. *Tel. 07413/8302. Admission: AS52 adults, AS30 children, AS150 family. Open Apr.–Oct., daily 9–5:30. Combination tickets available with Melk abbey and Schloss Schallaburg (see Tour 4, below).*

9 The Nibelungenau ends at **Persenbeug,** a small town with an important castle (viewable only from the outside) and a number of attractive Biedermeier houses. The castle, which sits directly over the Danube, was the birthplace in 1887 of Austria's last emperor and still belongs to the Habsburg family.

10 About 19 kilometers (12 miles) upstream you'll come to **Grein,** a picturesque town with a castle set above the Danube. The river bend below, known for years as "the place where death resides," was one of the most dangerous stretches of the river until the reefs were blasted away in the late 1700s. In Grein, take time to see the intimate Rococo **Stadttheater** in the town hall, built in 1790 by the populace and still occasionally used for concerts or plays. *Rathaus, tel. 07268/680. Admission: AS20 adults, AS5 children. Tours Apr.–late Oct., daily 9, 10:30, 2:30.*

Time Out   **Kaffeesiederei Blumensträussl** (Stadtplatz 6) is a lovely spot for coffee and cake, amid the Viennese Biedermeier decor in winter or outdoors in the garden in summer. The *Mozarttorte* is renowned, as are the delicious goodies served during strawberry season. You can also get soup and snacks. *Closed Mon.*

⑪ At Dornach the road leaves the Danube, and about 6 kilometers (just under 4 miles) farther you'll find **Baumgartenberg,** which is worth a visit for its ornate Baroque parish church and the unusual chancel supported by a tree trunk.

Just before **Mauthausen** the road and the river again come together, and from the south the Enns river, one of six main tributaries, joins the Danube. Mauthausen, which has some interesting 16th-century houses, is better known today as the location of the Nazi concentration camp KZ Lager, northwest of the town. It has been preserved as a memorial to those who died here and in other such camps. *Marbach 38, tel. 07238/2269. Admission: AS15 adults, AS5 children. Open Feb.–Mar., daily 8–3; Apr.–Sept., daily 8–5; Oct.–mid-Dec., daily 8–3; closed mid-Dec.–Jan.*

⑫ From Mauthausen it's 27 kilometers (17 miles) to **Linz.** Route 3 takes you across the Danube south of the city and then into the center.

Tour 2: Linz

Numbers in the margin correspond to points of interest on the Linz map.

The capital of Upper Austria, set where the Traun river flows into the Danube, has a fascinating old city core and an active cultural life. In 1832 it had a horse-drawn train to Czechoslovakia that was the first rail line on the Continent. It is also the center of Austrian steel and chemical production, both started by the Germans in 1938. In the past, these industries made Linz a dirty city; with pollution controls now in place, Linz has been proclaimed cleaner than Vienna or Graz.

The heart of the city has been turned into a pedestrian zone; either leave the car at your hotel or use the huge new parking garage under the main square in the center of town. Distances are not great, and you can take in the highlights in the course of a two-hour walking tour.

⑬ Start at the tourist information office (Hauptplatz 34, tel. 0732/2393–1777, fax 0732/772873) and pick up the "Linz from A–Z" booklet in English. Here you're on the main square at the **Altes Rathaus,** the old city hall. Although the original 1513 building was mainly destroyed by fire and replaced in 1658–1659, its octagonal corner turret and lunar clock, as well as some vaulted rooms, remain, and you can detect traces of the original Renais-

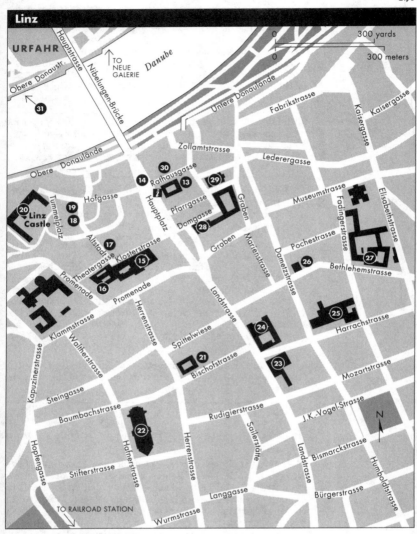

Alter Dom, **28**
Altes Rathaus (Old City Hall), **13**
Bischofshof, **21**
Carmelite Church, **23**
Deutschordens-kirche, **25**
Elisabethinen-kirche, **27**

Johannes Kepler House, **30**
Kremsmünsterer-haus, **19**
Landhaus, **16**
Linz Castle, **20**
Minorite Church, **15**
Mozart Haus, **17**

Neuer Dom, **22**
Nordico (City Museum), **26**
Pillar to the Holy Trinity, **14**
Pöstlingbergbahn, **31**
Stadtpfarrkirche, **29**
Ursuline Church, **24**
Waaghaus, **18**

sance structure on the Rathausgasse facade. The present exterior dates from 1824. The approach from Rathausgasse 5, opposite the Keplerhaus, leads through a fine arcaded courtyard. On the facade here you'll spot portraits of Emperor Friedrich III, the mayors Hoffmandl and Prunner, the astronomer Johannes Kepler, and the composer Anton Bruckner.

One of the symbols of Linz is the 20-meter (65-foot) Baroque **⑭ Pillar to the Holy Trinity** in the center of the square. Completed in 1723 of white Salzburg marble, the column offers thanks by an earthly trinity, the provincial estates, city council, and citizens, for deliverance from the threats of war (1704), fire (1712), and plague (1713). From March through October, there's a flea market here each Saturday (except holidays), from 7 to 2.

Turn right on the west side of the square into Klosterstrasse. **⑮** On your left at the end of the block is the **Minorite Church,** once part of a monastery. The present building dates to 1752–1758 and has a delightful Rococo interior with side altar paintings by Kremser Schmidt and the main altar by Bartolomeo Altomonte. *Open Oct.–June, Mon.–Sat. 7:30–11, Sun. 7:30–noon; July–Sept., daily 7:30–4.* The adjoining early Renaissance monastery buildings with the distinctive tower are now **⑯** the **Landhaus,** seat of the provincial government. Look inside to see the inner arcaded courtyard with the 1852 Planet Fountain and the Hall of Stone on the first floor, above the barrel-vaulted hall on the ground floor. The beautiful Renaissance doorway (1570) is made of red marble. Around the corner at **⑰** Altstadt 17 is the three-story Renaissance **Mozart Haus,** with a later Baroque facade and portal, where Mozart wrote his *Linz* symphony in 1783.

Heading down Altstadt toward the river, you'll pass the **⑱ Waaghaus,** bought by the city in 1524, at one time the public weighing office and now an indoor market. Emperor Friedrich **⑲** III is said to have died in the **Kremsmünstererhaus** (Altstadt 10) in 1493. The building was done over in Renaissance style in 1578–1580, and a story was added in 1616, with two turrets and onion domes. There's a memorial room to the emperor here; his heart is entombed in the Linz parish church, but the rest of him is in St. Stephen's cathedral in Vienna. *Tel. 0732/2393–1912. Open for groups by appointment.*

Just around the corner to your left, in Tummelplatz, you come to a massive four-story building with two inner courtyards, the **⑳ Linz Castle,** rebuilt by Friedrich III about 1477, literally on top of a castle that dates to 799. Note the **Friedrichstor,** the Friedrich gate, with the same *AEIOU* monogram we saw earlier in Krems. The castle houses the Upper Austrian provincial museum, with weapons, musical instruments, nativity scenes, Upper Austrian art, and prehistoric and Roman relics. *Tummelplatz 10, tel. 0732/774419. Admission: AS25. Open Tues.–Fri. 9–5, weekends and holidays 10–4.*

Up Herrenstrasse, at the corner of Bischofstrasse, you'll find **㉑** the **Bischofshof** (1721), with its fine wrought-iron gateway. **㉒** The massive **Neuer Dom** (new cathedral) in Baumbachstrasse is to your right diagonally across Herrenstrasse. The bishop of Linz in 1862 engaged one of the architects of the Cologne cathedral to develop a design in neo-Gothic French-cathedral style and ordered that its tower not be higher than that of St. Stephen's in Vienna. At 134 meters (440 feet), it is shorter by a scant 2 meters. The 1633 statues of St. Peter and St. Paul on the high altar came from the parish church in nearby Eferding. The crypt contains a large nativity scene. *Open daily 7:30–7.*

From Herrenstrasse, cross left through Rudigierstrasse and walk north one block in the pedestrian Landstrasse to Harrachstrasse, where magnificent Baroque churches sit on either side: the **Carmelite Church,** modeled on St. Joseph's in Prague (open daily 7–11:30, 3–6), and the **Ursuline Church,** with double-figured towers, one of the identifying symbols of Linz (open daily 8–6). Go down Harrachstrasse to see the former **Deutschordenskirche** (seminary church, 1723), a beautiful yellow and white Baroque treasure with an elliptical dome, designed by Johann Lukas von Hildebrandt, who also designed its high altar. *Open daily 8–6.*

Down Dametzstrasse, at the corner of Bethlehemstrasse, you'll find the **Nordico,** the city museum (1610), whose collection follows local history from pre-Roman times to the mid-1880s. *Bethlehemstr. 7, tel. 0732/2393–1912. Admission free, except for special exhibits. Open weekdays 9–6, weekends 3–5.*

Farther up Bethlehemstrasse is the **Elisabethinenkirche,** built in the mid-18th century. Note the unusually dynamic colors in the dome fresco by Altomonte. Turn down Elisabethstrasse and head west along Museumstrasse into Graben (straight ahead) to reach the Baroque **Alter Dom,** the old cathedral (1669–1678), whose striking feature is the single nave, together with the side altars. Anton Bruckner was organist here from 1856 to 1868. *Open daily 7–noon and 3–7.*

Continue around the corner in Domgasse to come to the **Stadtpfarrkirche** (city parish church), which dates to 1286 and was rebuilt in Baroque style in 1648. The tomb in the right wall of the chancel contains Friedrich III's heart. The ceiling frescoes are by Altomonte, and the figure of Johann Nepomuk (a local saint) in the chancel is by Georg Raphael Donner, in a setting by Hildebrandt. *Open Mon.–Sat. 8–7, Sun. 9–7.*

Head back toward the main square via Rathausgasse. At **No. 5,** the astronomer **Johannes Kepler** lived from 1622 to 1626; Linz's first printing shop was established in this house in 1745.

For a splendid view over Linz and the Danube, take the run up the **Pöstlingberg** on the electric **Pöstlingbergbahn.** To reach the base station for the railway, take streetcar line 3 across the river to Urfahr, Linz's left bank. The cars take 16 minutes for the 2.9-kilometer (nearly 2-mile) trip, making a 255-meter (840-foot) climb. When it was built in 1898, it boasted the steepest incline of any noncog railway in Europe. In summer, the old open-bench cars are used. *Tel. 0732/2801–7002. Round-trip fare: AS35 adults, AS17 children 6–15, two children under 6 free. Combined ticket with streetcar line 3: AS40 adults, AS20 children. Service daily all year, every 20 min, 5:30 AM–8:20 PM.*

A treat at the top for children is the fairy-tale-grotto railroad, which runs through a colorful imaginary world. *Admission: AS30 adults, AS15 children under 15. Open Sat. before Palm Sunday–Apr., Oct., daily 9–4:45; May–Sept., daily 9–5:45.*

The twin-towered Baroque pilgrimage church (1748) at the summit is another Linz landmark. The zoo on Pöstlingberg is still in the development stage, but it has some 600 animals.

Windflachweg 19, tel. 0732/237180. Admission: AS15 adults, AS5 children. Open Oct.–Mar., daily 10–4; Apr.–Sept., daily 10–6; closed Dec. 24–26, 31, and Jan. 1.

Also in Urfahr is the exceptional **Neue Galerie,** one of Austria's best modern-art museums, which has a fine, well-balanced collection, mainly by contemporary artists. *Blütenstr. 15, Urfahr, tel. 0732/2393–3600. Admission: AS40 adults, AS20 children. Open May–Oct., Mon.–Wed., Fri. 10–6, Thurs. 10–10, Sat. 10–1; Nov.–Apr., Fri.–Wed. 10–6, Thurs. 10–10.*

Tour 3: Short Excursions from Linz

Numbers in the margin correspond to points of interest on the Danube Valley maps.

The **Mühlviertel** (mill district in the agricultural, not industrial, sense) north of Linz to the Czech border is made up of meadows and gentle wooded hills interspersed with towns whose appearance has changed little since the Middle Ages. To the west of Linz, south of the Danube, lies the **Innviertel,** named for the Inn river (which forms the border with Germany before it joins the Danube), a region of broad fields and meadows, of enormous woodland tracts, ideal for cycling, hiking, and riding. To the south, the hilly landscape with its many streams and forested areas begins the foothills of the Austrian Alps.

㉜ To get to **Freistadt,** a preserved walled city in the eastern part of the Mühlviertel, cross the Danube to Linz–Urfahr and turn right onto Freistädter Strasse (Route 125/E55).

Freistadt developed as a border defense city on the salt route into Bohemia (now the Czech Republic), which accounts for the wall, towers, and gates. Look at the Late Gothic **Linzertor,** the Linz gate, with its steep wedge-shaped roof, and the **Böhmertor,** on the opposite side, leading to Bohemia. Walk around the wall to get an impression of how a city in the Middle Ages was conceived and defended; it will take you about a half hour. The city's central square, aglow with pastel facades, is virtually the same as that of 400 years ago, with no jarring modern buildings; only the parked cars intrude into the picture.

Wander through the alleys behind the central square and note the architectural details; many of the arcades contain interesting small shops. The 15th-century parish church of St. Catherine's was redone in Baroque style in the 17th century but retains its slender tower, whose unusual balconies have railings on all four sides. The Late Gothic castle to the northeast of the square now houses the Mühlviertel district museum (Heimathaus); the display of painted glass (for which the nearby town of Sandl is famous) in the chapel and the hand tools in the 50-meter (163-foot) tower are especially interesting. *Tel. 07942/2274. Admission: AS10 adults, children free. Guided tours only: May–Oct., Tues.–Sat. 10 and 2; Sun., holidays, 10; Nov.–Apr., Tues.–Fri. 10; Tues. and Thurs. also at 2.*

㉝ On the way back from Freistadt, detour slightly east to **Kefermarkt,** about 10½ kilometers (6½ miles) south. Here in the Late Gothic St. Wolfgang's church is one of Europe's great anonymous art treasures, a 13-meter- (42-foot) high winged altar intricately carved from linden wood and completed in 1497.

About 26 kilometers (16¼ miles) west of Linz on Route 129 lies
③④ **Eferding,** a centuries-old community with an attractive town
square. The more adventuresome route to Eferding is via the
LILO (Linzer Lokalbahn) interurban railway from Christian-
Coulin-Str. 30 (tel. 0732/654376), near the main rail station. In
the town itself, the double door in the south wall of the 15th-
century church of St. Hippolyte is a gem of Late Gothic stone-
cutting, with the madonna and child above flanked by Saints
Hippolyte and Agyd. Inside, note the Gothic altar with its five
reliefs and the statues of Saints Wolfgang and Martin. Visit the
Spitalskirche (originally built in 1325) and note the Gothic frescoes in the Magdalen chapel, which date to about 1430.

Take Route 130 north from Eferding to Pupping, and follow
signs for the turnoff on the left to **Schaunberg's** castle ruin.
Otherwise, continue 3 kilometers (2 miles) up the road from
③⑤ Pupping to the parish church at **Hartkirchen,** to see fine Baroque wall and ceiling frescoes that create the illusion of space
and depth. And 2 km (1 mi) farther (Route 131), on the Danube,
③⑥ is **Aschach,** a small village that was once a river toll station,
with gabled-roof burgher houses, a castle, and a Late Gothic
church.

③⑦ Southeast of Linz lies **St. Florian,** best known for the great abbey where the composer Anton Bruckner (1824–1896) was organist for 10 years and where he is buried. Take the road south
to Kleinmünchen and Ebelsberg, or for a most romantic approach, try the **Florianer Bahn,** a resurrected electric interurban tram line, which runs museum streetcars on Sunday and
holidays 6 km (nearly 4 mi) from Pichling to St. Florian (tel.
0732/485323, 0732/236107, or 07224/4333; departures 11:10,
2:10, 3:10, 5:10). Guided tours include a magnificent figured
gate encompassing all three stories, a large and elegant staircase leading to the upper floors, major rooms grouped around
the inner courtyard, and the imperial suite. In the splendid abbey church, where the ornate decor is somewhat in contrast to
Bruckner's music, the Krismann organ (1770–1774) is one of
the largest and best of its period. *Tel. 07224/8903–10. Admission: AS50 adults, AS15 children. Guided tours only, 1½ hrs.
Apr.–Oct., daily at 10, 11, 2, 3, 4.*

Take Route 139 southwest (or the train) from Linz to the vast
③⑧ Benedictine abbey at **Kremsmünster,** established in 777, one of
the most important cloisters in Austria. Inside the church is
the Gothic memorial tomb of Gunther, killed by a wild boar,
whose father, Tassilo, duke of Bavaria, vowed to build the abbey on the site. There are magnificent rooms: the **Kaisersaal**
and the frescoed library with more than 100,000 volumes, many
of them manuscripts. On one side of the **Prälatenhof** courtyard
are four elegant fish basins amid splendid Baroque statuary,
and opposite is the **Abteitrakt,** whose art collection includes the
Tassilo chalice, from about 765. The eight-story observatory
houses an early museum of science. The "mosque" garden
house from 1640 has Oriental decoration. *Tel. 07583/275216.
Admission to rooms and art gallery: AS45 adults, AS20 children. Guided tours daily (minimum 5 persons), Easter–Oct.
10, 11, 2, 3, 4; Nov.–Easter 11 and 2. Observatory: Admission
with tour AS50 adults, AS20 children; tours daily (minimum 5
persons), May–Nov. 10, 2 (July–Aug. at 4 also).*

Where Route 139 joins Route 122, cut south to **Bad Hall,** known
for its saline-iodine curative springs. Tassilo, who founded

Kremsmünster, gave the springs to the abbey in 777, but the town is now an independent spa.

About 17 kilometers (10½ miles) farther along Route 122, at the confluence of the Steyr and Enns rivers, you'll come to **Steyr,** a stunning Gothic market town. Today the main square is lined with pastel facades, many with Baroque and Rococo trim, all complemented by the castle that sits above. On the Enns side, steps and narrow passageways lead down to the river. So many of the houses are worthy of attention that you have to take your time and explore. The **Bummerlhaus** at No. 32, in its present form dating to 1497, has a Late Gothic three-story effect. The Steyrertalbahn, a narrow-gauge museum railroad, wanders 17 kilometers (10½ miles) from Steyr through the countryside. (For information, tel. 07252/46569 or 0732/250345.)

Tour 4: The South Bank of the Danube, the Wachau

South of the Danube is a district of gentle countryside crossed by the valleys of rivers that rise in the Alps and eventually feed the Danube. Little evidence remains today, in this prosperous country of small-industry and agriculture, that the area was heavily fought over in the final days of World War II.

The return trip east starts at **Enns.** A settlement has existed continuously here at least since AD 50; the Romans set up a major encampment shortly after that date. From 1945 to 1955, the Enns river east of the city marked the border between the Soviet occupation zone and the U.S. zone.

Enns is dominated by the 56-meter (184-foot) square city tower (1565–1568) that stands in the town square. A number of Gothic buildings in the center have Renaissance or Baroque facades. Visit the **St. Laurence basilica,** built on the foundations of a far earlier church, west of the town center, to view the glass-encased layers of earlier civilizations discovered by archaeologists. And outside, look for the Baroque carved-wood Pontius Pilate disguised as a Turk, alongside a hand-bound Christ, on the balcony of the old reliquary.

Take the A1 autobahn or Route 1 east from Enns to just before Amstetten, where Route 121 cuts south paralleling the Ybbs river and the branch rail line for about 25 kilometers (16 miles) to **Waidhofen an der Ybbs.** This appealing river town developed early as an industrial center, turning Styrian iron ore into swords, knives, sickles, and scythes. These weapons proved successful in the defense against the Turks in 1532; in remembrance, the hands on the north side of the town tower clock remain at 12:45. In 1871, Baron Rothschild bought the collapsing castle and assigned Friedrich Schmidt, architect of the Vienna city hall, to rebuild it in neo-Gothic style. Stroll around the two squares in the Altstadt to see the Gothic and Baroque houses, and to the Graben on the edge of the old city for the delightful Biedermeier houses and the churches and chapels.

Make your way back to the Danube via Routes 31 and 22 east, then Route 25 north through the beer-brewing town of Wieselburg to **Ybbs an der Donau.** Or retrace your steps up Route 121 and take the autobahn. Floods and fires have left their mark here, but many 16th-century and Renaissance houses remain, their courtyards vine-covered and shaded. The parish church of St. Laurence has interesting old tombstones, a gorgeous gilded organ, and a Mount of Olives scene with clay figures dating to 1450.

From Ybbs, backtrack 2 kilometers (1 mile) on Route 25 to Route 1, then head northeast for about 1½ kilometers (1 mile) until you come to a road on the left marked to Sarling and Sausenstein. Follow it to **Pöchlarn**, the birthplace (in 1886) of the artist Oskar Kokoschka, whose dramatic and colorful oils are in museums around the world. His birthplace is now a museum that has special exhibits every year. *Regensburger Str. 29, tel. 02757/7656. Admission: AS30. Open mid-May–Sept., Tues.–Sun. 9–noon and 2–5.*

Continuing eastward through Pöchlarn brings you back to Route 1. About 4 kilometers (2½ miles) on, you'll glimpse the **㊸** magnificent **Melk** abbey ahead, on its promontory above the river, one of the great views in all Austria. The ideal time for this approach is mid- to late afternoon, when the sun sets the abbey's ornate yellow facade aglow.

Melk by any standard is a Baroque masterpiece. Here the story of Umberto Eco's historical novel and film *The Name of the Rose* took place, and in fact as in fiction, the monastery did burn in 1297, in 1683, and again in 1735. The Benedictine abbey was established in 1089; the building you see today dates to 1736, although earlier elements are incorporated. A tour of the building will include the main public rooms: the magnificent library, with more than 70,000 books, 2,000 manuscripts, and a superb ceiling fresco by the master Paul Troger; the marble hall, whose windows on three sides enhance the ceiling frescoes; the glorious spiral staircase; and the church of Saints Peter and Paul, an exquisite example of Baroque. Note the side altars and the portraits of the saints; the artist Paul Troger was active here, too. *Abt. Berthold Dietmayr-Str. 1, tel. 02752/2312. Admission: AS45 adults, AS20 children; with guided tour, AS55 adults, AS30 children. Open Apr.–Sept., daily 9–5 (guided tours hourly); Oct., daily 9–4; Nov.–Mar., by tour only at 11 and 2. Tours last about 50 min. Combination tickets available with Schloss Artstetten (see Tour 1, above) and Schloss Schallaburg (see below).*

Time Out The **Stiftsrestaurant** here offers standard fare, but the abbey's excellent wines elevate a simple meal to an experience—particularly on a sunny day on the terrace. The roast chicken is good with the dry white wines. *Closed Nov.–Apr.*

From Melk, a road south marked to Mank and **Schloss Schallaburg** will bring you to this restored Protestant castle (dating from 1573) with an imposing two-story arcaded courtyard, the finest example of Renaissance architecture in the area. The warm brown terra-cotta decoration is unusual and ornate. The yard served as a jousting court. The Romanesque living quarters include an ornate Gothic chapel, and the castle now houses changing special exhibits. *Tel. 02754/6317. Admission: AS50 adults, AS15 children, AS30 senior citizens, AS80 family. Guided tours AS20 per person extra. Combined tickets with Melk abbey: AS75; with Schloss Artstetten: AS87. Open mid-May–Oct., weekdays 9–5, weekends and holidays 9–6.*

From Schallaburg, return to Melk. Take Route 33 along the south bank, and you're back in the Wachau again. About 4 kilometers (2½ miles) along, you'll come to **Schönbühel an der Donau,** whose unbelievably picturesque castle, perched on a cliff overlooking the Danube, is unfortunately not open to visitors.

Past **Aggsbach Dorf** you'll spot, on a hill to your right, the romantic ruin of 13th-century Aggstein castle, reportedly the lair of pirates who preyed on river traffic.

Mautern, opposite Krems, was a Roman encampment mentioned in the tales of the Nibelungen. The old houses and the castle are attractive, but contemporary Mautern is known for one of Austria's top restaurants, in an inn run by Lisl Bacher; in nearby Klein-Wien there's another—also superb—run by her sister (*see* Dining and Lodging, *below).*

44 You're bound to have seen **Stift Göttweig** as you came along the riverside road: The vast Benedictine abbey high above the Danube valley watches over the gateway to the Wachau. To reach it, go along Route 33, turn right into the highway south (marked to Stift Göttweig and St. Pölten), and turn right again (marked to Stift Göttweig) at the crest of the hill. Göttweig's exterior was redone in the mid-1700s in classic style, which you'll note from the columns, balcony, and relatively plain side towers. Inside, it is a monument to Baroque art, with marvelous ornate decoration against the gold, brown, and blue. The stained-glass windows behind the high altar date to the mid-1400s. The public rooms of the abbey are splendid, particularly the Kaiserzimmer (emperor's rooms), in which Napoleon stayed in 1809, reached via the elegant emperor's staircase. Depending on the schedule of exhibitions, rooms may or may not be open to view. In postwar years, surprising treasures turned up in the Göttweig library, including original musical scores by Haydn and Mozart. *Furth bei Göttweig, tel. 02732/855810. Admission: AS35 adults, AS20 children. Guided tours only (minimum 8 persons), Easter–Oct., daily at 10, 11, 2, 3, and 4.*

Time Out The terrace of the **Stiftsrestaurant** on the abbey grounds offers not only good local cuisine but, on a fine day, a spectacular view. It's a great spot for lunch, coffee, or a drink. You might try—and buy by the bottle—the excellent wines produced by the abbey.

45 You may want to make a detour 20 kilometers (12½ miles) south to **St. Pölten,** Lower Austria's capital. The old center of the city, now mainly a pedestrian zone, shows a distinctly Baroque face: The originally Romanesque cathedral on Domplatz has a rich Baroque interior; the Rococo Franciscan church at the north end of the Rathausplatz has four altar paintings by Kremser Schmidt. The Institute of English Maidens (a former convent) in nearby Linzer Strasse is one of the finest Baroque buildings in the city. The church contains frescoes by master Paul Troger.

Take Wiener Strasse (Route 1) out of St. Pölten headed east for 12 kilometers (8 miles) to Kapelln, then turn left to **Herzogenburg.** In the great Augustine cloister here, the buildings date mainly to the mid-1700s. Fischer von Erlach was among the architects who designed the abbey. The church, dedicated to Saints George and Stephen, is ornate Baroque. *Tel. 02782/3112. Admission: AS40 adults, AS10 children.*

Open daily Apr.–Oct. Guided tours only (about 1 hr) on the hr, 9–noon and 1–5.

Head north on Route S33 or the parallel road, marked to Traismauer, and pick up Route 43 east. If you're ready for back roads (too well marked for you to get lost), cut off to the left to Oberbierbaum (Upper Beer Tree!) and then on to Zwentendorf (there's a fascinating black madonna in the side chapel of the parish church here). If you follow Route 43, it will land you on Route 1 at Mitterndorf; drive east and after 4 kilometers (2½ miles), turn left off Route 1 onto Route 19, marked for Tulln.

46 At **Tulln,** you'll spot a number of charming Baroque touches in the attractive main square. There's a new museum to honor the artist Egon Schiele (1890–1918), who was born here. *Donaulände 26, tel. 02272/4570. Admission: AS30 adults, AS15 children. Open Tues.–Sun. 9–noon and 2–6.*

The Romanesque parish church of St. Stephen on Wiener Strasse is noteworthy for its west door and the six figures carved in relief circles on each side (presumably the 12 apostles). Beside the church, the unusual combined chapel (upstairs) and charnel house (below) is in a structure that successfully combines late Romanesque and early Gothic.

Drive east on Route 14 and turn left at St. Andrä-Wördern to hug the Danube shoreline en route to **Greifenstein.** Atop the hill, another castle with a spectacular view looks up the Danube and across to Stockerau. Its earliest parts date to 1135, but most stems from a thorough but romantic renovation in 1818. The view is worth the climb, even when the castle is closed. *Kostersitzgasse 5, tel. 02242/32353. Currently closed.*

47 As you come down into **Klosterneuburg,** the great Augustine abbey dominates the scene. It has changed many times since it was established in 1114, most recently in 1892, when Friedrich Schmidt, architect of Vienna's city hall, added neo-Gothic features to its two identifying towers. Klosterneuburg was unusual in that until 1568 it had both men's and women's orders.

In the abbey church, look for the carved wood choir and oratory and the large 17th-century organ. Among Klosterneuburg's treasures are the beautifully enameled 1181 Verdun Altar in the Leopold chapel, stained-glass windows from the 14th and 15th centuries, Romanesque candelabra from the 12th century, and gorgeous ceiling frescoes in the great marble hall. In the wine cellar there's a huge cask over which people slide. The exercise, called *Fasslrutsch'n,* is indulged in during the *Leopoldiweinkost,* the wine tasting around St. Leopold's day, November 15. *Stiftsplatz 1, tel. 02243/621–0212. Admission: AS40 adults, AS15 children; guided tours only (about 1 hour) every half-hour, Mon.–Sat. 9–11 and 1:30–5; Sun. and holidays 11, 1:30–5.*

Time Out | Stop at **Café Veit** (Niedermarkt 13) for coffee (house-roasted), or tea (25 varieties). Try the potato soup or the semolina dumpling soup and finish with an excellent apple strudel.

About 3 kilometers (2 miles) down the road, off to the right tucked under Leopoldsberg, is the charming small vintners' village of **Kahlenbergerdorf,** an excellent spot to stop and sample the local wines. And you're now on the outskirts of Vienna, where our trip began.

What to See and Do with Children

Burg Kreuzenstein (*see* Tour 1, *above*).

The trip up the **Pöstlingberg** (*see* Tour 2, *above*) to the fairy-tale grotto and the zoo.

The museum at **Schloss Ebelsberg** in Linz (take Wiener Strasse from Blumauerplatz near the main rail station, or streetcar 1 to Simonystrasse and change to bus 11 to Ebelsberg) shows weapons, from the breech loader to the automatic rifle, and has a collection of old-time cars and motorcycles. *Schlossweg 7, Ebelsberg, tel. 0732/307632. Admission: AS40 adults, AS25 children. Open June–Oct., weekends and holidays 10–noon, 1–5.*

The **Florianer Bahn** from Pichling to St. Florian (*see* Tour 3, *above*).

The **Steyrertalbahn** (*see* Tour 3, *above*).

The castle at **Kremsegg,** on Route 139 near Kremsmunster, has a collection of old-fashioned cars and motorcycles. *Tel. 07583/ 247–14. Admission: AS70 adults, AS30 children. Open Sat. 1–5, Sun., holidays 10–noon, 1–5; July–Aug., daily 10–noon, 1–5.*

In a moated castle north of **Pottenbrunn,** 6½ kilometers (4 miles) east of St. Pölten, there's a museum *(Zinnfiguren-museum)* of tin soldiers. Imagine a bird's-eye view of entire armies in battle; you'll see thousands of soldiers, at their places in the battles of Leipzig (1813), Berg Isel (Innsbruck, 1809), Vienna (1683), and World War I. *Pottenbrunner Hauptstr. 77, tel. 02785/2337. Admission: AS40 adults, AS15 children, AS80 family. Open mid-Apr.–Oct., Tues.–Sun. 9–5.*

The **Feuerwehrmuseum** (Firefighters' Museum) in St. Florian displays equipment from the Baroque era to the present day. St. Florian, the patron saint of firefighters and the guardian against fire, is easily recognized in Austrian churches as a figure pouring water from a bucket over a blazing house. *Stiftstr. 3, tel. 07224/219. Admission: AS25 adults, AS15 children. Open May–Oct., Tues.–Sun. 9–noon, 2–4.*

Off the Beaten Track

There's a marvelous *Heuriger* (wine garden) at Hollenburg, 1 kilometer (½ mile) up the hill after the intersection of Routes 33 and S33, southeast of Krems, then about 5½ kilometers (3½ miles) east—the turnoff is marked to Thallern. The setting is on a hill above the Danube, and there's even a castle ruin. The **Ruinenheuriger** is one of those seasonal places that's open when it's open, so call ahead. The wines come from the Geymüller vineyards; nearly everybody in the town appears to be a vintner. *Tel. 07239/2287.*

Steyr has an intriguing section of abandoned industrial buildings along the Steyr river (take Gaswerkgasse and turn down to the river). In the same area, you'll see workers' housing of 100 years ago.

Shopping

If you want to shop for wine, you're in the ideal area. St. Pölten has more standard items, and you will find good local souvenirs in Krems and Enns. Linz is a good place to shop; prices are generally lower than those in resorts and other large cities, and selections are good. The major shops are found in the main square and the adjoining side streets, in the old quarter to the west of the main square, in the pedestrian zone of the Landstrasse and its side streets, and in the Hauptstrasse of Urfahr, over the Niebelungen bridge across the Danube. For local handmade items and good-quality souvenirs, try **Ö.Ö. Heimatwerk** (Landstr. 31, Linz, tel. 0732/773–3760), where you'll find silver, pewter, ceramics, fabrics, and some clothing. Items from clothing to china are sold at the **Flea Market** (March–mid-November, Saturday 7–2) on the Hauptplatz (main square). In winter the market moves across the river next to the new city hall. The state-run "Dorotheum" auction house is at Fabrikstrasse 26 (tel. 0732/773132).

For antiques go to the old city, on the side streets around the main square. Try **Otto Buchinger** (Bethlehemstr. 5, tel. 0732/770117), **Richard Kirchmayr** (Bischofstr. 3a, tel. 0732/276–9843), **Kunsthandlung Kirchmayr** (Herrenstr. 23, tel. 0732/774667), **Ute Pastl** (Wischerstr. 26, Urfahr, tel. 0732/237306), and **Heinz Roland** (Khevenhüllerstr. 25, tel. 0732/663003). For jewelry, try **Pfaffenberger** (Landstr. 42, tel. 0732/772495) or **Wild** (Landstr. 49, tel. 0732/774105).

Sports and the Outdoors

Participant Sports

Bicycling The trail along the Danube must be one of the great bicycle routes of the world. For much of the way (the exception being the Korneuburg–Krems stretch) you can take this trip by bike on either side of the river. For details and information, *see* Getting Around, By Bicycle, above. Get the folder "Danube Cycle Track" (in English, from Niederösterreich-Information, Heidenschuss 2, A–1010 Vienna, tel. 0222/533–4773, fax 0222/535–0319) for hints on what to see and where you'll find "cyclist-friendly" accommodations, repairs, and other services. Some small hotels will even pick up you and your bike from the cycle path. You'll find bicycle rentals at Aggsbach–Markt, Dürnstein, Grein, Krems, Mautern, Melk, Persenbeug-Gottsdorf, Pöchlarn, Schönbühel/Aggsbach Dorf, Spitz, Weissenkirchen, and Ybbs.

The terrain around Linz is relatively level, and within the city there are 89 kilometers (55 miles) of marked cycle routes. Get the brochure "Cycling in Linz" from the tourist office. You can rent a bike through Fahrradzentrum B7 (Bischofstr. 7, tel. 0732/771986, open Mon.–Fri. 8–6). In the areas of Eferding, St. Florian, through the Enns river valley, and around Steyr, the territory is generally good for cycling, with gentle hills and special routes. Bicycles can be rented at the railroad stations in Freistadt (tel. 07942/2319) and Steyr (tel. 07252/5950), or privately in Kremsmünster (tel. 07583/7498 or 07583/304).

MCI brings Europe and America closer together.

Call the U.S. for less with MCI CALL USA®

It's easy and affordable to call home when you use MCI CALL USA!

- Less expensive than calling through hotel operators
- Available from over 80 countries and locations worldwide
- You're connected to English-speaking MCI® Operators
- Even call 800 numbers in the U.S.[†]

†Regular MCI CALL USA rates apply to 800 number calls.

Call the U.S. for less from these European locations.

Dial the toll-free access number for the country you're calling from.
Give the U.S. MCI Operator the number you're calling and the method of payment: MCI Card, U.S. local phone company card or collect. Your call will be completed!

Austria	022-903-012	Hungary	00*-800-01411	Poland	0*-01-04-800-222
Belgium	078-11-00-12	Ireland	1-800-551-001	Portugal	05-017-1234
Czech/Slovak	00-42-000112	Italy	172-1022	San Marino	172-1022
Denmark	8001-0022	Liechtenstein	155-0222	Spain	900-99-0014
Finland	9800-102-80	Luxembourg	0800-0112	Sweden	020-795-922
France	19*-00-19	Monaco	19*-00-19	Switzerland	155-0222
Germany	0130-0012	Netherlands	06*-022-91-22	United Kingdom	0800-89-0222
Greece	00-800-1211	Norway	050-12912	Vatican City	172-1022

* Wait for 2nd dial tone.
Collect calls not accepted on MCI CALL USA calls to 800 numbers.
Some public phones may require deposit of coin or phone card for dial tone.

Call 1-800-444-3333 in the U.S. to apply for your MCI Card® now!

6/93

Spend your
vacation
touring
castles.
Not train
stations.

© 1993 Budget Rent a Car Corporation

Vacation Cars. Vacation Prices. Wherever your destination
in Europe, there is sure to be one of more than 1,000 Budget locations near
Budget offers considerable values on a wide variety of quality cars, and if
you book before you leave the U.S., you'll save even more with a special
rate package from the Budget World Travel Plan[SM] For information and
reservations, contact your travel consultant or call Budget in the U.S. at
800-472-3325. Or, while traveling abroad, call a Budget reservation cente

THE SMART MONEY IS ON BUDGET.

We feature Ford and other fine cars.   *A system of corporate and licensee owned locatio*

Canoeing The Danube in general is fast and tricky, so you're best off sticking to the calmer waters back of the power dams (at Pöchlarn, above Melk, and near Grein). You can rent a canoe at Pöchlarn. You can also canoe on an arm of the Danube near Ottensheim, about 8 kilometers (5 miles) west of Linz. For information call Ruderverein Donau (tel. 0732/236250) or Ruderverein Ister-Sparkasse (tel. 0732/774888).

Fishing This is splendid fishing country. Check with the town tourist offices about licenses and fishing rights for river trolling and fly-casting in Aggsbach–Markt, Dürnstein, Emmersdorf, Grein, Kleinpöchlarn, Krems, Mautern, Mauthausen, Persenbeug–Gottsdorf, Pöchlarn, Schönbühel/Aggsbach Dorf, Spitz, Waidhofen/Ybbs, and Ybbs. In Linz, check **Fischereiverband** (Kärntnerstr. 12, tel. 0732/650507) or **Weitgasser** (Figulystr. 5, tel. 0732/656566).

In the streams and lakes of the area around Linz, you can fly-cast for rainbow and brook trout and troll for pike and carp. For details, contact the tourist offices or the numbers listed below: Aschach (Dreihann-Harrach'sche Gutsverwaltung, tel. 07273/6312), Attersee (Franz Zotter, tel. 07666/334), Bad Hall (Gasthof Schröck "Hofwirt," hotel guests only, tel. 07258/2274), Freistadt (Sportgeschäft Gutenbrunner, tel. 07942/2720; Sportgeschäft Juch, tel. 07942/2532), Grein (Sparkasse Mauthausen, tel. 07268/203), Kremsmünster (Gerhard Fleck, tel. 07583/6103), Steyr (Angelsportverein Steyr, tel. 07252/615443).

Golf An 18-hole, par-72 course at **Tillysburg,** near St. Florian, is open April to November, but you'll have to caddy for yourself. *Tillysburg, St. Florian bei Linz, tel. 07223/2873. Greens fee: AS480 Mon.–Thurs., AS580 Fri.–Sun.* A number of other clubs have opened in the area, among them an 18-hole par-72 championship course in Bad Hall. *Golfclub Herzog Tassilo, Blankenbergerstr., tel. 07258/5480. Greens fee: AS400 weekdays, AS500 weekends.* There are additional courses in Bad Ischl, Mondsee, and Wels.

Health and Fitness Clubs To keep fit in Linz, try **Olympic** (Rudigierstr. 1, tel. 0732/776156; open weekdays 10–9, Sat. 2–6, Sun. 10–2) or **Sportstudio California** (Landwiedstr. 119, tel. 0732/341157; open weekdays 10–9, weekends 10–2).

Hiking You could hardly ask for better hiking country: From the level ground of the Danube valley, hills rise on both sides, giving great views when you reach the upper levels. There are *Wanderwege* (marked hiking paths) virtually everywhere; local tourist offices have maps and route details, and in Linz you can get the booklet "Urban Hiking Paths in Linz." Around the city you might retrace the route of the Linz–Budweis horse-drawn tramway, Continental Europe's first railway, or wander from one castle to another. You can arrange to hike in the Mühlviertel from Freistadt to Grein (information: tel. 0732/235020) and even get your pack transferred from hotel to hotel.

Jogging Runners also use the bicycle trail along the Danube. The place to jog in Linz is along the river bank on the far side of the Danube (Urfahr).

Skating Linz is an ice-skating city; from late October to late February, there's outdoor skating daily 2–5 and 6–9 (no evening skating on Thursday), weekends and holidays also 9–noon, and indoors from late September to April, Wednesday 9–noon, Saturday 2–5, Sunday 10–noon, 2–5, 6–9. *Untere Donaulände 11, tel. 0732/778513.*

Tennis You'll find tennis courts—indoors and out—in nearly every town. Ask at the tourist offices in Aggsbach–Markt, Dürnstein, Grein, Krems, Maria Taferl, Mautern, Persenbeug–Gottsdorf, Pöchlarn, Spitz, Waidhofen/Ybbs, and Weissenkirchen. In Linz, contact the Upper Austrian Tennis Association (Waldeggstr. 16, tel. 0732/7651250). The Novotel also has two clay courts (Wankmüllerhofstr. 37, tel. 0732/347281).

In the country around Linz, there are courts in Bad Hall (Kurverwaltung, tel. 07258/20310), Freistadt (UTC Union, tel. 07942/2570), Kremsmünster (Tennishallenbetrib, tel. 07583/395, and Tennis-Center Stadlhuber, tel. 07583/7498), and Steyr (Tennishof Rottenbrunner, tel. 07252/61219).

Water Sports and Swimming Water sports are available all along the Danube (check with the tourist offices in Krems, Mautern, and Pöchlarn), but the Danube is not for swimming. Virtually every town has an outdoor pool, and some have them indoors as well. You'll find large pools at Artstetten, Dürnstein, Grein, Krems, Maria Taferl, Mauthausen, Melk, Pöchlarn, Schönbühel/Aggsbach–Dorf, Spitz, and Waidhofen/Ybbs. All are family facilities, with changing rooms and lockers; most have snack bars or restaurants, too. In Linz, the Kral Waterskiing School offers waterskiing and other water sports (Talgasse 14, 0732/231494). The closest swimming is at the Pleschinger lake; to get there, take the No. 1 tram to Urfahr/Reindlstrasse and the No. 32 bus to the lake. This is a pleasant spot for family swimming, although it tends to be crowded on sunny, warm weekends.

Spectator Sports

Soccer matches are played in Linz in the **Stadion** (Roseggerstr. 41, tel. 0732/656055 or 0732/660670). Tennis matches and other sports events are held at the adjacent **Stadthalle** (tel. 0732/657311). Hockey and skating competitions are held in the **Eishalle.** Buy tickets for sports events at Kartenbüro Ruefa (Landstr. 67, tel. 0732/662–6810, fax 0732/662681–33; open weekdays 8:30–noon, 2–6; Sat. 8:30–noon).

Dining and Lodging

Dining

The restaurants in this chapter are varied; they range from sophisticated and stylish to plain. Where possible, they capitalize on the river view, and outdoor dining is common. Many of the towns along both sides of the Danube will have country inns with dining rooms rather than separate restaurants. Prices include tax and a service charge, but it is customary to leave a small additional tip.

Highly recommended restaurants are indicated by a star ★.

Category	Cost*
Very Expensive	over AS500
Expensive	AS300–AS500
Moderate	AS200–AS300
Inexpensive	under AS200

per person for a typical three-course meal with a glass of house wine

Lodging

On this trip you might stay in a castle hotel, a standard city hotel, or a country inn. Distances are short between tours, so you can easily stay in one place and drive to another to try a different restaurant. Room rates include taxes and service and almost always breakfast (except in the most expensive hotels), but it is wise to ask. It is customary to leave a small (AS20) additional tip for the chambermaid.

Highly recommended lodgings are indicated by a star ★ .

Category	Cost*
Very Expensive	over AS1,500
Expensive	AS1,000–AS1,500
Moderate	AS700–AS1,000
Inexpensive	under AS700

All prices are for a standard double room, including tax and service.

Aschach/Feldkirchen

Dining and Lodging
★

Faust Schlössl. Once a toll-collection station belonging to the Schaunberg family (ruins of the family castle are nearby), this castle, on the river directly across from Aschach, is said to be haunted and to have been built by the Devil in a single night for Dr. Faustus. Ignore the tale and enjoy simple but modern comfort in the converted castle among the towers and turrets. *Oberlandshaag 2, A–4082 Feldkirchen, tel. 07233/7402. 25 rooms. Facilities: restaurant (closed Tues.), outdoor pool, bicycle rental, fishing. No credit cards. Moderate.*

Zur Sonne. The welcome of the bright yellow facade carries over to the comfortable traditional decor inside. You're right on the Danube here, and the best rooms have a river view. The popular restaurant offers regional and traditional specialties and, of course, fish, including fresh trout. *Kurzwernhartplatz 5, A–4082 Aschach/Donau, tel. 07273/6308. 12 rooms with bath or shower. Facilities: restaurant (closed Fri. Oct.–Easter). No credit cards. Moderate.*

Bad Hall

Dining and Lodging
★

Schlosshotel Feyregg. You'll be in an exclusive setting in this Baroque castle just outside town, the elegant summer residence of an abbot. The comfortable, spacious guest rooms on the ground floor are furnished in period style. *A–4540 Bad Hall/*

Feyregg-Pfarrkirchen, tel. 07258/2591. 14 rooms. Facilities: restaurant, bar, garage. No credit cards. Very Expensive.

Herzog Tassilo Kurhotel. The yellow exterior of this turn-of-the-century house reflects the friendly attitude within. Rooms are comfortable if not luxurious, but the main attractions are the vast park in which the hotel is set and the opportunity to "take the cure" under medical supervision for eye, heart, or circulation complaints. Minimum half-board is required. *Parkstr. 4, A-4540 Bad Hall, tel. 07258/26110, fax 07258/2611–5. 53 rooms in main building, 30 in two adjacent villas. Facilities: restaurant, café, bar, indoor pool, sauna, solarium, fitness room, garage. AE, DC, MC, V. Very Expensive.*

Dürnstein

Dining **Loibnerhof.** Here, in an idyllic setting on the banks of the Danube, you'll dine on interesting variations on Austrian themes: ravioli with blood-sausage filling and various grilled fish or lamb specialties. The garden is enchanting in summer, but on weekends it's packed, and service tends to suffer. The excellent wines come from the restaurant's own vineyards. *Unterloiben 7, tel. 02732/82890. Reservations advised on weekends. Dress: casual. No credit cards. Closed mid-Jan.–mid-Feb. and Mon.–Tues. Very Expensive.*

Zum Goldenen Strauss. A onetime post station, long a simple *Gasthaus*, now has ambitions to be something more. You'll be offered substantial portions of very good Austrian fare, with a flair that helps compensate for the occasionally slow service. Try the garlic soup followed by *Tafelspitz.* The dining rooms inside are cozy, the terrace a delight. *Tel. 02711/267. No reservations. Dress: casual but neat. No credit cards. Closed Tues. and mid-Jan.–mid-Mar. Moderate.*

Lodging **Richard Löwenherz.** The superb vaulted reception and dining rooms of this former convent are beautifully furnished with antiques. Though spacious and comfortable, the balconied guest rooms in the newer part of the house are more modern in decor and furnishings. A terrace overlooking the Danube offers stunning views. The restaurant is known for its regional specialties and local wines. *A-3601, tel. 02711/222, fax 02711/222–18. 40 rooms. Facilities: restaurant, bar, outdoor pool, parking. AE, DC, MC, V. Closed Nov.–mid-Mar. Very Expensive.*

★ **Schlosshotel Dürnstein.** If there's to be one big fling on your trip, it might well be here. This 17th-century early Baroque castle, on a rocky terrace with exquisite views over the Danube, offers dream accommodations, surrounds you with genuine elegance and comfort, and has a particularly friendly and helpful staff. The best rooms look onto the river, but all are unusually bright and attractive; of moderate size, they have pillows, comfortable chairs, and country antiques throughout. Half-board is required. The kitchen has a good reputation, and wines are from the area. Dining on the terrace is a memorable experience. *A-3601, tel. 02711/212, fax 02711/351. 37 rooms. Facilities: restaurant (reservations advised, jacket and tie advised), bar, indoor and outdoor pools, sauna, solarium, garage. AE, MC, V. Closed Nov.–Mar. Very Expensive.*

Sänger Blondel. Behind the yellow facade is a very friendly, typical, traditional family hotel, with elegant country rooms of medium size that have attractive paneling and antique decorations. The staff is particularly helpful and can suggest several excursions in the area. The hotel is known for its restaurant, which features local specialties and a wide range of salads and lighter dishes. You can even buy a loaf of the house bread or a jar of the apricot marmalade. *A–3601, tel. 02711/253, fax 02711/253–7. 16 rooms. Facilities: restaurant (reservations advised on weekends, jacket advised, closed Sun. eve., Mon.), bicycle rental, garage. No credit cards. Restaurant and hotel closed mid-Nov.–Mar. Moderate.*

Eferding

Dining **Dannerbauer.** Two kilometers (1¼ miles) north of Eferding on the road to Aschach, right on the Danube, is one of the area's best restaurants. It serves species of fish you probably never heard of, poached, grilled, broiled, or fried. Many of the fish come from the river; some are kept in the house tanks, to ensure freshness. There are meat dishes, too, and game (delicious wild hare) in season, and the soups (try the nettle soup) are excellent. The place has a pleasant outlook with lots of windows. *Brandstatt bei Eferding, tel. 07272/2471. Reservations advised. Jacket suggested. AE, DC. Closed Mon., Tues., and Feb. Expensive.*

Dining and **Zum Goldenen Kreuz.** The golden facade indicates a typical
Lodging country-style hotel, simple but with the charm of a family-run establishment. You'll sleep on fluffy featherbeds. The restaurant is known for its good regional cuisine, and there are occasional specialty weeks. *Schmiedstr. 29, A–4070, tel. 07272/ 42470, fax 07272/4249. 21 rooms. Facilities: restaurant (closed Sat. and Sun. night). AE, DC, MC. Closed a few days at Christmas. Moderate.*

Enns

Dining and **Lauriacum.** You might overlook this plain contemporary build-
Lodging ing, set as it is among Baroque gems in the center of town, but it's the best place to stay. The bright rooms offer modern comfort, and the quiet garden is a welcoming spot. *Wiener Str. 5–7, A–4470, tel. 07223/2315, fax 07223/2332–29. 30 rooms. Facilities: restaurant, bar, sauna, parking. MC, V. Expensive.*

Freistadt

Dining and **Deim/Zum Goldenen Hirschen.** This romantic 600-year-old
Lodging house full of atmosphere fits perfectly into the old city and is a
★ wonderful place to stay. The rooms are up-to-date and attractive. The stone-arched ceiling adds to the elegance of the dining room, where you'll find international and local specialties and game in season. *Böhmergasse 8, A–4240, tel. 07942/2258, 07942/2111, fax 07942/2258–040. 23 rooms, 19 with bath. Facilities: restaurant (closed Fri. in winter). DC. Expensive.*

★ **Zum Goldenen Adler.** Here you'll be in another 600-year-old house; it has been run by the same family since 1807, so tradition runs strong. The medium-size rooms are modern and full of country charm; hotel service is exceptionally accommodating. The newly renovated garden, with a piece of the old city wall as background, is a delightful oasis. The restaurant can be variable, but is known for regional specialties such as *Böhmisches Bierfleisch,* a cut of beef cooked in beer. The desserts are outstanding. *Salzgasse 1, A–4240, tel. 07942/2112, 07942/2556, fax*

072112–44. 30 rooms. Facilities: restaurant, pub, outdoor pool, solarium, sauna, fitness room. AE, DC. Moderate.

Göttweig/Klein Wien

Dining ★ **Schickh.** This restaurant, tucked away among lovely old trees below the north side of the Göttweig abbey, is worth looking for. The variety of dishes, from lamb to lobster, is astonishing for a small place, and the creative ideas that come out of the kitchen have made it a draw for knowledgeable diners. (It's in friendly competition with Bacher in nearby Mautern; the two are run by a pair of sisters.) In summer you'll dine in the garden, probably rubbing elbows with the Viennese elite. There's a handful of guest rooms available for overnights. *Avastr. 2, A–3511 Klein-Wien/Furth bei Göttweig, tel. 02736/218, fax 02736/218–7. Reservations required. Jacket and tie advised. No credit cards. Closed Wed., Thurs. Very Expensive.*

Klosterneuburg

Dining **Stiftskeller.** The main dining rooms are on the ground floor, but the atmospheric underground rooms in a historic part of the abbey are an authentic cellar in every sense of the word: Some of the fine wines carry the Klosterneuburg label. You can sample them along with standard Austrian fare, from Wiener schnitzel to rump steak with onions. *Albrechtsberggasse 1, tel. 02243/2070. Dress: casual but neat. Reservations advised on weekends. No credit cards. Moderate.*

Korneuburg

Dining **Tuttendörfl.** This rustic-modern restaurant is attractive, if just for the terrace right on the Danube. The kitchen turns out a long list of standard Viennese fare, good but unexciting, and there's game in season. To get here, look for the turnoff left from Route 3 (*not* the A22 autobahn) marked "Tuttendörfl," about 1½ kilometers (1 mile) west of the Bisamberg intersection and traffic light. *Tuttendörfl 6, tel. 02262/2485, fax 02262/61535. Reservations suggested on weekends. Jacket advised. No credit cards. Closed Sun., Mon., and Jan. Expensive.*

Krems/Stein

Dining and Lodging ★ **Alte Post.** You're allowed to drive into the pedestrian zone to this romantic old house in the heart of the old town, next to the Steinener Tor (west gate). The rooms are in comfortable country style, but the real feature here is dining on regional specialties or having a glass of local wine in the arcaded Renaissance courtyard. The staff is particularly friendly, and cyclists are welcome. *Obere Landstr. 32, A–3500 Krems, tel. 02732/82276. 25 rooms, 5 with bath. Facilities: restaurant, bicycle rental, garage. No credit cards. Moderate.*

Am Förthof. An inn has existed on the riverside site of this modern hotel for hundreds of years. The rooms are comfortable and balconied; those in front have a view of the Danube and Göttweig abbey across the river—and the sounds of the traffic. The dining room offers exceptionally good regional cuisine, and breakfasts are particularly recommended. *Förthofer Donaulände 8, A–3500, tel. 02732/83345, 02732/81348, fax 02732/83345–40. 22 rooms. Facilities: restaurant, outdoor*

pool, sauna, solarium, bicycle rental. DC, MC, V. Closed Fri.
lunch. Restaurant: Expensive. Hotel: Moderate.

Langenlebarn

Dining **Zum Roten Wolf.** In an unpretentious but attractive rustic res-
★ taurant (one of Austria's top 20), the stylishly elegant table settings complement the outstanding food. Try any of the lamb
variations or the breast of duck. The service is especially
friendly; ask for advice on the wines. You can get here by local
train from Vienna; the station is virtually at the door. *Bahnstr.*
58, tel. 02272/2567. Reservations required. Jacket and tie rec-
ommended. AE, DC, MC, V. Closed Mon., Tues. Expensive.

Linz

Dining **Kremsmünsterer Stuben.** In a beautifully restored house in the
★ heart of the old city you'll find an attractive wood-paneled restaurant offering everything from regional specialties to a sev-
en-course dinner. You might choose from saddle of hare or fillet
of venison as a main course as you relax in the comfortable, traditional ambience of the city's best restaurant. *Altstadt 10, tel.*
0732/782111, fax 0732/784130. Reservations advised. Jacket
and tie required. AE, DC. Closed Mon., two weeks in Jan., two
weeks in Aug. Very Expensive.
Vogelkäfig. In 1992 Georg Essig moved his restaurant, exotic
bird cages and all, from an idyllic suburban location into town;
the one trace of country remaining is the lovely garden under
chestnut trees. But the kitchen is still imaginative, featuring
such dishes as the "best from veal," with various selected cuts.
The setting and presentation help compensate for inconsisten-
cies in the kitchen. *Holzstr. 8, tel. 0732/770193. Reservations*
recommended. Jacket and tie advised. AE, DC, MC, V. Closed
Sat., Sun. Very Expensive.
Stadtwirt. Here you can expect first-class regional food in a colorful, genuinely local atmosphere (since 1622) unspoiled by
frills, and at remarkably reasonable prices. If you long for a
proper veal schnitzel, try it here. The house strudels are outstanding. *Landstr./Bismarckstr. 1, tel. 0732/773165. Reserva-*
tions useful. Jacket and tie advised. No credit cards. Closed
Sun. Moderate.
Tautermann. Downstairs you can choose from the café's
prizewinning cakes and pastries and enjoy them with coffee at
the wrought-iron tables upstairs. *Klammstr. 14, tel. 0732/*
779686. No reservations. Dress: casual but neat. No credit
cards. Closed Tues. Moderate.
★ **Traxlmayr.** This is one of Austria's great coffeehouses in the
old tradition, with the patina of age, where you can linger all
day over one cup of coffee, reading the papers in their bentwood
holders, and then have a light meal. All Linz gathers on the terrace in summer. Ask for the specialty, *Linzer Torte,* with your
coffee. *Promenade 16, tel. 0732/773353. Reservations unneces-*
sary. Dress: casual but neat. No credit cards. Closed Sun.
Moderate.
Zum Klosterhof. This complex in the former Kremsmünster abbey gives you a choice of upstairs and downstairs rooms that
range from fairly formal to rustic-country to completely informal. The fare is traditional Austrian, and the beverage of
choice is Salzburger Stiegl beer. *Landstr. 30, tel. 0732/773–*
3730, fax 0732/773373–21. Reservations usually not neces-

sary. Dress: jacket or casual, depending on the room. AE, DC, MC, V. Moderate.

Dining and Lodging

Schillerpark. This very modern complex (glass outside, marble inside) puts you close to the south end of the pedestrian zone but still reasonably near the center and the sights. The casino is in the same building. The rooms have clean lines, with contemporary furnishings. *Rainerstr. 2–4, tel. 0732/69500, fax 0732/ 69509. 111 rooms. Nonsmoking floor. Facilities: 2 restaurants (1 in the casino), 2 bars (1 in the casino), café, sauna, solarium, garage. AE, DC, MC, V. Very Expensive.*

Spitz. This ultramodern neo–Art Deco hotel in Urfahr is an easy walk across the bridge from the city center. The rooms are smallish but comfortable, and some have a view over the new city hall to the main city. Paladino, its restaurant, is earning a good reputation. *Karl-Fiedler-Str. 6, tel. 0732/236–4410, fax 0732/230841. 56 rooms. Facilities: restaurant (closed Sun.), bar, sauna, solarium, garage. AE, DC, MC, V. Very Expensive.*

Dom-Hotel. Behind the plain facade on a quiet side street near the new cathedral and the city center is a modern hotel with its own garden. The rooms are compact but attractive, in natural woods and shades of blue. *Baumbachstr. 17, tel. 0732/778441, fax 0732/775432. 44 rooms. Facilities: restaurant, bar, sauna, solarium, parking. AE, DC, MC, V. Expensive.*

Drei Mohren. This has been an inn since 1595, and the rooms are well worn, but they have up-to-date baths. It's all in the heart of the old city within a block of the pedestrian zone. *Promenade 17, tel. 0732/772626, fax 0732/772626–6. 27 rooms, 24 with bath. Facilities: restaurant, bar. AE, DC, V. Expensive.*

Prielmayerhof. This attractive, traditional house is not central, but bus No. 21 will take you the eight blocks to the pedestrian zone or the main rail station. The Oriental-carpeted rooms are larger than those in the newer hotels, and the baths are fully up to standard. *Weissenwolfstr. 33, tel. 0732/774131, fax 771569. 32 rooms, 30 with bath. Facilities: restaurant, bar. AE, DC, MC, V. Expensive.*

Trend. You'll be directly on the Danube in this multistory modern hotel, next to the Brucknerhaus concert hall and within reasonable walking distance of the center. The rooms are compact-modern, air-conditioned, and attractively decorated; ask for an upper room on the river side for the superb views. The excellent restaurant is packed with businesspeople at lunchtime. *Untere Donaulände 9, tel. 0732/76260, fax 0732/76262. 176 rooms. Facilities: restaurant, bar, nightclub, café, indoor pool, sauna, solarium, fitness room, garage. AE, DC, MC, V. Expensive.*

★ **Wolfinger.** This charming, traditional hotel in an old building in the heart of the city is a favorite of regular guests, in part because of the friendly staff. You couldn't be more central. The medium-size rooms have been recently modernized, with comfortable new furniture and bright fabrics. Those on the front are less quiet but give you a first-hand view of city activities. *Hauptplatz 19, tel. 0732/773–2910, fax 0732/773291–55. 27 rooms, 23 with bath. AE, DC, MC, V. Moderate.*

Zum Schwarzen Bären. This fine, traditional house near the center of the old city, a block from the pedestrian zone, was the birthplace of the tenor Richard Tauber (1891–1948). The rooms are smallish and well worn, but the baths (most with shower) are modern, if compact. *Herrenstr. 9–11, tel. 0732/772–4770,* *fax 0732/772477–47. 36 rooms, 29 with bath. Facilities: restaurant, bar, wine stube. AE, DC, MC, V. Moderate.*

Maria Taferl

Dining and Lodging **Krone–Kaiserhof.** Two hotels under the same family management share each other's luxurious facilities. The Krone looks out over the Danube valley, the Kaiserhof has views of the nearby Baroque pilgrimage church. Both have rooms done a bit slickly in country style. Every Sunday in July and August there's a buffet with live dance music, on Wednesdays a *Heuriger* buffet (new wine and cold dishes) with zither music. *A–3672 Maria Taferl, tel. 07413/63550 or 07413/6358, fax 07413/6355–83. 65 rooms. Facilities: 2 restaurants, bar, indoor and outdoor pools, sauna, solarium, fitness room, minigolf, garage. No credit cards. Expensive.*

Mautern

Dining ★ **Landhaus Bacher.** Lisl Bacher's creative, light cuisine has elevated this attractive country restaurant to one of the top dozen in the country. The light-flooded rooms are elegant but not stiff, and there's an attractive garden. A recent menu offered crabmeat salad, roast suckling pig, and spring lamb. Ask for advice on wines; the choice is wide. There are a few small and cozy rooms for overnight guests in an adjoining guest house. *Südtirolerplatz 208, tel. 02732/829370 or 02732/85429, fax 02732/74337. Reservations required. Jacket and tie advised. DC, V. Closed Mon., Tues. lunch May–Oct.; Mon., Tues. Nov.–Apr.; and from mid-Jan. to mid-Feb. Very Expensive.*

Melk

Dining and Lodging **Stadt Melk.** This traditional hotel in the heart of town offers plain but adequate accommodations in smallish rooms, but the main feature here is the excellent and attractive restaurant. The cuisine ranges from regional traditional to creative light; try one of the cream soups and stuffed chicken breast to enjoy the contrasts; dishes here are individually prepared. *Hauptplatz 1, A–3390, tel. 02752/2475, fax 02752/2475–19. 16 rooms. Facilities: restaurant (reservations advised, jacket advised; closed Mon. lunch Nov.–Feb.), garage. MC, V. Restaurant: Expensive. Hotel: Inexpensive.*

Goldener Ochs. Here in the center of town you're in a typical village *Gasthof* with the traditional friendliness of a family management. The rather small rooms were renovated in 1990, and the restaurant offers solid standard fare. *Linzer Str. 18, A–3390, tel. 02752/2367, fax 02752/2367–6. 35 rooms, 25 with bath. Facilities: restaurant (closed Sat., Sun. Nov.–Apr.), wine cellar, sauna. AE, DC, MC, V. Moderate.*

Mühldorf

Lodging **Burg Oberranna.** This 12th-century castle has been successfully turned into a charming and comfortable hotel, great as a base for hiking and perfect for those who just want to get away. Rooms include a kitchenette. *Oberranna 1, A–3622, tel. 02713/8221, fax 02713/8366. 11 rooms and apartments. Facilities: restaurant. AE, DC, MC, V. Closed Nov.–Apr. Very Expensive.*

Persenbeug

Dining **Donaurast.** The dining room has views over the Danube, about 2 kilometers (1 mile) below Persenbeug, as you dine. Various river fish are specialties here, as are interesting meat dishes such as wild boar, roast chicken, or Tafelspitz. Finish up with any of the excellent desserts or the selection of Austrian cheese. There are rooms as well, should you decide to stay overnight. *Wachaustr. 28, Persenbeug/Metzling, tel. 07412/52438. Dress: informal. Reservations not required. No credit cards. Closed Tues. in Nov. and Dec., also Wed. in Mar.–May, Oct.; closed mid-Jan.–end Feb. Moderate.*

St. Pölten

Dining **Galerie.** Stock from the antique shop next door flows over to lend atmosphere to this stylish small restaurant. In contrast to the antiques, the kitchen strives to do new things—generally successfully—with Austrian standards like pork fillet. *Fuhrmanngasse 1, tel. 02742/51305. Reservations advised. Jacket and tie advised. AE, DC, MC, V. Closed Sun., Mon., and a week each in Jan., Apr., and Oct. Expensive.*

Spitz

Dining **Mühlenkeller.** You're really in an old mill here, and the cellar rooms go back to the 11th century. This is as much a *Heuriger* as it is a restaurant, open mainly in late afternoon and evening; wines come from neighboring vineyards. In summer you've the choice of the inside courtyard or the garden. Huge portions are served of local specialties like roast pork and Tafelspitz. *Auf der Wehr 1, tel. 02713/2352. No reservations. Dress: informal. No credit cards. Closed Wed., mid-Dec.–mid-Jan. Moderate.*

Dining and Lodging **Wachauer Hof.** This appealing traditional house, set near the vineyards, has been under family management for generations. You can enjoy the wines in the *Gaststube*, the shaded garden, or the restaurant, which offers basic Austrian fare. The medium-size rooms have comfortable chairs, ample pillows, and rustic decor. *Hauptstr. 15, A–3620, tel. 02713/2303, fax 02713/2912. 30 rooms, all with bath or shower. Facilities: restaurant. AE, MC. Closed mid-Nov.–Palm Sunday. Moderate.*

Steyr

Dining **Rahofer.** You'll have to search out this intimate Italian restaurant in one of the passageways off the main square down toward the river. The choice is limited but of excellent quality; try the saltimbocca. Soups and desserts are praiseworthy. *Stadtplatz 9, tel. 07252/54606. Reservations advised. Dress: casual but neat. AE, DC, MC, V. Closed Sun., Mon. Moderate.*

Dining and Lodging ★ **Minichmayr.** From this traditional hotel the view alone—out over the confluence of the Enns and Steyr rivers, up and across to Schloss Lamberg—will make your stay memorable. Add to that the especially homey rooms, a friendly staff, and an excellent restaurant offering creative, light cuisine and regional specialties, and there's little more to want, except easier parking. Ask for rooms on the river side. The hotel is one of the Romantik Hotels group. *Haratzmüllerstr. 1–3, A–4400, tel.*

07252/534190, fax 07252/482–0255. 51 rooms. Facilities: restaurant, sauna, solarium. AE, DC, MC, V. Expensive.

★ **Mader/Zu den Drei Rosen.** In this very old family-run hotel with small but pleasant modern rooms, you're right on the picturesque town square. The restaurant offers solid local and traditional fare, with outdoor dining in a delightful garden in the ancient courtyard. *Stadtplatz 36, A–4400, tel. 07252/533580, fax 07252/533506. 53 rooms. Facilities: restaurant (closed Sun.), garage. AE, DC, MC, V. Moderate.*

Tulln

Dining and Lodging
★

Zur Rossmühle. Starting with the cheerful yellow facade, elegance is the byword in this attractively renovated hotel on the town square. From the abundant greenery of the reception area to the table settings in the dining room, you'll find pleasing little touches. The rooms are in modern Baroque decor. For sheer pleasure, take lunch in the courtyard garden; here, as in the more formal dining room, you'll dine on Austrian standards and ambitious creations by the aspiring young chef. You'd do well with any of the excellent open wines on the list. *Hauptplatz 12–13, A–3430, tel. 02272/2411, fax 02272/2539. 55 rooms. Facilities: restaurant (reservations advised, jacket and tie advised), bar, sauna, riding. AE, DC, MC, V. Restaurant closed Mon.; hotel and restaurant closed last two weeks in January. Restaurant: Expensive. Hotel: Moderate.*

Waidhofen an der Ybbs

Dining

Türkenpfeiferl. Family atmosphere is served at this attractive, family-run restaurant, along with excellent creative, light cuisine and regional standards. Try the breast of chicken or lamb in a spiced crust. Note the attention to details: The bread is house-baked. The garden is particularly pleasant for summer dining, and children are welcome. *Hoher Markt 23, tel. 07442/ 3507. Reservations recommended. Jacket advised. DC, MC. Closed Mon. and first week in July. Moderate.*

Weissenkirchen

Dining
★

Florianihof. This is one of those restaurants that's packed on pleasant weekends; come during the week if possible. The dark-wood paneling in the succession of rooms is imposing and lends an illusion of elegance to this simple place. Try the *Rostbraten* (rump steak), roast pork, or grilled chicken. *Wösendorf 74, tel. 02715/2212. Reservations advised. Dress: casual but neat. No credit cards. Closed Wed., Thurs., and mid-Jan.–mid-Feb. Very Expensive.*

★ **Jamek.** Josef Jamek is known for his outstanding wines, his wife, Edeltraud, for what she and her chefs turn out in the kitchen of this excellent restaurant, which is, in fact, their home. The combination makes for memorable dining in a rustic-elegant atmosphere. You dine in one of several tastefully decorated rooms with 18th-century touches. Creative variations on typical Austrian specialties are emphasized; lamb and game in season are highlights. *Joching 45, tel. 02715/2235, fax 02715/2483. Reservations required. Jacket and tie advised. No credit cards. Closed Sun., Mon.; mid-Dec.–mid-Feb.; first week in July, but check, as this may vary. Expensive.*

Kirchenwirt. The fare here is dependably Austrian: You'll find tafelspitz, roast pork, *Kaiserfleisch* (corned pork), and other standards, all well prepared and served in the cozy rooms. *Weissenkirchen 17, tel. 02715/2332. Reservations advised on weekends. Dress: casual but neat. No credit cards. Closed Mon., Tues. in winter; closed mid-Dec.–mid-Jan. Expensive.*

Prandtauerhof. The Baroque facade is the work of Jakob Prandtauer, the architect responsible for many buildings in the area. Ornate details are carried over into the cozy guest rooms and the inner court; a sense of history pervades the house. The kitchen delivers excellent traditional cuisine with such creative touches as pork medaillons in a light Gorgonzola sauce. You'll find fish and game in season, and the wines come from the house vineyards. *Joching 36, tel. 02715/2310, fax 02715/ 2310–9. Reservations recommended. Jacket and tie advised. No credit cards. Closed Tues., Wed., and mid-Feb.–mid-Mar. Expensive.*

Lodging **Raffelsbergerhof.** This stunning Renaissance building (1574),
★ once a shipmaster's house, has been tastefully converted into a hotel with every comfort. The rooms are attractively decorated without being overdone. The family management is particularly friendly, and there's a quiet garden to complement the *gemütlich* public lounge. *A-3610 Weissenkirchen, tel. 02715/2201. 12 rooms. MC. Closed Nov.–Apr. Expensive.*

The Arts and Nightlife

In the smaller towns and cities covered in this chapter, the arts tend to come to life in summer. Nightlife is not bad in Linz and St. Pölten, and each town or group of towns has a hangout where the crowd gathers, but this is family country for vacationers, and nightlife will usually consist of sitting around a table with a glass of wine. In Linz, don't overlook the casual wine gardens set under huge trees on the north bank of the Danube (Urfahr district), west of the new city hall. This is anything but tourist territory, and you'll toast the friendly Linzers with mugs of wine on pleasant summer afternoons and evenings.

The Arts

In Linz, the tourist office's monthly booklet "Was ist los in Linz und Oberösterreich" (What's On in Linz and Upper Austria) will give you details of theater and concerts. Two ticket agencies are **Linzer Kartenbüro** (Herrenstr. 4, tel. 0732/778800) and **Ruefa** (Landstr. 67, tel. 0732/662–6810, fax 0732/662681–33).

Music Summer concerts are held in June and July at the abbeys at Kremsmünster and St. Florian (tickets: Domgasse 12, tel. 0732/776127). A chamber-music festival takes place at Schloss Tillysburg in July (tel. 0732/775230). In July and August, a series of concerts on the Bruckner organ is given on Sunday afternoons at 4 in the church at St. Florian (tel. 07224/8903). Melk also offers a series of concerts around Pentecost, and concerts are held at Grafenegg during the summer. Get details and dates from the town or regional tourist offices.

In Linz, concerts and recitals are held in the **Brucknerhaus,** the modern hall on the banks of the Danube. From mid-September to early October, it's the center of the International Bruckner Festival. *Untere Donaulände 7, tel. 0732/775230, fax 0732/ 783745. Box office open weekdays 10–6.*

The biggest multimedia event in the area is the **Ars Electronica** in Linz in mid-June, combining a musical and laser-show spectacle (Brucknerhaus, Untere Donaulände 7, tel. 0732/775230, fax 0732/783745).

Opera From June through August, the operetta festival in **Bad Hall** presents a series of lighter works (tel. 07258/2255–35 or 07258/2031).

The **Linz** opera company is excellent and often more willing to mount venturesome works and productions than those in Vienna or even Graz. Most performances are in the **Landestheater** (tel. 0732/7611–100), some in the Brucknerhaus.

The **Stadttheater** (tel. 02742/520260 or 02742/541830) in **St. Pölten** includes operetta and occasionally opera in its repertoire. Check with the tourist office for schedules and times.

Theater In **Linz,** plays (in German) in the classical tradition and some operas are performed at the **Landestheater;** in the **Kammerspiele** you'll find more contemporary plays. Several smaller "cellar" theaters also offer drama; the tourist office will have information. *Landestheater: Promenade 39, tel. 0732/7611–100. Box office open Mon.–Fri. 10–6, Sat. 10–12:30, and 1½ hrs before performances. Kammerspiele: Promenade 39, tel. 0732/7611–102. Box office open same hours as Landestheater.*

The theater in **St. Pölten** is quite good for a provincial house; classical and contemporary plays in German are presented. *Stadttheater, Rathausplatz 11, tel. 02742/520260 or 02742/541830. Box office open Tues.–Sun. 11–1, 5–6:30, and 1 hr before performances.*

Summer theater is held on the grounds next to the abbey in **Melk** during July and August, and **Grein** puts on a summer festival; call the tourist office for details.

Nightlife

Linz is a far livelier town than most Austrians realize, and the local population is friendlier than in Vienna or Salzburg and much less cliquish than in the top resort towns.

Cabaret Linz has no cabaret in the Viennese tradition, but there's striptease at **Moulin Rouge** (Wiener Str. 217, tel. 0732/344272) until 6 AM.

Casinos The Linz casino, with roulette, blackjack, poker, and slot machines, is in the **Hotel Schillerpark;** the casino complex includes a bar and the **Rouge et Noir** restaurant. *Rainerstr. 2–4, tel. 0732/54487, fax 0732/54487–24. Open daily except Good Friday, Nov. 1, and Dec. 24, 3 PM–3 AM. Admission: AS210, includes five AS50 tokens. Passport required. Jacket and tie advised.*

Bars and Lounges Linz has not lagged behind other Austrian cities in developing its own "Bermuda triangle." Around the narrow streets of the old city (Klosterstrasse, Altstadt, Hofgasse) are dozens of fascinating small bars and lounges, and as you explore, you'll probably meet some Linzers who can direct you to the current "in" location. The area, however, has acquired a somewhat unsavory reputation in recent months; it's a good idea to avoid arguments and stick to bars that seem peaceful.

Discos St. Pölten is the place for disco activity, and the **Fabrik,** with its bars and pizzeria, continues to pack in crowds from as far away as Vienna (Radlberger Hauptstr. 60, tel. 02742/65521, nightly from 9). You might also try **Bellini** (Mühlweg 67, tel. 02746/66407). The vast Fabrik is a perennial favorite, but otherwise the mortality rate of St. Pölten's clubs and discos is high.

Jazz Clubs Linz is developing a tradition for good jazz, and it's worth checking activities at **17er Keller** (Hauptplatz 17, tel. 0732/779000) and **Kasper-Keller** (Spittelwiese 1, tel. 0732/773692).

Index

Personal Itinerary

Departure *Date*

Time

Transportation

Arrival *Date*   *Time*

Departure *Date*   *Time*

Transportation

Accommodations

Arrival *Date*   *Time*

Departure *Date*   *Time*

Transportation

Accommodations

Arrival *Date*   *Time*

Departure *Date*   *Time*

Transportation

Accommodations

Personal Itinerary

Arrival *Date*   *Time*

Departure *Date*   *Time*

Transportation

Accommodations

Arrival *Date*   *Time*

Departure *Date*   *Time*

Transportation

Accommodations

Arrival *Date*   *Time*

Departure *Date*   *Time*

Transportation

Accommodations

Arrival *Date*   *Time*

Departure *Date*   *Time*

Transportation

Accommodations

Personal Itinerary

Arrival *Date*   *Time*

Departure *Date*   *Time*

Transportation

Accommodations

Arrival *Date*   *Time*

Departure *Date*   *Time*

Transportation

Accommodations

Arrival *Date*   *Time*

Departure *Date*   *Time*

Transportation

Accommodations

Arrival *Date*   *Time*

Departure *Date*   *Time*

Transportation

Accommodations

Personal Itinerary

Arrival *Date*   *Time*

Departure *Date*   *Time*

Transportation

_____

_____

_____

Accommodations

_____

_____

_____

Arrival *Date*   *Time*

Departure *Date*   *Time*

Transportation

_____

_____

_____

Accommodations

_____

_____

_____

Arrival *Date*   *Time*

Departure *Date*   *Time*

Transportation

_____

_____

_____

Accommodations

_____

_____

_____

Arrival *Date*   *Time*

Departure *Date*   *Time*

Transportation

_____

_____

_____

Accommodations

_____

_____

_____

Personal Itinerary

Arrival *Date*   *Time*

Departure *Date*   *Time*

Transportation

Accommodations

Arrival *Date*   *Time*

Departure *Date*   *Time*

Transportation

Accommodations

Arrival *Date*   *Time*

Departure *Date*   *Time*

Transportation

Accommodations

Arrival *Date*   *Time*

Departure *Date*   *Time*

Transportation

Accommodations

Addresses

Name	*Name*
Address	*Address*
Telephone	*Telephone*
Name	*Name*
Address	*Address*
Telephone	*Telephone*
Name	*Name*
Address	*Address*
Telephone	*Telephone*
Name	*Name*
Address	*Address*
Telephone	*Telephone*
Name	*Name*
Address	*Address*
Telephone	*Telephone*
Name	*Name*
Address	*Address*
Telephone	*Telephone*
Name	*Name*
Address	*Address*
Telephone	*Telephone*
Name	*Name*
Address	*Address*
Telephone	*Telephone*

Addresses

Name	*Name*
Address	*Address*
Telephone	*Telephone*
Name	*Name*
Address	*Address*
Telephone	*Telephone*
Name	*Name*
Address	*Address*
Telephone	*Telephone*
Name	*Name*
Address	*Address*
Telephone	*Telephone*
Name	*Name*
Address	*Address*
Telephone	*Telephone*
Name	*Name*
Address	*Address*
Telephone	*Telephone*
Name	*Name*
Address	*Address*
Telephone	*Telephone*
Name	*Name*
Address	*Address*
Telephone	*Telephone*

Addresses

Name

Address

Telephone

Name

Address

Telephone

Name

Address

Telephone

Name

Address

Telephone

Name

Address

Telephone

Name

Address

Telephone

Name

Address

Telephone

Name

Address

Telephone

Name

Address

Telephone

Name

Address

Telephone

Name

Address

Telephone

Name

Address

Telephone

Name

Address

Telephone

Name

Address

Telephone

Name

Address

Telephone

Name

Address

Telephone

Fodor's Travel Guides

Available at bookstores everywhere, or call 1–800–533–6478, 24 hours a day.

U.S. Guides

Alaska

Arizona

Boston

California

Cape Cod, Martha's Vineyard, Nantucket

The Carolinas & the Georgia Coast

Chicago

Colorado

Florida

Hawaii

Las Vegas, Reno, Tahoe

Los Angeles

Maine, Vermont, New Hampshire

Maui

Miami & the Keys

New England

New Orleans

New York City

Pacific North Coast

Philadelphia & the Pennsylvania Dutch Country

The Rockies

San Diego

San Francisco

Santa Fe, Taos, Albuquerque

Seattle & Vancouver

The South

The U.S. & British Virgin Islands

The Upper Great Lakes Region

USA

Vacations in New York State

Vacations on the Jersey Shore

Virginia & Maryland

Waikiki

Walt Disney World and the Orlando Area

Washington, D.C.

Foreign Guides

Acapulco, Ixtapa, Zihuatanejo

Australia & New Zealand

Austria

The Bahamas

Baja & Mexico's Pacific Coast Resorts

Barbados

Berlin

Bermuda

Brazil

Brittany & Normandy

Budapest

Canada

Cancun, Cozumel, Yucatan Peninsula

Caribbean

China

Costa Rica, Belize, Guatemala

The Czech Republic & Slovakia

Eastern Europe

Egypt

Euro Disney

Europe

Europe's Great Cities

Florence & Tuscany

France

Germany

Great Britain

Greece

The Himalayan Countries

Hong Kong

India

Ireland

Israel

Italy

Japan

Kenya & Tanzania

Korea

London

Madrid & Barcelona

Mexico

Montreal & Quebec City

Morocco

Moscow & St. Petersburg

The Netherlands, Belgium & Luxembourg

New Zealand

Norway

Nova Scotia, Prince Edward Island & New Brunswick

Paris

Portugal

Provence & the Riviera

Rome

Russia & the Baltic Countries

Scandinavia

Scotland

Singapore

South America

Southeast Asia

Spain

Sweden

Switzerland

Thailand

Tokyo

Toronto

Turkey

Vienna & the Danube Valley

Yugoslavia

Special Series

Fodor's Affordables

Caribbean

Europe

Florida

France

Germany

Great Britain

London

Italy

Paris

**Fodor's Bed &
Breakfast and
Country Inns Guides**

Canada's Great
Country Inns

California

Cottages, B&Bs and
Country Inns of
England and Wales

Mid-Atlantic Region

New England

The Pacific
Northwest

The South

The Southwest

The Upper Great
Lakes Region

The West Coast

The Berkeley Guides

California

Central America

Eastern Europe

France

Germany

Great Britain &
Ireland

Mexico

Pacific Northwest &
Alaska

San Francisco

**Fodor's Exploring
Guides**

Australia

Britain

California

The Caribbean

Florida

France

Germany

Ireland

Italy

London

New York City

Paris

Rome

Singapore & Malaysia

Spain

Thailand

Fodor's Flashmaps

New York

Washington, D.C.

Fodor's Pocket Guides

Bahamas

Barbados

Jamaica

London

New York City

Paris

Puerto Rico

San Francisco

Washington, D.C.

Fodor's Sports

Cycling

Hiking

Running

Sailing

The Insider's Guide
to the Best Canadian
Skiing

Skiing in the USA
& Canada

**Fodor's Three-In-Ones
(guidebook, language
cassette, and phrase
book)**

France

Germany

Italy

Mexico

Spain

**Fodor's
Special-Interest
Guides**

Accessible USA

Cruises and Ports
of Call

Euro Disney

Halliday's New
England Food
Explorer

Healthy Escapes

London Companion

Shadow Traffic's New
York Shortcuts and
Traffic Tips

Sunday in New York

Walt Disney World
and the Orlando Area

Walt Disney World
for Adults

**Fodor's Touring
Guides**

Touring Europe

Touring USA:
Eastern Edition

**Fodor's Vacation
Planners**

Great American
Vacations

National Parks
of the East

National Parks
of the West

**The Wall Street
Journal Guides to
Business Travel**

Europe

International Cities

Pacific Rim

USA & Canada

WHEREVER YOU TRAVEL, *H*ELP IS NEVER FAR AWAY.

From planning your trip to providing travel assistance along the way, American Express® Travel Service Offices* are always there to help.

Austria

GRAZ
American Express Travel Service
Hammerlinggasse 6
43-316-817010

INNSBRUCK
American Express Travel Service
Brixnerstrasse 3
43-512-582491

KLAGENFURT
Reiseburo Springer
Wiesbadener Strasse 1
43-463-33520

LINZ
American Express Travel Service
Buergerstrasse 14
43-732-669013

SALZBURG
American Express Travel Service
5 Mozartplatz
43-662-842501

VIENNA
American Express Travel Service
Kaerntnerstrasse 21/23
43-222-51540